The Just Shall Live by Faith Series

Transformation!

HOW SIMPLE BIBLE STORIES PROVIDE IN-DEPTH ANSWERS FOR LIFE'S MOST DIFFICULT PROBLEMS

Dr. Troy Reiner

Reiner **Publishing**

Unless otherwise noted, Scripture quotations in this book are taken from the King James Version of the Bible.

Scripture references marked AMP are taken from The "Amplified" trademark is registered in the United States Patent and Trademark Office by The Lockman Foundation. Use of this trademark requires the permission of The Lockman Foundation.

Scripture references marked NLT are taken from Holy Bible. New Living Translation copyright © 1996 by Tyndale Charitable Trust. Used by permission of Tyndale House Publishers.

Scripture references marked NIV are taken from the Holy Bible, New International Version, Copyright © 1973, 1978, 1984 by the International Bible Society. Used by permission of Zondervan Publishing House. The "NIV" and "New International Version" trademarks are registered in the United States Patent and Trademark Office by International Bible Society.

Scripture references marked WEY are taken from Weymouth: The Modern Speech New Testament by Richard F. Weymouth, 3rd Edition (1912), Revised & edited by E. Hampden-Cooke.

ISBN 978-0-9903856-1-5
Library of Congress Catalog Card Number: 2005905980

Table of Contents

Introduction

In this book, I will develop a new, biblical narrative approach to Christian counseling and in-depth answers for counseling many of life's most difficult problems. This approach is different from previously proposed Christian counseling methods because it is derived directly from the Bible, relies on the overall direction of the Holy Spirit and employs biblical narrative stories to teach psychological principles. These stories provide simple, yet comprehensive answers to many of the most challenging psychological issues confronting the church today, including dysfunctional relationships, abuse, addictions, codependency, homosexuality and many others. These types of problems require more than just a few words of wisdom or solution-focused therapy; they require a life transformation. The Bible is filled with stories of people with difficult problems whose lives were transformed through faith and who achieved victory over the enemies that confronted them. It is from these stories that we can find the answers for transforming our lives today. Because it was directly derived from the Bible, this method of counseling and the models for treating specific problems can be easily applied within the church for pastoral ministry, lay counseling, professional Christian counseling, and support groups.

There are several reasons why this book is sorely needed at this specific time. The church has been failing for years to meet many of the deepest needs of the large number of emotionally hurting and dysfunctional people coming to its doors. It has been referring many of these people with the most difficult psychological problems to secular counselors and psychologists outside of the church. Even the question of what Christian counseling in the church should be remains unresolved. I believe that this state of affairs is, in part, the result of a lack of a simple, truly biblical counseling method and a lack of thorough biblical answers for dealing with these complex and challenging psychological problems.

This leads us to a basic, fundamental question: Does the Bible really claim to provide in-depth answers for life's really difficult problems? Many suggest that the Bible deals primarily with spirituality and, therefore, is not a counseling manual and should not be expected to provide help with psychological problems. I cannot agree with this assumption. First, the spiritual and psychological realms are so interwoven that they cannot be easily separated. Second, God's plan for salvation, the main theme of the Bible, implies the achievement of complete wholeness—spirit, soul and body. This is clearly seen in the Greek word *sozo*, which is translated salvation in the Bible. It means, "to heal, preserve, save, do well, be whole." (Strong, 1890, Greek dictionary, p. 70). Psychology is the study of the soul—the mind, emotions and will—which is the basis of the human personality. Christianity attempts to bring healing to the whole person, including the soul and the spirit. The Bible itself says that God has provided everything that we need for life and Godliness.

2 Pe 1:3 According as his divine power hath given unto us <u>all things</u> that [pertain] unto <u>life and godliness</u>, through the knowledge of him that hath called us to glory and virtue:

2 Ti 3:16 All scripture [is] given by inspiration of God, and [is] profitable for doctrine, for reproof, for correction, for instruction in righteousness:

17 <u>That the man of God may be perfect</u>, thoroughly furnished unto all good works.

Consequently, we should expect the Bible to address at least the most common psychological problems. Since the Bible and the direct revelation of the Holy Spirit are the primary sources of Godly knowledge (and revelation is to be judged by the Bible), we should expect the Bible to provide much more than is currently understood and applied in the area of Christian counseling.

It is the hypothesis of this book that the Bible provides exactly what is needed: a comprehensive, integrated counseling theory, specific insights into these problems, and models for effectively resolving them. Clearly, just as no secular counseling manual can cover every specific issue of every possible problem, exactly what is covered in the Bible and in what depth it is covered awaits further investigation. However, if we should expect the Bible to address these issues, where is this exhaustive, untapped counseling information in the Bible? As I asked God this question, He began revealing the answers as I needed them, over a number of years, as I faced these specific issues in my own counseling practice.

My first clue came over twenty years ago when I heard on audio tape a series of messages on "Restoring the Sin-Scarred Personality" by Dr. Jack Hayford, pastor of *Church on the Way*. He related the rebuilding of Jerusalem under Nehemiah to the rebuilding of a sin-scarred personality. During my discipleship days, Pastor Ronald Jones at *Victory World Outreach* in Colorado Springs, Colorado, taught a Sunday school class on the spiritual meanings of the tribes of the land of Canaan from the book, *Giants or Grasshoppers* (1982) by Reginald Klimionok. Later as a pastor, I extensively used the "types and shadows" interpretation of the Bible for help in understanding the spiritual applications of the Old Testament and New Testament stories. However, it was not until my ministry became focused on Christian counseling that I began to see the true significance of these stories for therapy.

I have always attempted to base everything that I do in counseling on a solid biblical foundation. Consequently, when I read Dr. Hemfelt, Minirth, Meier, and Newman's book, *Love is a Choice* (1989), I asked the Lord, "Where are the codependents in the Bible?" If all that was said in their book was true and this problem was as prevalent as many suggested, I suspected that it must be addressed somewhere in the Bible. A few days later while I was jogging, the Holy Spirit gave me my first answer. As clear as a person speaking to me, God said to my spirit, "King Saul." That was the first of the almost uncountable number of revelations that our Lord has provided since that time concerning codependency and numerous other complex problems buried in the biblical stories of the Old and New Testament.

I am not alone in this discovery. Quite a number of years ago, at a seminar by Malcom Smith, I was introduced to the struggle for worth in Adam and the codependency in the children of Israel—especially Aaron. In preparation for a counseling course I was teaching on biblical models at Word of Life Institute, I found the book, *The Way Out of the Wilderness* (1991), in which Dr. Henslin exposes David, Solomon and Abigail as codependents. Throughout this course, the Lord continued to show me additional biblical models for dealing with a number of other complex counseling problems. For me, the Bible has now become a veritable encyclopedia of counseling information and counseling models waiting to be discovered and understood.

Someone experienced in Bible interpretation may ask, "How can you be sure of your interpretation using types and shadows since many commentators even disagree on some of the clearest examples in the Bible?" This is a valid question. Even Walter Lewis Wilson, author of *Wilson's Dictionary of Bible Types,* divides his types into three groups: 1. Pure types plainly described as such and referred to as such in the Scriptures. 2. Those that seem to be types because of their use and because of the evident meaning they convey. 3. Passages in which there is a question as to whether or not they are types. (1957, p. 5) In addition, the exact meaning of names and places sometimes varies even between respected scholars of the original languages. As much as possible, I have tried to rely on pure types and clearly understood meanings of names and places in the Bible. However, as with anything that leans upon revelation for its ultimate understanding, the final answer must rest in the product. Does the revelation fit together with and not contradict existing scriptural knowledge? Does it fit with actual experience? Do others sensitive to the Spirit confirm it? Does it produce positive biblical results? I do not claim to have unique or even complete revelation on any of these subjects. Therefore, I invite the reader to closely and thoroughly examine this work and judge it based on these criteria and to accept or reject it according to their best judgment following the biblical injunction, "Let every man be fully persuaded in his own mind." (Romans 14:5)

Psychological problems fall into three main categories: 1. Those which are common to every person. 2. Those which are considered dysfunctional and affect large numbers of people. 3. Those which are considered mental disorders. Because of the limited length of this book and the large number of complex counseling problems involved, I will address only those problems commonly found within the church. I have used the biblical meaning of words and common terminology rather than technical psychological terms so that this book can be easily understood without a graduate counseling degree. For example, although lust today is primarily associated with sexual sin, I have used it more generally as it is used in the Bible to mean a strong desire of any type. Furthermore, instead of the more technical term "alcohol dependence" I have used the word that is more common "alcoholic." I have included illustrations that I use in counseling, quick reference charts, and a listing of Christian counseling resources that I use in conjunction with these models. Stories of actual clients are presented to give modern-day examples of each type of problem but these stories have been modified and names have been changed to protect the confidentiality and the identity of each client.

This book is part of a complete system for implementing salvation-based therapy within the church. The remaining three books in the series – *Faith Therapy, Revelations That Set You Free*, and *Principles for Life* – provide an in-depth understanding of the process of salvation by faith, tools for applying faith in counseling, a comprehensive roadmap for psychological and spiritual growth, and an in-depth method for building counseling plans from biblical principles.

I want specifically to thank all of my clients and students, my wife, Nancy, my mother, Hildegard, my daughter, Sarah, and our assistant administrator, Loretta Goetting for their contributions in preparing this manuscript for publication. My gratitude also goes to Athena Dean and all the other wonderful people at Pleasant Word Publishing for their patience and assistance in publishing this book.

All Bible references are from the Authorized Version (AV) of the King James Bible. The King James Bible is quoted as originally written and therefore spelling, grammar and capitalization may not agree with modern usage. For example, in my writing I have chosen to capitalize all references to God. This is not done in the King James Version of the Bible. Greek, Hebrew, Bible translations, and biblical dictionary references are obtained and quoted directly from The Online Bible Millennium Edition (2000) by Larry Pierce.

I believe that God is calling us, as Christians, to demonstrate to the world that "Jesus is the answer," even to life's most demanding problems, and that His Word is sufficient to provide the basis for "healing the broken hearted and setting the captive free." It is my hope that this book will stimulate the reader to take up the quest of developing and applying better biblically based Christian and pastoral counseling to bring healing to the psychological and emotional problems that are so prevalent in our churches and society today.

PART I

A Biblical Foundation

Chapter 1

The Need for In-depth Biblical Answers

The evidence is all around us that we are in desperate need of simple, yet in-depth, biblical answers for the many complex and difficult problems of life. Although most churches provide at least some level of pastoral counseling, the large majority refer the most complicated problems to counselors outside the church. Most of these counselors rely heavily on experientially derived secular methods and counseling theories when treating complex problems. By referring outside of the church and relying primarily on secular methods, we have implicitly agreed with the world that the church does not have the answers to these difficulties.

It took only one experience to convince me that what I was taught in the church and my best efforts were inadequate for the kind of problems we are facing in our society today. Before the Lord called me into the field of Christian counseling, I was in the United States Air Force stationed in the mid-west and an active member of an evangelistic church. Two days earlier new neighbors had moved in next door, but we had not yet met them. About five in the evening, our doorbell began frantically ringing. It was one of the neighbor's teenage sons. He asked us to call an ambulance. His mother had just plunged a six-inch knife into his father's chest! My wife Nancy dialed 911 and I ran to the neighbor's house to find Ron sitting propped up on the floor. His face was extremely gray from loss of blood. Fortunately, when the paramedics arrived one was able to give him intravenous liquids while they rushed him to a nearby hospital. The attending physician told us that if Ron had arrived at the hospital twenty minutes later he would have died!

We did what we could to befriend them and eventually led them to Christ. Our families spent much time together. Although they even attended our church for a while, their problems with alcohol often resulted in domestic violence. Although we did our best to counsel them from the scriptures and encourage them to give up their drinking, their problems remained. Once Connie asked us to visit her in the hospital, because she had "broken her arm falling on the ice." Another time her face was heavily bruised. His job provided secular counseling, but it did not seem to change the situation. We told them that Jesus was the answer, listened to their problems and encouraged them to get more involved in a church.

They moved to another part of town. About six months later, they called and invited us over for a barbecue. When we arrived, we saw that they had a brand new truck and all new furniture! After the usual pleasantries and dinner, they explained what had happened. They had gone to a bar several months earlier. After Connie had too much to drink, she became jealous over the attention some other women were giving to Ron. She incited some men at the bar to pick a fight to get back at Ron. They went outside and in his inebriated state; he tried to fight with several men at once. One of them kicked his eye out and he was now blind in one eye. Their sudden wealth was due to an insurance payment for his lost eye. Without any understanding of codependency, we recommended the obvious. If they were unable to quit destroying each other, they should separate for at least a short time while they could work on their problems and grow spiritually. That was one of the last times we saw them. They were obviously too attached to each other to even consider such a suggestion. They no longer wanted our advice and we were left wondering if there was something, we could have really done to help them. For these kinds of problems, our knowledge and the simple application of Christian principles just did not seem to be enough.

The Danger of Referring Outside of the Church

Referring a church member for psychological counseling outside the church does not insure that they will receive effective help. Even clinics and hospitals started by Christian denominations employ doctors and psychologists who are not Christians and almost all use secular psychological theories and techniques, many of which contradict biblical principles. Only under the very best circumstances are prayer and the client's faith even accepted in this environment. Much of secular counseling, especially associated with hospitals, is based on the "medical disease model" which almost totally ignores the concept of sin and the spiritual dimension. Increasingly, the secular psychological answer to difficult problems is the prescription of psychoactive drugs. These might bring short-term relief but generally do not resolve the underlying problem. In the current managed care environment, rapid and cost-effective resolution of the presenting problem is the primary goal of treatment. Many times this results in the treatment of the symptoms rather than the actual underlying problem. Even though Alcoholics Anonymous began as a Christian movement, this and other associated 12-Step programs have been secularized by the use of a "higher power" rather than Jesus Christ. Real life change and the true power of the Holy Spirit are usually missing. In addition, because most 12-Step, self-help groups are led by the members of the group, almost anything "helpful" can be shared and a biblical standard is rarely, if ever, evoked.

Unfortunately, there is no such thing as value-free counseling. Secular philosophy and political correctness, such as the women's liberation movement and the acceptance of homosexuality as an alternate lifestyle, are generally promoted in the secular counseling community. In fact, using any theory or technique, including new age and Eastern religious meditation, is considered ethical if the counselor believes that it will help the client. Consequently, sending a person for secular help will, at the least, result in confusion between Christian and secular values and concepts.

In summary, the problems faced by our society are increasing; and the church continues to refer difficult problems outside the church. The real underlying issue is that we have not had a biblically based method for counseling or an understanding of the biblical answers for these life-dominating psychological problems that can be easily applied in the church. Most pastors or lay leaders simply have not had the answers or the training necessary to deal with these issues. It is the goal of this book to provide these answers as they have been revealed to us through a deeper study of the lives of prominent characters of the Bible whose lives were transformed through faith.

Chapter 2

A New Source of Answers
for Biblical Therapy

So far, I have discussed the problems that occur from referring complex and difficult problems outside of the church. I believe that this situation continues to exist due to a lack of an understanding of the clear, simple, in-depth biblical answers for addressing these more-difficult problems of life. I have suggested that if a solid biblical counseling theory and answers to these problems were available, many of these hurting people could be effectively helped within the church. I believe the answers that we are looking for lie in a types and shadows analysis of the lives of many of the more prominent characters in the Bible. I realize that the reader might think that this approach is too simplistic to yield real answers, but I request that you withhold judgment until I am able to demonstrate the depth of what the Bible has to offer using this method. In order to access this information, a basic understanding of the interpretation of the Bible using types and shadows is required.

Students of the Bible have long known that the Bible is a veritable, unending source of revelation and that all scripture contains the directions necessary for living a Godly life.

2 Ti 3:16 All scripture [is] given by inspiration of God, and [is] profitable for doctrine, for reproof, for correction, for instruction in righteousness:
17 That the man of God may be perfect, thoroughly furnished unto all good works.

On the surface, the Bible gives us a history of the Jewish nation and God's wonderful plan of salvation through Christ. On a deeper level, these examples provide us principles for living and an understanding of the process of salvation or achieving wholeness. Finally, at the deepest level it provides symbolic and analogical clues to understanding spiritual and psychological truth. The Bible itself says that this is true.

1 Co 10:1 Moreover, brethren, I would not that ye should be ignorant, how that all our fathers were under the cloud, and all passed through the sea;

2 And were all baptized unto Moses in the cloud and in the sea;

3 And did all eat the same spiritual meat;

4 And did all drink the same spiritual drink: for they drank of that spiritual Rock that followed them: and that Rock was Christ.

5 But with many of them God was not well pleased: for they were overthrown in the wilderness.

6 Now these things were our examples, to the intent we should not lust after evil things, as they also lusted.

7 Neither be ye idolaters, as [were] some of them; as it is written, The people sat down to eat and drink, and rose up to play.

8 Neither let us commit fornication, as some of them committed, and fell in one day three and twenty thousand.

9 Neither let us tempt Christ, as some of them also tempted, and were destroyed of serpents.

10 Neither murmur ye, as some of them also murmured, and were destroyed of the destroyer.

11 <u>Now all these things happened unto them for ensamples: and they are written for our admonition, upon whom the ends of the world are come</u>.

From these verses, it is very clear that if we do not pay attention to the character stories of the Bible and learn from them, God considers us ignorant. Unfortunately, few pastors and counselors in our day have diligently applied themselves to understand these stories in the depth necessary to use them effectively in the field of counseling. These verses state that these Bible stories provide insights concerning many different areas of our lives including at the least lusting after evil things, idolatry, fornication, tempting God (challenging His authority), and murmuring. In these verses, God admonishes us to take particular heed to this story of the exodus of the children of Israel. It provides the spiritual truths by which we are to live.

Probably, the most familiar examples of this method of understanding spiritual realities are the parables of Jesus.

Lu 8:9 And his disciples asked him, saying, What might this parable be?

10 And he said, <u>Unto you it is given to know the mysteries of the kingdom of God</u>: but to others in parables; that seeing they might not see, and hearing they might not understand.

11 Now the parable is this: The seed is the word of God.

12 Those by the way side are they that hear; then cometh the devil, and taketh away the word out of their hearts, lest they should believe and be saved.

13 They on the rock [are they], which, when they hear, receive the word with joy; and these have no root, which for a while believe, and in time of temptation fall away.

14 And that which fell among thorns are they, which, when they have heard, go forth, and are choked with cares and riches and pleasures of [this] life, and bring no fruit to perfection.

15 But that on the good ground are they, which in an honest and good heart, having heard the word, keep [it], and bring forth fruit with patience.

Over the years, many people have pondered Luke 8:10. It is clear that these analogies make the principles simple and clear when they are correctly interpreted, but why does God shroud His truth in mysteries that must be uncovered? I once heard a sermon in which the preacher stated that God only gives us hints concerning Him. He has given us only one book, the Bible, rather than a complete library of books revealing Him. The Apostle John suggests in John 21:25 that the world itself could not contain all the books that would need to be written just to tell of all the things that Jesus did. God wants us to desire Him, to seek Him diligently, and to know Him in a deeper way. However, He does not want to push Himself or His wisdom onto us. He provides hints in the creation, hints in His dealings in our lives, and hints in His Word so that only those who are really interested in knowing Him will truly receive the riches of His wisdom. Those who really do not deeply desire to know Him will "not see," and if they hear "will not understand."

Since Christ is no longer on this earth to help us understand these "mysteries," as He did His disciples, we must rely on the Bible and the revelation of the Holy Spirit to help us discover them. One of the means for understanding these mysteries is the interpretation of the Bible through the types and shadows of the detailed accounts provided in the Bible. Some of these types are clearly stated in the Bible. Others can be understood by comparing one scripture with another in order to identify the type. In many cases, the original meanings of names and places in the Bible will give us collaboration. Each type must also fit within context and be confirmed by the Holy Spirit.

One thing that is clear, however, is that not all cases of types and shadows interpretation of the Bible are equally certain. As I briefly discussed in the introduction, most authorities identify at least three levels of clarity. First, there are clear types, which are specifically mentioned in the Bible. For example, we are told that the story of Noah and the flood is a type of our spiritual salvation.

1 Pe 3:20 Which sometime were disobedient, when once the long-suffering of God waited in the days of Noah, while the ark was a preparing, wherein few, that is, eight souls were saved by water.

21 The like figure whereunto [even] baptism doth also now save us (not the putting away of the filth of the flesh, but the answer of a good conscience toward God,) by the resurrection of Jesus Christ:

Second, there are probable types like the fig tree which Jesus cursed for producing no fruit. (Mark 11:13-20) Most scholars believe that the fig tree represents the nation of Israel. If this is true, then Jesus' actions foretold the destruction of the nation of Israel in 70 AD because it had not produced spiritual fruit. The third category is possible types, which must be confirmed through context and the revelation of the Spirit. Possibly Absalom's hair (which probably resulted in his head being caught in an oak tree as he attempted to escape from Joab. 2 Samuel 18:9) stands for pride. We can corroborate this idea by the description of its beauty in 2nd Samuel Chapter 14. Others might disagree.

A clear Old Testament example of types and shadows is the building of the tabernacle. C. W. Slemming, in his book *Made According to Pattern* (1974), demonstrates that every dimension, every color, and every item in the tabernacle are types of Christ dwelling in the heart of man, the new tabernacle. God warned that every part of the tabernacle should be made according to the pattern provided! Today it provides us a model for approaching God in worship and helps us understand all that Christ has done for us.

Just as we would not think of ignoring the parables of Jesus, we need to be careful not to take the meanings of the other types and shadows in the Bible lightly. When Moses violated God's intended type of Christ by striking the rock twice at Meribah, (Christ was to die only once for our sins) God took this act so seriously that Moses was forbidden from entering the Promised Land. (Numbers 20:11-13) I believe that if we neglect this significant source of information that God intended us to have, we risk failing to enter our own land of promises and achieve the abundant life that was secured for us through Christ's death.

The application of this method of interpretation will become clear, as I apply it in the chapters and counseling models that follow. Although I do not expect the reader to agree with every type and shadow that I suggest, I do believe that the preponderance of the evidence presented in the remainder of this book will convince the reader of the validity of this approach.

Chapter 3

A Narrative Approach to Christian Counseling

In His teaching, Jesus told at least 30 stories or parables in order to simply and clearly illustrate His most important principles. Trench, in his *Notes on the Parables of our Lord*, states, "The parable is constructed to set forth a spiritual truth." (1961, p. 3) The parable is not a fable, myth, proverb, or allegory. It differs in that it teaches spiritual truth, never transgresses the actual order of natural things, and is necessarily figurative. (p.5) Trench continues by saying,

> …We may assume as certain, that the general aim of our Lord in teaching by parables, was wither to illustrate or to prove, that thus to make clearer, the truths which he had in hand. (p.7) Had our Lord spoken naked spiritual truth, how many of His words would have entirely passed away from the hearts and memories of His hearers. But being imparted to them in this form, under some lively image, or in some brief but interesting narrative, they awakened attention, and excited inquiry; …When the Spirit brought all things to their remembrance, He quickened the forms of truth, which they already possessed, with the power and spirit of life. Gradually, the meanings of what they had heard, unfolded themselves. And thus must it ever be with all true knowledge, which is not the communication of information, but the planting seeds of truth, which shall take root in the new soil, and striking roots downward, and sending their branches upward, shall grow into goodly trees. (p.11)

Clearly, the type and shadow narratives of the Bible are intended to teach spiritual truth and are not just fables, myths or allegories but are actual truths that are both physical and spiritual. Since this is the case, I believe they also possess most of the other characteristics and benefits of the parables of Jesus.

From a counseling point of view, it is clear that the truth that we learn from personal experience or the experiences of others generally has more power to transform us than the truth that we simply comprehend with our minds. This is especially true for those who seem to think in a more pictorial fashion. This difference of perception is the challenge discussed by McGee and Morrison in *From Head to Heart* (1997). Until truth finds its way from our mind into our spirit, we are seldom significantly changed by it. We call truth in the spirit, revelation. When we have a revelation of something, it changes how we perceive our world; and how we perceive our world dictates how we think, act, and feel. Another way to understand this process is that the nonverbal right side of our brain is more strongly associated with our experiences and our choices. Until the information from our verbal or left side of our brain becomes experiential, it has much less effect on our choices. Directly approaching the right or nonverbal side of the brain with stories, narratives and pictures, which more nearly approximate our experiences, therefore, tends to be more effective in influencing change in our lives.

It is interesting to note that only as recently as the 1980's, the power and benefits of narrative pictures have found their way into Marriage and Family Therapy in the form of narrative therapy. Unfortunately, this power has been applied to attempt to pull down absolute narratives such as Christianity and reconstruct personal narratives in their place. Although deconstructing negative narratives is justified in some cases—such as narratives describing a client as the "black sheep" of the family or as a descendant of slaves who are ostracized by society—this method has also been used as a tool of postmodernist counselors to foster relativism. (Cameron, 2001, p. 17) In response to this growing trend, Robert Piehl states,

> Narrative therapy is best viewed as neither all good nor all bad, but as one more therapy modality that, if understood critically and used properly, can facilitate the important goal of emotional healing. …Narrative therapists assert that because they are necessarily suspect, all metanarratives should be deconstructed during consultation. Clearly, this imperative is contrary to esteeming the story of the Bible as our authoritative metanarrative. (2001, p. 27)

According to Piehl, "A metanarrative is a comprehensive explanation of the cosmos and the role of human beings within it. Other names for metanarratives are master narratives, cultural stories, and worldviews." (2001, p. 25) In reality, the metanarratives of the Bible are the primary tools for change in the process of salvation by faith. It is our faith in our position in Christ, our faith in His death and resurrection, our faith in the grace and forgiveness of God, and our faith that God loves us and will actively intervene in our lives to meet our needs that overcomes our insecurity and transforms us into the image of Jesus. This paradigm shift in the way we look at life is the basis of the Christian worldview. Piehl continues,

> …The major difference between narrative therapy's postmodern and a Christian worldview is that Christians derive their new identity by connecting to a larger story—one that they did not make up for themselves. Indwelling this metanarrative brings possibilities for grace, forgiveness, and deeper connection. Christian counselors should keep this fundamental distinction in mind as they, from a position of faith, employ narrative therapy techniques. (p.28)

When we realize the importance of narrative methods to Christianity as a whole, the possible benefits from their use, and the emphasis placed on them by Jesus himself, it is clear that they should be applied in Christian counseling to help our clients. The smoke screen that secular counselors have discovered and are now using narrative counseling should in no way deter our use along biblical guidelines. In fact, it should further encourage us since if these techniques had not proven themselves effective, they would not have become widely accepted as a new type of Marriage and Family Therapy.

First, let us investigate how narrative methods are used in a biblical manner. John 8:32 states "And ye shall know the truth, and the truth shall make you free." It is our faith in the truth that provides the foundation for God's process of salvation by faith, which makes us whole. The truth is God's metanarrative. We learn and build our faith in the truth by reading it in the Word of God, through hearing the preaching of the Word of God, through the example of Jesus (Who is the Truth), through the examples of those who have gone before us, and through direct spiritual revelation. The objective of the use of the narrative form in the parables, the example of the life of Jesus, and the examples of the biblical characters in the Old and New Testament is to reveal the truth in the simplest and most effective form.

We should realize that secular counselors or researchers sometimes do stumble onto some of the truth of God and derive methods to employ it. Therefore, let us briefly review the basic methods of secular narrative therapy so that they can be compared to biblical methods. Narrative therapy attempts to free the client by removing accepted cultural stories that hold the client in bondage and substitute new personally derived narratives in their place. Techniques are divided between "story deconstruction" and "story reconstruction." In the first phase, the counselor challenges the authority of the story that he thinks may create a problem for the client. The majority of these stories deal with gender, race or class. As an example, the problem "story" may be that no one ever gets out of the ghetto without "becoming white," or "females are expected to submit—even to domestically violent husbands." The counselor shows the client that the story has unfairly entrapped them and is not actually supported by fact. He challenges the unexamined assumptions behind the story or suggests different assumptions than those accepted by the client. In doing so, he frees the client from "false and abusive belief systems" that cause suffering. Externalizing the problem makes more interventions possible, lessens the pain of failure and expands the range of responses to the problem. As an example, the counselor might ask, "How it is that 'Anorexia' tricked you into starving yourself and hating nutritional food?" or "how has the client let 'Depression' talk him out of having hope?" The counselor is also looking for times that the client's actions did not meet the expectations of the prior narrative. These are called "unique outcome questions" and are used to demonstrate that the client is actually free from the enslaving narrative. Story reconstruction begins by helping the client decide how he (or she) wants the story to turn out. The client is to design a story and claim a new identity that leads to the desired outcome. He is then to "thicken" the story by telling others about who he really is and recruiting them to support his new identity. Any achievements are then made public. (Piehl, 2001, p. 26)

Although there are obviously some concerns here, there are also numerous parallels to well-known biblical methods. Clearly, it is not up to us to decide and make up new narratives about our future outside of the will of God for our lives. Nevertheless, the Bible reveals all that we need in the way of positive narratives for our lives. Furthermore, it provides validity to the methods just described when implemented from a Christian metanarrative or worldview. It is the lies of this world and of Satan that are embedded in false narratives provided by the world and sometimes by our family or friends. Narratives that support feelings of low self-worth, ideas that we are failures, or are stupid, need to be debunked from God's Word. Narratives from the world that homosexuals cannot recover need to be shown as false. These should be replaced by biblical models that declare the power and grace of God that can overcome every problem. These new narratives are then "thickened" through confession and through acting in accordance with the truth, which build faith in the Word of God. We do not attempt to provide a "shame-free" way of looking at the problem. God has already provided for the confession and forgiveness of sins through the narrative and experience of Jesus' death and resurrection.

In fact, what we see in the methods of narrative therapy are simply parts of the model for Christian counseling. This will be further developed directly from the Bible in the next chapter. This model is derived from the story of the exodus of the children of Israel from Egypt. The abusive metanarrative that the children of Israel were to be the slaves to the Egyptians had to be deconstructed by the miracles of God. It also had to be replaced by a metanarrative of freedom and the power to overcome the giants of the land of Canaan. As they built faith in this second narrative, it led them systematically to victory over the slavery in their lives.

Clearly, the basic tenants of narrative therapy have a strong resemblance to the methods used by Jesus and those suggested throughout the Bible. The power of narrative therapy is that it provides a pictorial view that changes how the client perceives life and provides a framework through which everything else is perceived. Whether this view of life is based on the truth or on a lie will significantly affect how the client thinks and acts. Thinking and acting according to the truth is the very basis of renewing of the mind (Romans 12:2). Even secular narrative therapy has proven to be effective in causing a paradigm shift in the way the client views his world. Therefore, I believe using biblical narrative therapy—which is based on the absolute truth of the Bible—embodies an even greater potential for change and growth in our clients.

PART II

A Comprehensive Model

Chapter 4

A Model for Biblical Therapy
(The Children of Israel)

In order to develop a model for biblical narrative therapy, we must learn more about the overall process of salvation (or wholeness), and how it is actually carried out by the Chief Counselor, the Holy Spirit. Although other models for counseling might suffice for dealing with problems of a less complex nature, we need a comprehensive model that focuses on the entire person when attempting to address the complex difficult problems addressed in this book. The Bible gives us exactly what we need. Possibly the best known, most extensive, and clearest type and shadow in the Bible is that of the story of the children of Israel's exodus from Egypt and their journey through the wilderness to the Promised Land.

Where is our client in his spiritual journey? What obstacles does he need to overcome? How can we help him overcome these obstacles on his journey into the land of God's promised wholeness? These are questions that each counselor needs to ask in order to apply this important model for Christian counseling. Because of the multitude of verses associated with this and subsequent models, I will quote only those verses, which are essential to an understanding of each problem.

The story of the exodus of the children of Israel is found in the Bible in the books of Exodus through Joshua. When understood in-depth, it provides us with an almost unfathomable wealth of information concerning the process of salvation by faith, the types of psychological struggles that Christians can expect to encounter, and a method for overcoming these severe problems.

Deliverance from Egypt

The first step in the journey toward complete wholeness is the acceptance of Jesus Christ as savior. A significant number of clients seen at Christian counseling centers are not "saved" and definitely have not yielded the direction of their lives to Christ. Therefore, one of the first steps toward wholeness is the initiation of the basic process of salvation. In most cases, a trusting therapeutic relationship with the counselor must first be established through empathetically listening to the client's presenting problems. Then the counselor will be in a position to demonstrate to the client that salvation is essential to his full recovery. This need for salvation will become extremely clear once the problem is isolated, and the process for dealing with the problem is explained.

The process of this first step is seen in the story of the children of Israel's struggle to leave Egypt (which stands for the world with its riches and opportunities). I believe Moses represents the Holy Spirit, whose job it is to lead us out of the world. I believe that Aaron, whose name means "enlightened," represents the enlightened Christian counselor who is called to speak for Moses to assist in the deliverance of God's people. God defines the relationship between Moses and Aaron in Exodus 4:16: "And he (Aaron) shall be thy spokesperson unto the people: and he shall be, even he shall be to thee (Moses) instead of a mouth, and thou shalt be to him instead of God."

The first job of the Christian counselor (Aaron) is to build hope and faith in the client. The Bible uses the Greek word *paramutheo,* which means "to speak close" or "comfort," to describe this style of counseling. Comforting begins by telling the client of God's plan of deliverance.

Ex 4:29 And Moses and Aaron went and gathered together all the elders of the children of Israel:

30 And Aaron spake all the words which the LORD had spoken unto Moses, and did the signs in the sight of the people.

31 And the people believed: and when they heard that the LORD had visited the children of Israel, and that he had looked upon their affliction, then they bowed their heads and worshipped.

The signs referred to in verse 30 are the signs given by God to Moses in Exodus 4:4-9. They are: 1. When he cast down his rod, it became a snake and when he picked it up again it became a rod. 2. When he put his hand into his bosom it became leprous, and when he put it back again it became whole. 3. When he poured water from the river onto the land, it became blood. I believe these three examples stand for what Christ has done for us. The snake or sin, when picked up by the tail, was transformed into a rod of authority. Christ, who was made sin for us, has given Christians this authority over Satan. The hand (or our actions) that was leprous or sinful because of the selfishness of our hearts is made whole through God's power. This is accomplished through the forgiveness of our sins and our sanctification through faith. Finally, the water from the river poured out on the land, stands for the outpouring of the Spirit, which brings life (represented by the blood) to the whole world. We, as counselors, are to bring hope by demonstrating through our own lives and the lives of others that God has power over Satan, has provided the forgiveness of sins, and has given us His abundant life through the power of God's Spirit.

The second job of the Christian counselor is to confront the world and Satan who hold the client captive. The word in Colossians 1:28 translated as "warn" is *noutheteo, which* means "to warn or confront." Jay Adams (1973) has based his entire style of counseling on this principle. Here we have a definite application of that style.

Col 1:28 Whom we preach, warning every man, and teaching every man in all wisdom; that we may present every man perfect in Christ Jesus:

Confrontation is accomplished by challenging the ways of the world used by the client and demonstrating that these ways do not work. Many times this is quite easy in a counseling setting, because the client has come to counseling after realizing that what he is doing does not work. This openness to new ways of dealing with life is one of the reasons that counseling is such an effective tool for evangelism. However, we must not expect Satan to give up easily. **In fact, the client's problems may initially increase when he decides to quit relying on his worldly ways of coping with life.** This is exactly what happened to the children of Israel in Exodus Chapter 5. Pharaoh increased the amount of work required of the Israelites by refusing to give them straw. We should also not be surprised if the client, his family, and friends blame us for these increased problems just as the children of Israel did when they blamed Moses and Aaron.

The judgments and miracles of God in Egypt represent this type of confrontation with the world's system. As I have noted below, each was a specific challenge to one or more of the gods of Egypt. (See Missler, 2000)

1. Aaron cast down his rod and it became a snake. The Egyptians magicians also cast down their rods and they became snakes, but Aaron's snake swallowed up their snakes. The cobra was the symbol of Egyptian sovereignty. The snake is also the symbol of Satan and sin. This sign demonstrated that the authority and power of Christ (the rod) is greater than that of world and Satan (the magician's rods). The effectiveness of Christian counseling today demonstrates that the power and methods of Christ are greater than the secular theories and methods of the world.

2. <u>When Aaron struck the Nile River with his rod it turned to blood killing all of the fish in the river</u>. The Egyptians worshipped the Nile as the source of life. Osiris, the chief god of the Nile River, was one of the most respected gods of Egypt. Those who worship the god of this world will find out that the world's life only results in the death of the very things they need most in their lives (the fish). The world cannot and will not truly meet the client's needs. Nonetheless, worldly people (the Egyptians) usually just ignore their own selfish ways and see their struggles as just a natural part of life; not a clear indication of their need for God.

3. <u>The land was covered with frogs</u>. One of the chief goddesses of the land was Hekt, the wife of the "creator of the world." She was represented by a frog. Egypt's worship of frogs prevented them from destroying the frogs that polluted the land. I believe the frogs stand for the dishonorable habits and the addictions of life. The world uses its addictions and habits as a way of coping with life. All of us agree that these habits and addictions make life stink and that the world is not capable or completely willing to eradicate them. The frogs that remained in the river show that as long as the client relies on the god of this world, he will not escape his addictions. It is interesting to note that even many secular addiction therapy programs today use Alcoholics Anonymous' 12-step program. This treatment process was originally derived from biblical principles because most other secular therapy programs are less effective. Unfortunately today, reliance on Jesus Christ has been replaced with a "higher power" in order to appeal to our secular society.

4. <u>The dust became lice on man and beast</u>. What the King James Bible translates as "lice" were most probably sand flies. (Missler, 2000) Since these sand flies came from the soil, they were a great embarrassment to Geb, the Egyptian god of the earth, to whom the Egyptians gave offerings for the bounty of the soil. Man was created from the dust. Man has no answers to explain his origin and the end of life, but the question bothers man like sand flies or lice bothered the Egyptians and beasts in the Bible story. It is almost impossible to get rid of these thoughts about life and death. Evolution, which is a poor theory without reasonable support, is man's best attempt to address this question. This is the first miracle to which the Egyptians had no answer, and the client must see that, without God, he does not have an answer either.

5. <u>The swarms afflicted the Egyptians</u>. These were probably the scarab beetle. Amon-Ra, the king of the Egyptian gods, had the head of a beetle. These swarms stand for the evil and selfish deeds of others that afflict every person and society in the world. They did not bother the Israelites living in the land of Goshen, which means "drawing near." Christians who draw near to God through faith are set free from their selfishness and evil deeds and are protected from the deeds of others. If they will turn to God for help, God is able to deliver the client from evil just as He took away the swarms of flies from the Egyptians when they asked for help.

6. <u>The flocks were destroyed in Egypt</u>. Apis was the bull god and Hathor was the cow-headed goddess of the deserts. These gods were so prominent that the Israelites later made a golden calf in the wilderness to represent the gods of Egypt. The wealth and resources of the world are destroyed by catastrophes and problems like plagues, earthquakes, famines, and floods; but Christians who draw near to God (live in Goshen) are delivered.

7. <u>The ashes of the furnace became boils upon man and beast</u>. This was a challenge to Thoth, the god of intelligence and medical learning. It was the custom of the priests to throw the ashes of their human sacrifices into the air, which would be carried by the wind over the worshippers. These boils stand for the shame that results from sin. It brings inner pain and results in the ego defenses constructed by all sinners. The Christian who draws near to God (lives in Goshen) receives forgiveness, not condemnation and toxic shame. The only hope for dealing with toxic shame is the change received through confession and accepting the forgiveness provided by the death of Christ on the cross. A sinner can even feel conviction by just being in the presence of righteous people.

8. <u>The hail killed all men and beasts that did not take shelter</u>. Egypt was sunny without much rain. Where were Shu the wind god and Nut the sky god that should have protected them? This hail represents God's judgment on the earth for sin. Even the sinner can take heed of the warnings and choose to escape judgment by accepting Christ, or he will eventually be judged for his sin.

9. <u>The locusts brought by the East wind devoured all the good things of Egypt</u>. The locusts were a challenge to Nepri, the grain god, Ermutet, the goddess of crops, and Anubis, the jackal-headed guardian of the fields. These stand for the problems of life (the devourer of Malachi Chapter three) that are inevitable and which devour the client's blessings. God alone can heal and protect the client from life's problems, as He did for the Israelites that lived in the land of Goshen.

10. <u>A thick darkness covered Egypt for three days</u>. The thick darkness was a challenge to Ra, the god of the sun, Aten, the sun's disc, Ankh, the symbol of life from the sun, Horus, the god of the sunrise, Tem, the god of the sunset, and Shu, the god of light. The world does not have any true purpose or direction for life. It cannot predict the future, and its knowledge is so limited that it is truly darkness. If the client tries to direct his own life, he will stumble and will be unable to accomplish anything of eternal significance.

11. <u>The death of the firstborn of Egypt</u>. The fact that the firstborn were killed on a night with a full moon was a challenge to Thoth, the moon god. (*Moses and the Gods of Egypt*, Wade Cox, 2000) The world has no answer for eternity and life after death . The Egyptians built huge monuments and mummified their leaders in order to provide for life after death. All die eternally, except for those saved because of Christ and His blood sacrifice for sins. When the bitterness of death comes to the firstborn of the world, the need for salvation and eternal life becomes most apparent. How many have been led to the Lord with the question, "If you died tonight, would you go to heaven?" Possibly this miracle was also in retribution for all the sons of Israel that the Egyptians had ordered to be killed in their effort to subjugate the Israelites.

12. <u>The victory over Pharaoh through the miracles and the Red Sea</u>. The final sign is that Pharaoh (Satan) and his forces could not follow the Israelites through the Red Sea, which stands for baptism. When an individual decides to follow Christ, trusts in His power and submits the direction of his life to God, he will be delivered from all the power of Satan.

Building Faith in the Wilderness

<u>The third job of the Christian counselor is to help the client build faith, as they pass through the wilderness</u>. The newly saved person who still knows little about spiritual warfare, Christian principles and faith is extremely vulnerable to spiritual attack. It is in the wilderness that the client is led by his circumstances to rely on God, build faith and die to self. The Greek word *parakaleo* means "to come along side of, or to console." It is also the word for "comforter" which is used to refer to the Holy Spirit (the Chief Counselor). In Exodus Chapter 13, it is made clear that God took the children of Israel through the wilderness to prepare them for spiritual warfare.

> Ex 13:17. And it came to pass, when Pharaoh had let the people go, that God led them not [through] the way of the land of the Philistines, although that [was] near; for God said, Lest peradventure the people repent when they see war, and they return to Egypt:
>
> 18 But God led the people about, [through] the way of the wilderness of the Red sea: and the children of Israel went up harnessed out of the land of Egypt.

In the verses that follow in the scriptures, we see the presence of God manifested in the cloud by day and the pillar of fire by night. The first step in the process of salvation occurs in baptism and was symbolized when the children of Israel passed through the Red Sea. Baptism is an outward manifestation of the inward commitment of the client to die to self, separate from the world, and look for God to direct his life.

Although baptism is essential to the process of salvation, it is many times neglected in the Christian counseling process. Moses commanded the children of Israel in Exodus 14:13 "Fear ye not, stand still, and see the salvation of the LORD."

To the extent that the new convert is still overly dependent on himself, others, and/or the world, and is not willing to forsake his sin and die to himself (as is typified by baptism), he is still an idolater or, in the language of recovery, a codependent. This term and its biblical application will be discussed in more detail in later chapters as one of the complex problems blocking salvation or wholeness. All of the children of Israel struggled with this problem of codependence due to their experiences as slaves in Egypt. Everyone is codependent and will manifest codependent symptoms to the degree they still excessively rely on the world to meet their needs. Problems relating to relationships with codependents account for much of the interpersonal conflict in the church. It is the counselor's job to come along side the codependent, allow him to learn from his own choices and consequences, and help him develop enough faith to enter God's "land of promises." This is no easy task. Moses and Aaron became extremely frustrated as they attempted to lead the children of Israel through the wilderness. Let us see what we can learn about this part of the salvation process.

1. Clients must appropriate for themselves what Christ did on the cross. The waters of Marah were bitter. They were made sweet when Moses cast a tree into the water. The tree represents the cross of Christ. The client must apply Christ's crucifixion to his life, which will bring forgiveness and make it sweet. Simply having our spirit saved is not enough. Our flesh must be "crucified with Christ." Continuing to try to meet our own basic needs in our own strength will only make life bitter.

2. Clients can only escape the problems of life by trusting God to heal them. In Exodus 15:26, God declares himself as "the LORD that healeth thee." He promised that if the Israelites would obey, He would put none of the diseases of the Egyptians upon them. As already discussed, the diseases of the Egyptians were not only physical illnesses, but also the psychological consequences of trying to meet their needs through the world which has no answers.

3. To have the abundant life, clients must accept God's government of their life by making Jesus their Lord or boss, not just their Savior. At Elim the Israelites found 12 wells of water and 70 palm trees. Elim means "palms," which stands for radiant believers living under austere conditions (Wilson, p. 476) The number 12 stands for the government of God, and the number 70 stands for God's complete provision in Christ. God limits Himself in His ability to help those who refuse to completely submit themselves to Him, because they will not obey His directions.

4. They must learn to trust God for all their needs even in hard times. God provided the manna in the wilderness. The Israelites complained that what they ate in Egypt under slavery was better than what they were getting in the wilderness. For most clients there is a time of having a pity-party or acting as victims when they remember the pleasures of sin—their old coping mechanisms and addictions. The counselor must help them find Christ Who is the true manna that will always be available in the wildernesses of life and which truly satisfies the soul. They must learn to desire the spiritual feeding of the Word daily in order to develop the faith necessary to come into even greater provisions of the promises of God (the land of Canaan).

5. Client must learn to use God's authority to meet their needs. Moses smote the rock in Horeb and water came out. Complaining in the desert (Horeb) of life is not the answer. When clients ask if "the Lord is among us or not," they must be taught to use God's authority (rod) to retrieve water (life) from the rock that was smote (Christ). Getting needs met though Christ must become a reality. Many times clients will fail to do their part by not using the authority given to them by Christ.

6. The war between the flesh and the Spirit must be won. The decision to choose the spiritual answer instead of the fleshly one is critical. In Exodus 22, in the battle with Amalek (the flesh), Joshua (Jesus) had to do the fighting, but the battle was determined when Aaron (the counselor and the person's

intellect) and Hur (the person's spirit) held up Moses' hand which held the rod of authority. Jesus has already won the victory over the flesh, but it must be worked out in the client's life by the constant correct use of God's authority (the rod) assisted by his right mental choices (with counselor's inputs) and his reliance on the Holy Spirit. We are warned that although God (Jehovah-Nissi) has promised to lead us in the battle against Amalek (the flesh), this battle will continue to be fought "from generation to generation." We should be encouraged that God promises us the final victory in that He "will utterly put out the remembrance of Amalek (the flesh) from under heaven" when we are received into His heavenly kingdom. (Exodus 17:14)

7. <u>Clients must be led and directed by the Holy Spirit</u>. This, of course, requires that they learn to discern the direction of the Holy Spirit. In Exodus Chapter 23, God states that He will send his angel or messenger to lead the children of Israel into the Promised Land. We are told that God's method of change is slow, rather than fast. Transformation occurs as we replace our old ways of coping with the new spiritual ways of meeting our innermost needs. The Holy Spirit is not in a hurry during this process.

    Ex 23:29 I will not drive them out from before thee in one year; lest the land become desolate, and the beast of the field m-ultiply against thee.

    30 By little and little I will drive them out from before thee, until thou be increased, and inherit the land.

8. <u>God's first method of motivation is the law</u>. Clients must get to know God's law as a mirror to convict of sin, not as a solution to life's problems. In it, Christians will find God's directions for living a good life and the fact that, without faith, they are powerless to obey the law. They must learn that they can be saved only through God's grace and power. When Moses delivered the law, they all agreed to obey it. However, as soon as they felt let down by God (Moses was gone 40 days), they quickly returned to the gods of Egypt. Unfortunately, so did Aaron, our model counselor. **We, as Christian counselors must be careful that our own codependency and need to be successful does not lead us to return to worldly solutions for our clients!**

9. <u>God's second method of motivation is allowing clients to learn from the consequences of their decisions</u>. In order to learn, clients must be allowed to make their own choices and reap the associated consequences. Options, not advice, should be given. The children of Israel had returned to worshipping the gods of Egypt by making the golden calf. Moses broke the tablets of the law, confronting them with the fact that they had broken the law by making and worshipping the golden calf. He made them drink the powder of their idol after he had the gold the calf was made of burned, ground up and sprinkled into their drinking water. Three thousand men were killed by the Levites, they were filled with shame because of their nakedness and they now faced the possibility of being separated from God. Neither Moses nor Aaron attempted to protect them from these consequences. Finally, Moses entreated God asking that His presence would again accompany them to the Promised Land. In the same way, we as counselors are to allow our clients to face their own consequences for their sins but continue to reassure them of God's forgiveness for their sins, His unconditional love, and His acceptance.

10. <u>God's third method of motivation is judgment</u>. If clients will not learn from their consequences, eventually more direct discipline from God will be required. Clients must learn that continually lusting after worldly things brings judgment. In Numbers Chapter 11, the children of Israel began lusting for meat like they used to have when they lived in Egypt. God gave them more than they could possibly eat, but along with it came a plague that killed so many that the place was named Kibrothhattaavah, which means "the grave of lust."

11. <u>The counselor must be careful not to take sides with his clients prematurely</u>. This is especially important if the issue is with a husband, wife, pastor or elder. The Bible warns never to judge something before hearing both sides (Proverbs 18:13) and that an accusation against an elder or pastor must be substantiated by at least two or three witnesses (1 Timothy 5:19). In Numbers Chapter 12, Aaron took sides with Miriam against the Ethiopian woman whom Moses had married. Miriam became leprous and Aaron had to appeal to Moses to ask God for her healing.

12. <u>Without faith the giants of life cannot be overcome, and God's promises cannot be claimed</u>. The consequence of not developing a strong faith in God is dying in the wilderness without appropriating God's abundant life here on earth. In Numbers 13, the ten spies (human infirmity) reported that the Promised Land was desirable, but that the giants in the land could not be defeated. Only Joshua and Caleb had enough faith in God to desire to enter the land of Canaan (low self-image) and drive out the giants (psychological problems). How many people in our churches have settled for a life in the wilderness, because they did not develop the faith to believe the promises of God and deal with their problems? Other attempts of clients to find their own way in life (like the children of Israel who tried to take the land without faith) are destined to fail again and again as clients are defeated by the flesh (the Amalekites) and the problems associated with their low self-image (the Canaanites).

Dying in the Wilderness

<u>The fourth job of the Christian counselor is to help those who have chosen, due to a lack of faith, to live as carnal Christians (in the wilderness)</u>. Clients must learn, through the consequences of their own decisions, to put off the immediate gratification offered by sin (die to self). This includes learning to deal with issues such as church splits, conflicts with church authorities, divorces and generational sin. These clients usually come to counseling only when life becomes unbearable and stay only long enough to get a little relief. Fortunately, even some of these clients can eventually find the faith to come out of the wilderness.

As the account of the children of Israel continues, we can clearly identify additional counseling principles for dealing with problems associated with unbelief.

1. <u>The counselor must help clients deal with forgiving others and themselves</u>. In Numbers 15, Moses was directed to provide specific sacrifices to make atonement for the sins that had been committed. Aaron was to assist with guilt sacrifices, just as the counselor is to assist clients in dealing with their guilt and shame through the forgiveness of sins, which was purchased by Jesus Christ. Those who were defiant were to be cut off from the congregation, just as those who refuse to repent, are to be excluded from the church.

2. <u>Through prayer, counselors should try to minimize the damage caused by rebellion</u>. In Numbers Chapter 16, Korah challenged Moses' and Aaron's leadership, and consequently, he and his followers were swallowed up by the earth. Moses and Aaron pleaded with the Lord not to consume the whole assembly, and Aaron took a censor (containing incense which represents prayer) among the congregation to stop the plague after 14,700 of the Israelites had been killed.

3. <u>If challenged, the counselor should allow the results of his counseling to speak as the proof of his anointing</u>. It is not necessary or desirable for us as counselors to defend our calling if we are challenged by clients. It is the client's choice to come to us, just as it was the Israelite's choice to follow Moses and Aaron. Many of these challenges to authority are the result of transference and should be dealt with directly by addressing the real issues. If we are an effective counselor called by God, the results of our work will validate our calling. The counselor must avoid the trap of trying to please clients instead of doing what is best for them. Aaron's rod budded, proving that he was chosen by God to do his calling. (Numbers 17:8) In extreme cases, when the client is very uncooperative, referral to another counselor is always an option.

4. <u>The counselor must closely follow the directions that God has given and not deviate from them</u>. In Numbers Chapter 20, at Meribah, instead of speaking to the rock, out of frustration Moses struck the rock (Christ) twice to produce water. Even though the technique worked before and it did produce the needed water, both Moses and Aaron were judged for their disobedience and were not allowed to enter the Promised Land. They did not trust God's direction about the method to use to meet the needs of the Israelites. **Using our own methods instead of what God directs us to do, even if our methods produce some success, will result in our own judgment for disobedience.**

5. <u>Counselors must avoid burnout through trusting God with their caseload</u>. If we, as counselors, believe that we are responsible for the recovery of the people that we counsel, if we try to fix them, or if we try to make their recovery happen in our own strength; we will eventually burn out and become as frustrated as Moses and Aaron. As counselors, we are warned to avoid getting frustrated with our clients, especially if this frustration leads us to try to do things our own way. **Because of this frustration, Moses and Aaron were not able to personally lead the Israelites into the Promised Land.**

6. <u>Faith in Christ is to be used to deal with impatience which eventually leads to sin and judgment</u>. In Numbers Chapter 21, rather than fight against Edom their brother, Israel was directed to take a longer way around Edom's territory. Because of impatience (wanting immediate need gratification), Israel sinned and was plagued by snakes (which represent sin). Impatience results in trying to make things happen our way, and this results in sin. The Israelites complained that they would die in the desert (God would not save them), that there was no bread (worldly pleasure), that there was no water (spiritual life), and that they detested the manna (the Word of God). These are symptoms of faithlessness. God's answer was to direct them to again put their faith in Christ (represented by the bronze snake on the pole, since Christ took our sins upon Himself). Consequently, we must direct the client to again place his faith in Christ when he becomes impatient and turns to sin in order to meet his needs.

7. <u>Contention must be decisively dealt with in relationships and in the church</u>. Contention must be resolved through counseling, or it will infect the church and destroy unity. The Moabites (lust) enlisted Midian (contention) to tempt the Israelites to commit fornication and worship Baal-Peor. Only the decisive action by Phinehas in Numbers Chapter 25 saved the Israelites from the consequences of their fornication, which had already resulted in the death of 24,000 Israelites.

8. <u>Support groups are important in the church as places of refuge for hurting people</u>. In Numbers Chapter 34, six towns were set aside to protect those who had accidentally killed someone. In the church, we need places of refuge from the abuse of the world. I believe that this is one of the most important functions of care groups and support groups in the church.

Entering the Promised Land

<u>The fifth job of the Christian counselor is to help clients defeat the psychological giants in their lives and appropriate the promises of God by faith</u>. I believe that the names of the tribes of the land of Canaan represent the major complex psychological problems that each of us may face to one degree or another in our lives. Through an understanding of the meanings of these Hebrew names, it is possible to identify the psychological problems associated with each. In a way, this is the biblical counterpart of the Diagnostic and Statistical Manual of Mental Disorders (DSM IV) used in secular psychology to categorize mental problems. Reginald Klimionok has made a good attempt at these meanings, but not as they relate to underlying psychological problems. As an example, he identifies the Amorites as the tongue since the word means "to speak against or boast publicly." I have identified the Amorites, which also means "prominence," as suggesting psychological problems with significance or prominence, which sometimes result in speaking against or boasting. He identifies the Canaanites, which means "lowland," or brought low by traffic or trade, as problems with greed and lust for material goods. I identify the Canaanites as low self-image problems, which

many times result in greed and lust. He identifies the Perizzites as the need for protection. In counseling, these are called "boundary problems." He identifies the Jebusites, which means "treading or trodden down," as condemnation. I suggest it means problems of abusing others, which result in condemnation of self and others. For the Girgashites, which are mentioned later in Joshua, Klimionok suggests backsliding—based on alternate meanings of turning back from a pilgrimage and dwelling on clay or muddy soil. I believe that the implication here is "getting stuck," turning back, or quitting, which in counseling is typified by emotional problems like depression, grief, and attempting suicide.

Except for these specific differences of interpretation that I have just discussed, I agree with Klimionok's suggested types for the remainder of these tribes. Here, to the best of my current understanding, are the giants of the land as they are listed in Exodus Chapter 23:

Ex 23:23 For mine Angel shall go before thee, and bring thee in unto the Amorites (prominence or significance problems), and the Hittites (terror and fear problems), and the Perizzites (problems relating to open country with unwalled towns or a lack of boundaries), and the Canaanites (humiliation or self-image problems), the Hivites (problems with life-giving or things we do to try to meet our needs including addictions and intimacy), and the Jebusites (treading down or threshing place, i.e. abusive behavior): and I will cut them off (deliver you from all these problems).

24 Thou shalt not bow down to their gods (be controlled or addicted to these things), nor serve them, nor do after their works: but thou shalt utterly overthrow them, and quite break down their images (false assumptions or lies that cause them)…

The analogy of tribes or organized forces is consistent with the idea that these represent groups of difficult problems, rather than individual disorders. In addition, I agree that spiritual forces take advantage of these psychological problems as suggested by Klimionok (p. 20). The psychological and the spiritual are so interwoven that all psychological problems probably have a spiritual component (Bufford, 1988, p. 51).

Because the Diagnostic and Statistical Manual of Mental Disorders (DSM IV, 1994) is the most recognized secular method for categorizing psychological problems, I will compare it to this biblical list of psychological giants. First, I believe that the biblical list is more general and includes a broad spectrum of common problems and dysfunctions as well as mental disorders. Conceptually DSM IV only addresses mental disorders (or mental illness). The categories of DSM IV have been empirically derived and have been significantly influenced by societal pressure and what is considered politically correct.

1. Amorites (prominence or significance problems)—This is what I call codependent independence. It results in excessive drive, performance self-worth, people pleasing, arrogance, pride, workaholism, imperativeness, desire for worldly prominence and rescuing. Because our society is so driven by a desire for prominence, this problem is not even identified in DSM IV as a psychological disorder. Some of the symptoms of prominence appear in the Histrionic and Narcissistic Personality Disorders.

2. Hittites (fear)—This is the basis of phobias of all types, anxiety disorders, panic attacks, shyness and withdrawal from relationships. Codependent avoidance is my recovery term for this disorder. When this problem becomes extreme, it is called Avoidant Personality Disorder in DSM IV. Other problems with fear are categorized as anxiety disorders, panic disorders, adjustment disorders and other types of personality disorders.

3. Perizzites (boundary problems)—This is classical codependent dependence with its people pleasing, inability to confront problems, staying in abusive situations, depression, angry outbursts, and enabling. When extreme, this problem sometimes results in Dependence Personality Disorder in DSM IV.

4. Canaanites (lowland or self-image problems)—This is low self-image that leads to passivity, codependency, addictions and dysfunctional relationships of all types. Low self-image is categorized as

"Problems Related to Abuse and Neglect," but may also be listed under almost all other areas because self-worth problems underlie most other problems.

5. <u>Hivites</u> (life-giving desires or lusts of the flesh)—This includes all addictions especially those relating to eating, intimacy and lust such as chemical dependency, alcoholism, eating addictions, romance addiction, relationship addiction, sexual addiction, and homosexuality. In DSM IV, these kinds of problems fall under substance abuse, sexual and gender disorders, and eating disorders. Homosexuality is not listed as a mental disorder in DSM IV.

6. <u>Jebusites</u> (to tread down, reject, trample down)—This includes all forms of control and abusive behavior including verbal, emotional, sexual, and physical abuse as well as domestic violence. Possibly the most appropriate category in DSM IV is Impulse Control Disorders and problems related to abuse or neglect. The only clear mental disorder identified by DSM IV in this area is Intermittent Explosive Disorder.

7. <u>Girgashites</u> (to be stuck in the mud or to turn back)—This includes all forms of emotional problems; especially depression, grief, and suicide. DSM IV lists these under mood disorders or bereavement.

God promised that the Spirit of Christ would go before the Israelites (Christians) and cut off all these problems from their lives. In the verses that follow, it is clear that this is to be done in a progression of victories by faith over time. All the land on which their feet trod was to be theirs, but it had to be taken one step at a time. Kenneth Hagin (1993) suggests that when a Christian is born again, his spirit is saved. The salvation of the soul is then the responsibility of the Christian. My experience is that almost no one is immediately delivered from all of the giants of the Promised Land. Unfortunately, many Christians seem to have missed this progressive plan of God and the reasons behind it, and therefore, expect that salvation will solve all their psychological problems immediately without great effort on their part. God understands that someone who has spent his life coping by worldly means will not immediately trust Him to supply all of his needs. Slowly these dysfunctional coping mechanisms must be replaced with spiritual ones. Faith and spiritual strength must be developed that is equal to the problems to be encountered.

> Ex 23:28 And I will send hornets (stinging or scourge—an inner sting of increasing guilt as we better perceive the holiness of God) before thee, which shall drive out the Hivite, the Canaanite, and the Hittite, from before thee.
>
> 29 I will not drive them out from before thee in one year; lest the land become desolate, and the beast of the field multiply against thee.
>
> 30 By little and little I will drive them out from before thee, until thou be increased, and inherit the land.

But God expects us to take all of the land and, in the end, totally replace our fleshly means with spiritual ones through faith. We are not to compromise with them even in the slightest way or let any remnant of them remain in our lives. If we do, they will cause guilt and shame that will eventually undermine our faith, which is the very basis of our salvation.

> Ex 23:31 And I will set thy bounds from the Red sea even unto the sea of the Philistines, and from the desert unto the river: for I will deliver the inhabitants of the land into your hand; and thou shalt drive them out before thee.
>
> 32 Thou shalt make no covenant with them, nor with their gods.
>
> 33 They shall not dwell in thy land, lest they make thee sin against me: for if thou serve their gods, it will surely be a snare unto thee.

As we prepare to continue our journey of faith into the Promised Land filled with these psychological giants, we must be careful to understand the strategy laid out for our clients and us. The fact that Moses and

Aaron did not accompany the children of Israel into the Promised Land is significant. At this point in the counseling process, clients must take responsibility for their own recovery. This is also clear because upon entering the Promised Land the manna stopped. Consequently, in the remainder of this story we must assume our own responsibility for our choices as we follow our Joshua (Jesus) to victory.

1. <u>We must yield totally to God's plan for taking the Promised Land by faith</u>. Joshua, whose name means "Jesus," is to be our leader. Moses directed the people to obey Joshua completely. His Spirit is to go before us. Joshua was warned in Joshua 1:7 to "turn not from it (God's direction) [to] the right hand or [to] the left, that thou mayest prosper whithersoever thou goest." One of the greatest difficulties in counseling is trying to get the client to decide to do what God requires to resolve the situation. Most clients feel far more secure trying to direct their own lives. Many a client has to be warned that if they keep doing the same thing, they will keep getting the same result.

2. <u>In order to have success, they must meditate day and night on the Word of God</u>. Joshua 1:8 makes this clear, "This book of the law shall not depart out of thy mouth; but thou shalt meditate therein day and night, that thou mayest observe to do according to all that is written therein: for then thou shalt make thy way prosperous, and then thou shalt have good success." The Bible is our main faith builder, and it is the blueprint of our campaign to conquer the Promised Land of complete wholeness and spiritual maturity.

3. <u>An assessment of the strongholds in the clients' lives is essential</u>. An important part in understanding these problems is determining whether clients are truly saved and to what extent they are relying on God to meet their needs. If they have not made a total commitment to follow Jesus (Joshua), they are not qualified to enter the Promised Land. Consequently, a true salvation experience needs to become a priority in the counseling plan. Rahab the harlot, who had faith, was told to put a red string in her window when Jericho was attacked. This stands for the application of the blood of Jesus. Without true salvation, where Jesus is Lord and boss, taking any of the promises of God by faith is impossible.

4. <u>God's method includes experiencing the baptism of the Holy Spirit through faith in order to enter the Promised Land</u>. The children of Israel had to follow the Ark of God through the Jordan River, which divided and backed up to the city of Adam (which stands for our human nature). Although some might disagree, I believe that the crossing through the Jordan River is the baptism of the Holy Spirit, just as crossing through the Red Sea is the baptism by water. My experience is that the baptism of the Holy Spirit equips the Christian for spiritual warfare and makes them more spiritually sensitive. Consequently, those so equipped, are more capable of overcoming the spiritual and psychological giants of the Promised Land. I believe that the Israelites who chose to dwell on the West side of the Jordan represent Christians who choose not to pursue the baptism of the Holy Spirit, but who are still required to fight the psychological giants of the land.

5. <u>Christians must do their part in order to get their needs met through the promises of God in the Promised Land</u>. On entering the Promised Land, the automatic provision of manna stopped. God will not do for us what we can do for ourselves. If He did, He would be enabling us, and God is not a codependent! While in the desert the manna was necessary for survival, but in the land of God's promises, all needs are to be met through faith. The "milk of the Word," manna, was easily available, but now we must learn to do our part and dig deeper into the Word of God (the meat of the Word) and believe its promises in order to meet our deepest needs. As a Christian counselor, we must realize that we cannot give out to our clients more than we have taken in from the Spirit of God. We will end up relying on ourselves instead of the Holy Spirit, and we will eventually "burn out" when our inner supply of the Spirit is exhausted.

6. <u>The flesh and sin must be set aside in order to prepare for the spiritual battle</u>. God commanded that all of the children of Israel (males of course) were to be circumcised, because the generation that grew up in the desert had never been circumcised. According to *Wilson's Dictionary of Bible Types* (1957), circumcision means "the act of reckoning one's self dead unto sin and of laying aside the desires of the flesh." (p. 113) Clients cannot hope to be victorious over psychological giants through the means of the flesh. Counseling can only weaken the flesh, not overcome problems through the flesh. It takes the power of the Spirit to overcome sin and the flesh.

7. <u>The church is God's designated base of operations for the good fight of faith</u>. The first camp for the children of Israel after crossing the Jordan River was Gilgal, which stands for the church. There they were commanded to keep the Passover, which in the New Testament is represented by the Lord's Supper. It was at this time that the manna was cut off, indicating that God expects the church to meet its needs though faith in the promises of God. It was near Gilgal, while scouting Jericho, that Joshua encountered the "Captain of the Hosts of the Lord." (Joshua Chapter 4-5) In the same way, it is in the church that God gives direction for taking the Promised Land. I believe it is extremely clear that the local church is to play a very significant part in God's plan for defeating the psychological giants in the lives of its members.

Conquering Jericho (Fear)

Jericho is the fortress of fear. Consequently, it represents our struggles to overcome the insecurity in our lives. We can verify that the city of Jericho represents fear by the fact that each time the city is mentioned, the people were living in fear. Rahab said that the inhabitants were in fear of the Israelites and that the gates were locked out of fear. (Joshua 2:9, 11, 6:1) The clients' fears are the first formidable challenge. We are later told that all the tribes were represented at Jericho. All sorts of psychological problems make their homes in the client's life based on fear. Probably the best-known types are fear of rejection, fear of failure, fear of shame, and fear of punishment. (McGee, 1990) Phobias, anxiety attacks, some panic attacks, obsessive-compulsiveness, codependency, domestic violence, and most other psychological disorders have their roots in fear.

The basis of overcoming simple fear by faith is outlined in this event:

1. <u>The first step in overcoming fear is to confront it</u>. In preparing to take Jericho, the Israelites marched around it for six days. They were not to speak at all. Negative self-talk and speaking about fear increases the power of fear. Marching around Jericho represents surveying the things that cause fear in our lives from a distance as we build our faith that we can conquer them. Six stands for man's sufficiency. Speaking about or relying on man's sufficiency is the basis of most fears. It takes faith in order to overcome fear. The client must get close enough to the thing that is feared; yet maintain his faith that, with God's help, it will not harm him.

2. <u>To overcome fear, we must trust God to meet our needs</u>. On the seventh day, they encompassed the city seven times. Seven stands for God's complete provision. They had to get to the point where they trusted God's complete provision so much that they were willing to openly declare and act on their faith.

3. <u>They were to confess their faith</u>. They blew on the ram's horn. The ram stands for Christ, the perfect sacrifice. The ram's horn stands for preaching. Faith comes by hearing. They were then to shout, or declare their faith in unison. When they did this, the walls or defenses of fear (Jericho) fell down. When we no longer believe the feared thing can harm us, it is defenseless. Hebrews 11:30 declares that, "By faith the walls of Jericho fell down after they were compassed about seven days."

4. <u>They had to physically occupy the territory of the fear</u>. The battle was not over until they actually killed the enemy and burned the city. Until we actually do the thing that is feared, we do not yet have complete victory.

5. <u>The credit for overcoming fear must go to God</u>. This was the first of ten cities and, as such, its wealth was the first tenth, or tithe. Joshua placed a curse on anyone who took anything from the city. If clients take credit for overcoming their fear, their fear will eventually return. This is because the clients are again relying on themselves. Self-reliance is the root problem underlying fear.

6. <u>The city of fear must never be rebuilt</u>. Joshua cursed anyone who would rebuild this city. The curse was that the children of those who rebuilt the city would die. (Joshua 6:26) Clients bring a curse on their posterity if they rebuild fear in their lives, since fear is transmitted from generation to generation. Unfortunately, this often happens because old patterns of thinking can easily return. (It is interesting to note that the first and last child of Hiel the Bethelite, the man who rebuilt Jericho, died (1 Kings 16:34)).

7. <u>Only those with faith will not be destroyed by fear</u>. Rahab, alone, was not destroyed with the people of Jericho. She believed that the Israelites would take Jericho. We need to believe that with God's help we can defeat all fear in our lives. (Hebrews 11:31 lists Rahab as one of the heroes of faith.)

If we take a close look at these events, we find the basis for a method for confronting fears that has been called systematic desensitization. It is possibly the most effective method of behavior modification for dealing with fear. First, the client is taught how to relax. Relaxation helps to alleviate fear. Because most persons cannot be relaxed and afraid at the same time, tension can also be used as an indicator of fear. Usually, clients are progressively exposed to fearful scenes in their minds in a hierarchical order (as they are able to remain relaxed and to overcome each fearful scene.) In this way, the client is slowly conditioned to be able to tolerate the feared stimulus. Finally, each of these situations is experienced in the same order in real life until clients can face even the most fearful situation that they can imagine. (Comer, 1995) When we examine the process of systematic desensitization, we find that it is no more than slowly developing faith that the feared situation can be overcome.

Secular systematic desensitization can only go so far. It can only help people with irrational fears. With faith in God, all worldly fears can be overcome; because we trust in His protection. My experience is that helping clients build a realistic faith in God, in combination with systematic desensitization, produces outstanding results in overcoming all fears and anxieties.

In dealing with generalized anxiety or anxiety attacks, faith in God is essential. The lies that clients believe need to be disputed and replaced with the truth. They do not live in a world which is dangerous and where everything goes wrong, but in a world where God works everything for their good (Romans 8:28). The confrontation of specific fears must be planned and carried out. The longer clients avoid their fears, the greater they grow.

If clients are experiencing panic attacks, both a renewed faith in God and dealing with the specific lies they believe is required. In most cases, a panic attack is triggered by some fear. The fear causes a physical response such as an increased heart rate. Clients focus on the physical symptoms and convince themselves that something is seriously wrong. This causes increased fear that in turn increases the physical symptoms until clients are convinced they have a very serious condition. At this point, many clients hyperventilate which causes them to feel faint. The cycle continues until they are convinced they are going to choke, faint, or die. Many persons subject to panic attacks are very suggestible and have irrational beliefs that trigger the attacks. Some of the lies they believe are that if their heart beats too fast they will have a heart attack, if they eat something they will choke, or because they are committing a particular sin they are going to go to hell. Helping them to quit hyperventilating, relax, and confront these lies with the truth usually brings rapid results.

Obsessive-compulsiveness is an attempt to feel in control when clients are actually feeling powerless. By concentrating on the problem or worrying and obsessing about it, clients do initially feel more in control. However, the more they obsesses about the problem the more serious it seems and, therefore, the more they need to concentrate on it to feel in control. Compulsiveness is an associated strategy in which clients concentrate on a particular repetitive action that they can control, in order to feel in control. Sometimes clients may have a fear that if they do not do a specific action something catastrophic is going to happen. The Bible directs that instead of worrying we are to trust God and pray. (Philipians 4:6) Compulsions must be confronted in the same way as other fears. When clients do what they fear and consequences do not result, they will gradually overcome them.

Overcoming Ai (Shame)

Ai was one of the most insignificant Canaanite cities. It means "heap of ruins." The word Canaanite means "low land" and represents our evaluation of ourselves. Here Ai represents the ruins of our lives due to sin, or our shame. It is one of the keys to the problem of low self-image. Guilt or shame, when not properly dealt with, turns to toxic shame. It changes from "I did a bad thing" to "I am a bad person." When Achan chose to take the gold and garments from Jericho, he did a bad thing. When he chose to hide them in his tent (ego defenses), his sin became part of him. He was relying on himself to meet his needs instead of God. The battle of Ai gives us the strategy for overcoming toxic shame, which, as we will see later, is the basis of addictions and codependency.

1. <u>Sin in the camp must die. We must repent of our life of sin</u>. Achan means "trouble" and that is exactly what sin brings us. As long as we choose to try to meet our own needs, our sin will cause our own defeat as it did for the Israelites at Ai. We cannot hide sin and defeat low self-worth (the Canaanites) at the same time. Achan sinned by taking some of the spoil of Jericho, and because he refused to deal with his sin and hid it, he was destroyed by it. Just as the Israelites were in fear of the other tribes because of their defeat at Ai, so shame makes it impossible for us to stand before or deal with the other psychological enemies in our lives.

2. <u>The shame must be drawn out and exposed</u>. Israel drew the soldiers of Ai away from the city and overthrew it with an ambush. The ambush that God has provided for us in order to defeat shame is the cross of Christ, which provides the forgiveness for every one of our sins. Jesus took our shame upon Himself. It is our job to admit our sins, accept His forgiveness, and trust Him to take away our shame.

3. <u>The entire city or foundation of shame must be destroyed</u>. The Israelites completely burned the city. In the same way, we must totally destroy our shame and the worldly evaluation of ourselves that is based on toxic shame. Our evaluation of ourselves based on our past actions must be exposed as a lie. It must be burned completely and replaced with our position in Christ and what Christ has done for us. The King of Ai, who I believe stands for pride (the defense of those struggling with low self-worth and shame), was hung on a tree and buried under a monument at the city gate. In the same way, our pride and shame are to die forever and be replaced with God's evaluation of us according to faith.

4. <u>Accomplishments and capabilities developed to overcome shame can be used for our good</u>. The cattle and spoil of the city were taken for use by the Israelites. Those struggling with low self-worth and shame are many times motivated to be over-achievers who accomplish and learn many things. These capabilities and the things that have been accomplished in a futile attempt to build a low self-image can still be used as a blessing.

5. <u>We must always be on guard against rebuilding shame</u>. Ai was to remain in desolation forever. We must be careful to confront and confess our sin and deal with it as soon as it is detected. Toxic shame, the result of hiding our guilt, must never be allowed to develop again. Pride must never be allowed again in our lives.

Subjugating Gibeon (Selfish Desire)

After dealing with fear and shame, we must confront our life-giving desires that we believe are the very basis of our lives. The name Hivite means "villager" from a root word meaning "life-giving or living place." Therefore I suggest that these are the things that we think improve the quality of our lives, make us feel better, help us cope more effectively with life, or meet our needs for love and acceptance. Because many of them (like drugs, alcohol, sex, and romance) do initially energize us and make us feel better they can easily lead to lust or an inordinate desire for them. They look like friends but are actually enemies because they divert us from the things of God that truly bring life. In the long run they lead to sin and death. This is made clear in James Chapter 1:

Jas 1:14 But every man is tempted, when he is drawn away of his own lust, and enticed.

15 Then when lust hath conceived, it bringeth forth sin: and sin, when it is finished, bringeth forth death.

The story of the subjugation of Gibeon seems confusing until we realize that Gibeon was a city of the Hivites, which stands for our deepest selfish, life-giving desires. It is clear that the complete destruction of Gibeon was God's perfect will. Instead, the Israelites were tricked into making an alliance with it. Unfortunately, very few Christians have been able to totally eradicate all of their deepest selfish desires and completely trust God to direct every aspect of their lives. These desires are so crafty that they look to most of us as something that God desires for us. We see this played out in the story of the subjugation of Gibeon beginning in Joshua Chapter 9.

1. <u>Our deepest selfish desires, sexual passions, and lusts are really our enemies</u>. They are under the influence of our flesh and, as such, are incapable of bringing life and carrying out the will of God. The inhabitants of Gibeon, who were Hivites (selfish life-giving desires), sent ambassadors to Israel. These ambassadors craftily deceived the Israelites into making a treaty with them. Gibeon means "feller of trees." Trees in the Bible often stand for men. Without doubt, selfish desires have caused the fall of many men. Our selfish desires fool us by making us think that they are no real threat to us and are something to be desired to meet our needs.

2. <u>We must submit our deepest desires to God</u>. The mistake of the Israelites was that they did not inquire of God before making a treaty with the people of Gibeon. Our desires have the same excuse that the Gibeonites had—they do not want to die. The Gibeonites even came to Gilgal, which represents the church. Unfortunately, many in the church have been fooled into making these deep selfish desires an ally without recognizing the danger or consulting with God. Lust is really unlimited, selfish, life-giving desire. Lust must be controlled and transformed into unselfish love, or it will lead to sin and spiritual death.

3. <u>Life-giving desires are subjugated by limiting their activities through boundary agreements</u>. Although God's original plan was the complete replacement of wrong desires with His will through faith, it is possible to subjugate these desires and use them for good. Because very few clients are anywhere near spiritual maturity, the counselor must many times settle for the subjugation of the client's desires. This is the establishment of self-boundaries. The Gibeonites agreed to become hewers of wood (Christian activities) and drawers of water (spiritual life) for the sanctuary. In the same way, the Christian is to limit his deepest desires to doing only the will of God and for the use of the Church.

4. <u>These desires must be turned into unselfish love and obedience</u>. The Gibeonites became loyal followers of God, and so can our desires. During the time of David, because Saul mistreated the Gibeonites; a famine came on the land. We also can learn to subjugate even sexual lust into a giving, loving marital relationship. Self-boundaries must be set on thought-life, fantasies, and sexual acting-out.

5. <u>We must defend our desires from the attack of prominence</u>. Probably one of the most insidious attacks on our selfish desires is the drive for prominence (Amorites). In Joshua Chapter 10, the five Amorite kings rose up to destroy the Gibeonites, because they had lost a strong ally. This is a victory that must be won, otherwise desires, which have been subjugated, will rise again as a multitude of lusts, leading to sin and ultimately spiritual death.

Defeating the Amorites (Prominence)

One of our basic psychological needs is our need for significance. This is not to be confused with our need for self-worth. Self-worth has to do with intrinsic value while significance has to do with our success in using that potential. In the world, prominence is the general measure of how significant others see us. The world is motivated by this desire for prominence. Almost anything will be done to achieve prominence. The "rat race" of life itself is based on the unlimited lust for more, fueled by a search for prominence in life. Our fleshly drive for prominence wants to take over our desires, which in the past have been strong allies. At stake in this battle with the Amorite kings (prominence) were the towns of Jerusalem (peace), Hebron (relationships), Jarmuth (worth), Lachish (invincibility), and Eglon (vigor). We must defeat the temptation to pursue our own prominence if we are to have peace, have healthy relationships, feel worthwhile, obtain the invincibility that only comes from God, and vigorously pursue the Kingdom of God. The real question is, are we going to trust God to meet our deepest desires or are we going to attempt to meet them through achieving prominence in this world through the flesh? The strategy for victory over prominence is this:

1. <u>We, as Christians, must recognize the threat of the drive for prominence in our lives</u>. This threat is revealed through our desires. The Gibeonites (life-giving desires) sent word to the camp at Gilgal that they were being attacked by the Amorites (drive for prominence). Every time we feel a desire to be first, best, or overly competitive, we should recognize the attack of prominence. Pride and selfishness are also clear signs of attack. Because many of us have been fooled into thinking that a desire for prominence is normal, the attack goes undetected, and our deepest desires are again made our enemies.

2. <u>The church must swiftly attack the drive for prominence using the Word of God</u>. The children of Israel took the Amorites by surprise and slew them with the sword (the Word of God). In the same way, the Word of God shows us that our desire for prominence is wrong and leads us to submit to God's plan of obedience and humility.

3. <u>God will judge our desire for prominence through consequences</u>. The Bible tells us that pride comes before a fall. (Proverbs 16:18) Eventually, everyone will reach the top of their ability and be forced to accept their human limitations. God used hailstones (judgment) to kill more of the escaping armies than those killed by the Israelites. The long-term consequences of our drive for prominence will eventually bring us to our knees if we refuse to let God deal with it. Jesus said that if we want to be great in the Kingdom of God we must be the servants of all. (Mark 9:35)

4. <u>If we ask and truly desire His help, God will even supernaturally suspend nature itself in order to assist us in this fight with prominence</u>. When Joshua took the authority given to him by God and commanded the sun and the moon to stop, they stopped their movement for an entire day in order to provide additional time to defeat the Amorites. (Joshua 10:12, 13) Probably **the most important part of this battle to overcome prominence is reaching a point where we completely submit ourselves to God's rule in our lives and desire only to please Him. Then He will "move heaven and earth" on our behalf.**

Taking the Remaining Land (Worldly Wisdom)

Once our fear, shame, selfish desires, and drive for prominence are defeated; our most significant enemies remain in our mind or intellect.

1. <u>We must recognize that our mind is the battlefield for overcoming most psychological enemies</u>. King Jabin (intellect) of Hazor (enclosure or castle) gathered all the enemies of the Israelites to the waters of Merom, which means "elevation." Intellectualism protected by closed-mindedness unites the remaining psychological enemies of self-pity (Jobab), strife (Madon), lack of motivation (Shimron), control (Achshaph), low self-worth (Canaanites), prominence (Amorites), fear (Hittites), boundary problems (Perizzites), abuse (Jebusites), and lust (Hivites).

2. <u>We Christians are not to be afraid of intellectual arguments or of challenging our intellectual assumptions</u>. Since the assumptions of life provide our worldview and our security, we seldom want to challenge our long-held assumptions. This is especially true of those premises of life held in our subconscious mind. Joshua was told not to be afraid of these enemies, but that God would deliver them into his hands slain. (Joshua 10:6)

3. <u>God's wisdom must be chosen over man's wisdom for the direction of our lives</u>. The battle was to be fought at the waters of Merom, which means "elevated." Man takes pride in his thoughts and intellectual achievements and thinks that they make him higher than others. We must decide to base our lives on God's wisdom—not man's—and choose to do the will of God instead of our own will.

4. <u>False premises are to be permanently disabled and logical arguments destroyed</u>. Jesus overcame His temptations by quoting the truth from the Word of God. (Luke 4:2-13) Wrong ways of thinking provide the basis of most psychological problems. Even our emotions are controlled by the way we look at situations. Joshua was ordered to hough (disable) the enemies' horses (premises) and to burn their chariots (arguments) to ensure that they would never be used again.

5. <u>The renewing of the mind is to be done quickly and completely</u>. The Israelites "suddenly" attacked the enemies at Merom and completely destroyed them. The Bible tells us that we are to think on good things (Philipians 4:8) and that out of the heart the mouth speaks. (Luke 6:45)

6. <u>Intellectualism and closed-mindedness must be completely destroyed by the Word of God</u>. Joshua then returned to Hazor (closed mindedness) and burned it, after killing King Jabin (intellectualism) with the sword (God's Word).

7. <u>Only worldly knowledge that opposes God's Word must be destroyed</u>. Hazor was burned with fire, but all the cattle were taken as plunder. This battle is not against the knowledge of the world, but the false knowledge of the world that opposes God's truth. The good things produced by intellectual pursuit are to be used for the Christian's good.

8. <u>The struggle for the supremacy of the Word of God over man's wisdom takes a long time</u>. The Bible tells us "Joshua made war a long time with all those kings." (Joshua 11:18) It also tells us that it was God's will that all the tribes of Canaan be completely destroyed.

9. <u>We must destroy all the remaining psychological giants</u>. The final battle was to eliminate the Anakins (giants) remaining in the mountains. I believe that these represent the more difficult and complex problems in each of the areas represented by these tribes. They will be addressed in detail in the following chapters.

10. <u>When the giants are finally eliminated from the land, the blessings of the promises of God are to be given as an inheritance to all</u>. Joshua was ordered to divide the land, allotting a part to each of

the children of Israel. This tells us that all of us will not necessarily receive every blessing, but that God Who "is able to do exceeding abundantly above all that we ask or think..." (Ephesians 3:20) has wonderful blessings awaiting each one of us who is willing to conquer our Promised Land by faith.

11. <u>One of the most important lessons that we must learn is how to fairly maintain personal boundaries</u>. The Israelites were to respect the boundaries that God established for them. Offenses come from violations of healthy boundaries. Without understanding personal boundaries, the commandment to love one another cannot effectively be carried out. In modern terms, we are said to be assertive when we have learned to maintain our own personal boundaries while respecting the boundaries of others.

12. <u>The final blessing is rest, which is the result of spiritual maturity</u>. Our psychological rest is based on our faith that God has and will always meet all of our needs according to His riches in glory. (Philippians 4:19) We can exit the rat race of life as we simply trust, obey and follow Him in all we have been called to do. This does not mean that we will no longer have any struggles, but that, because we are trusting in God for total victory in all we do, we will not be shaken by anything. Joshua 21:44-45 states, "And the LORD gave them rest round about, according to all that he sware unto their fathers: and there stood not a man of all their enemies before them; the LORD delivered all their enemies into their hand. There failed not ought of any good thing which the LORD had spoken unto the house of Israel; all came to pass." This is the fulfillment of our salvation and it is glorious!

As we examine what we have just learned, we can see a basic structure or plan for the conduct of Christian counseling. This model suggests a life-long developmental approach to counseling directed by the Holy Spirit as the Chief Counselor. It is He Who orchestrates the overall process. The client is brought to us so we can help him remove any hindrances to going forward into the next phase of the process of salvation by faith. The use of the narrative approach to teaching psychological truth simplifies the teaching process and continues to build faith in the client that God's truth, the Bible, can be trusted. Reliance on God's plan for salvation for the ultimate healing of the client is, and always will be, essential for long-term and lasting results. The basic steps of this plan are discussed below. I have indicated the origin of each step as they relate to the story of the exodus of the children of Israel in parenthesis. A complete case study using this method of counseling is presented in the last chapter of this book.

1. <u>Determine the problem</u>. (Identify the type of slavery.) While the process begins like most counseling intakes—determining the problem—the remaining steps are contingent on where the client is in his spiritual development. Determining the problem involves asking the client his reason for coming to counseling, gathering background information, analyzing the information, and attempting to fit the pieces of the puzzle together to form a hypothesis concerning the underlying cause. When dealing with complex problems, the counselor should attempt to determine if the problem fits one of the models developed later in this book. The problem of the children of Israel was that they were in slavery and afflicted by the cruel taskmasters of Egypt (the world). Before we are saved, we are the slaves of sin and the world and need to be delivered.

2. <u>Demonstrate that what the client is doing will not meet his needs and build hope that his problems can be overcome through Christ</u>. (Confront the gods of Egypt.) Until the client is convinced that his methods do not work, he will continue to do them and will get similar results. Moses had to demonstrate to Israel that the Egyptian's methods did not work before they were willing to leave Egypt. He also had to demonstrate that God's methods could deliver them from their slavery. I usually try to show my clients that the entire rat race in life makes no sense and that everyone is eventually promoted until they fail. Even all those who get to the top are eventually replaced and what they have accomplished has no lasting significance. In fact, without God, nothing they do will have

lasting value, and they do not have enough information even to attempt to direct their own lives. Life is but a vapor, and only God can make them eternally happy.

3. <u>Use the biblical principles and models to help the client perceive and understand the problem from a biblical perspective.</u> (Understand God's plan and repent.) Few clients will have an in-depth understanding of the problem identified in step one. Consequently, the counselor will need to use Bible principles or a narrative biblical model to help the client understand the problem from a biblical perspective. Moses had to help the Israelites understand that they were the chosen people of God; and that it was God's perfect will for them to live in the land of Canaan, not serve the Egyptian gods in Egypt.

4. <u>Determine where the client is in the process of salvation and, if appropriate, lead him to accept Christ, be baptized, yield the control of his life to God, and help him get established in a church.</u> (Cross the Red Sea.) After determining the problem, the counselor should locate where the client is in the overall plan for his salvation according to the model of the exodus of the children of Israel. The client must be saved, baptized and established in a good church to provide the support and a basis for this process of salvation or wholeness. When counseling someone who is not saved or who has a weak spiritual foundation, these initial four steps are essential. If a client has progressed beyond these steps, we must identify where they are in their spiritual walk in order to determine the next step to take.

5. <u>Help the client take responsibility for his own actions, not blame others or react to what they do, and do everything as unto God.</u> (Quit murmuring.) Most clients come to counseling blaming their parents, past events, or someone or something outside of themselves for the problem, just like the children of Israel did. Many times, they want the counselor to take the responsibility to "fix" them. They must understand that they are responsible for "working out their own salvation" (Philippians 2:12b) and that when they stand before God, He is not going to ask them what someone else did but how they responded to what others did. They must learn to do what is right in spite of what others do. The Israelites had to learn to quit murmuring, stop blaming Moses, and discontinue threatening to return to Egypt.

6. <u>Help the client grow in his personal relationship with Christ and build faith that, with God's help, he can overcome the problem.</u> (Build faith in the wilderness.) It is at this point that the first generation of Israelites, with the exception of Joshua and Caleb, failed. In order to trust God, the client needs to develop a personal relationship with Christ and build faith that God will help him overcome every aspect of his problem and meet all his needs. Without it, the client will not have the faith required to face his complex psychological problems. The client will fail if he tries to rely on himself, fix himself, or meet his own needs through the flesh.

7. <u>Assist the client in receiving the empowerment of the baptism of the Holy Spirit if he chooses to do so.</u> (Cross the Jordan River.) The baptism of the Holy Spirit received at Pentecost empowered the disciples to effectively move into the supernatural realm and trust God beyond anything they had yet experienced. Teen Challenge attributes much of their high success rate in helping to deliver incorrigible addicts from years of addiction to the enablement of the Spirit in their client's lives. However, just as not all the Israelites chose to permanently dwell in the land of Canaan, the counselor needs to respect the right of the client to skip this step; especially since the baptism of the Holy Spirit is still controversial or even spoken against in some churches. Faith is required to receive the baptism of the Holy Spirit. To have faith each client must be fully convinced in his own mind.

8. <u>Help the client apply the biblical principles or model to overcome the identified psychological problem.</u> (Conquer the giants.) Most clients come into therapy totally caught up in the methods and problems of the world. They are usually facing one of the giants of dysfunction, fear, codependency, abuse, addiction or depression. By this time in the therapeutic process, the client has

overcome most of the lies of the world system and realizes that he cannot overcome his problems by relying on his flesh. Now, the worldly lies that he has believed that underlie each of these strongholds needs to be replaced with the eternal truth of God. This is accomplished through the application of biblical principles or the application of complex models provided in the later chapters of this book.

9. <u>Determine the root cause of the difficulty and assist the client in developing faith to overcome this root problem.</u> (Conquering the cities of Canaan.) All counseling problems eventually can be traced to a basic need for love, security, worth or significance. In the story of the exodus of the children of Israel, Jericho stands for overcoming a lack of security or fear, Ai stands for overcoming low self-worth or shame, and Gibeon stands for overcoming the lusts of the flesh (fulfilling the need of love). The cities of the Amorites, Jerusalem (peace), Hebron (relationships), Jarmuth (worth), Lachish (invincibility), and Eglon (vigor), stand for overcoming problems with significance or trying to find worldly success in life. Finally, Hazor, which stands for the strongholds in the mind, must also be overcome. Through analysis, the counselor should help the client realize his needs, understand how he has been trying to meet them through the flesh, and help him begin to place his trust in God to meet them all. Without this step, a long-term resolution of the problem cannot be assured since the unmet needs will eventually re-assert themselves in another form. The Israelites had to fully defeat all of the tribes and cities of Canaan before final victory was assured.

10. <u>Release the client again to the care of the Holy Spirit so that He can continue to orchestrate the process of salvation by faith in the client's life.</u> (Enjoying the Promised Land.) We must remember that it is the Holy Spirit or Chief Counselor that orchestrates this entire process. Furthermore, Christ made it all possible; and we, as counselors, only have a small part in it. As the counseling process continues, it is our job to work ourselves out of a job. As the client finds greater and greater success, the counselor should require him to face more of his problems on his own (with God's help) or with the help of a support group. The client should be seen for counseling less frequently until the client only calls for an appointment if he is afraid he will relapse, or if he cannot resolve some problem on his own with God's help. Finally, God must be given all the glory and thanksgiving for the positive results that have been accomplished during the counseling process, and the client should again be released to the sole direction and care of the Holy Spirit.

A Biblical Plan for Christian Counseling

1. Determine the problem.

2. Demonstrate that what the client is doing will not meet his needs and build hope that his problems can be overcome through Christ.

3. Use the biblical principles and models to help the client perceive and understand the problem from a biblical perspective.

4. Determine where the client is in the process of salvation and, if appropriate, lead him to accept Christ, be baptized, yield the control of his life to God, and help him get established in a church.

5. Help the client take responsibility for his own actions, not blame others or react to what they do, and do everything as unto God.

6. Help the client grow in his personal relationship with Christ and build faith that, with God's help, he can overcome the problem.

7. Assist the client in receiving the empowerment of the baptism of the Holy Spirit if he chooses to do so.

8. Help the client apply the biblical principles or models to overcome the identified psychological problem.

9. Determine the root cause of the difficulty and assist the client in developing and applying faith to overcome this root problem.

10. Release the client again to the care of Holy Spirit to continue orchestrating this growth process of salvation by faith in his life.

PART III

The Canaanite Giants
Low Self-worth

Chapter 5

Feelings of Inferiority
(Leah)

Canaan means "low or lowland." As I have stated before, I believe that this stands for problems associated with low self-worth. This particular area of counseling has been hotly debated in Christian counseling for some time, probably due to the excesses in trying to deal with what is called "self-esteem" in secular psychology. The second major battle in Canaan was over Ai, which we have already discussed and identified as shame. Shame is one of the strongest feelings associated with low self-worth.

Low self-worth is the root problem or at least a contributing factor in most psychological disorders. According to the genealogy given in the Bible, Canaan was the father of the founders of the other tribes living in this geographical area. That is why this area was known as the land of Canaan. Consequently, the Bible suggests that low self-worth is a root cause of the remaining psychological problems that we will discuss.

Possibly, one of the most well known psychological problems is that of the "inferiority complex" popularized by Alfred Adler. (Morris, 1996, p. 459) There are many reasons why clients might perceive themselves as inferior to those around them. The core issues involved are those of self-worth and significance. Many times, it is the result of being put down by others or the experience of not measuring up in some aspect to those around them. Children treated as inferior will eventually believe that they are inadequate and will become self-conscious. Others may perceive them as artificial or socially inhibited. Sometimes, those that feel inferior will try to compensate for these feelings by acting just the opposite of how they feel and developing a strong drive to accomplish things or become great. They may come across as overbearing or arrogant. In any of these cases, their actions will actually work against the very acceptance that they so desperately seek, and they will find themselves increasingly rejected and insecure, fulfilling what they believe about themselves. Although feeling inferior is characteristic of low self-image and codependency, it can be, in itself, a common, yet significant complex psychological problem.

Stacey was good-looking and intelligent, and seemed to have everything going for her. In High School, she struggled with what she called the "cliques" and worldly ways of the other students but seemed always to have at least one good friend and several others that she did things with from time to time. She spent hours shopping and trying on clothes, so that she looked just right. Because of her high grades, she was accepted at a very well known girl's school on the East Coast. This is where her troubles seemed to begin. Possibly, because of the reputation of the school or the fact that a student had to be in the "top five percent" to get in, she perceived herself as inferior to the other girls. (Many of which were the daughters of nationally known politicians or celebrities.) She did everything she could to "be popular," but the more she tried, the more artificial she felt, and the less she seemed to be accepted. The more she "succeeded" the more she became self-conscious, and the more she wondered whether the other girls liked her, the more she perceived herself as not fitting in. Even going to the cafeteria was a traumatic experience; since, it was possible she would not be able to find a friend to go with her. When she would see most of the other students sitting and chatting with their friends, she would feel envious of them and become depressed. When she became depressed, she would withdraw to her room and when she felt more accepted, she would again chase popularity and neglect her homework. She just could not seem to find a balance, end the chaotic feelings in her life or get organized. She became convinced that it was all her fault and that because she had blown her chance for acceptance, she would be better off just quitting school and starting over at another college. She was a typical person struggling with feelings of inferiority.

The clearest biblical example of this problem is found in the story of Leah, the oldest daughter of Laban. From the very first references concerning Leah in Genesis Chapter 29, we are told that Leah had a problem.

1. The underlying basis of this problem is that the client is convinced that she is, in some way, inferior to others. The Bible tells us that Leah was "tender eyed" but that her sister Rachel was beautiful. In many societies, looks can make all the difference, especially when young women are compared one to another. The Hebrew word for eye, *ayin*, can also be interpreted as "how one sees themselves mentally." Therefore, we are told that Leah viewed herself as weak, tender or inferior in some way. Since we are told that her sister Rachel was beautiful and well favored, we can conclude that the inferiority was based on external looks.

    Ge 29:16 And Laban had two daughters: the name of the elder was Leah, and the name of the younger was Rachel.

    17 Leah was tender eyed; but Rachel was beautiful and well favoured.

2. Because she sees herself as inferior, the client protects herself from the possibility of rejection through certain self-defeating behaviors. Leah's name in the Hebrew means "to be weary, to be impatient, to be grieved, to be offended, or to be tired of something." The root of this word comes from *rakak*, which means "to be tender, to be soft, to be weak, to be timid, or to be fearful." Therefore, we see a picture of a client suffering from an inferiority complex. Because she sees herself as inferior, she becomes timid and afraid of rejection. The stress of constant vigilance to determine if she is liked results in weariness, impatience, grief, and becoming easily offended. As a result, she often becomes tired and weary of life itself.

3. The client who feels inferior usually determines her worth by what others say, how others treat her, and how she compares herself to others. Inferiority is a matter of comparison. The same person may feel superior in one situation and inferior in another depending on how she views the evaluations of other people. When Laban deceived Jacob by giving him Leah instead of Rachel in marriage, Leah clearly understood that Jacob considered her inferior to Rachel. This virtually guaranteed that Leah would feel inferior, at least in her marriage to Jacob. Being promoted too rapidly or being hired into a job above one's ability can also lead a client to struggle with feelings of inferiority.

    Ge 29:23 And it came to pass in the evening, that he took Leah his daughter, and brought her to him; and he went in unto her.

    25 And it came to pass, that in the morning, behold, it was Leah: and he said to Laban, What is this thou hast done unto me? did not I serve with thee for Rachel? wherefore then hast thou beguiled me?

4. One of the results of feeling inferior is often depression. Leah was given Zilpah as her handmaid. Her name means "to trickle or droop" which is the overall impression one has of a person who believes herself to be inferior in the company of others or is depressed. The character of relatives and others in a person's life usually indicates something about her character also.

    Ge 29:24 And Laban gave unto his daughter Leah Zilpah his maid for an handmaid.

5. <u>The client may actually be perceived as inferior by others based on the world's standards</u>. Without question, the Bible tells us that Jacob loved Rachel more than he loved Leah. Consequently, she would most certainly feel inferior to Rachel because of Jacob's demonstrated favoritism.

   Ge 29:30 And he went in also unto Rachel, and he loved also Rachel more than Leah, and served with him yet seven other years.

6. <u>God is on the side of the person who is treated as inferior or rejected by others</u>. Jesus Himself was rejected even though He was perfect in every way. God values all of His children as equals and never rejects anyone, or treats anyone as inferior.

   Ge 29:31 And when the LORD saw that Leah was hated, he opened her womb: but Rachel was barren.

7. <u>The person who feels inferior usually desperately seeks to be loved and accepted, and wants others to see them as worthwhile</u>. Helping the client find an area in her life in which she can perform competently can help. Leah named her firstborn son Reuben, which means "behold a son." The word translated from the Hebrew as behold means "to perceive, to respect, to regard, to learn, to discern." She was hoping that Jacob would now value, love, and accept her as the mother of his oldest son, who in the Jewish culture was considered so valuable that he was supposed to receive half of the entire inheritance.

   Ge 29:32 And Leah conceived, and bare a son, and she called his name Reuben: for she said, Surely the LORD hath looked upon my affliction; now therefore my husband will love me.

8. <u>One of the keys to overcoming feelings of inferiority is for the client to believe what God says about her—that she is not inferior and is fully accepted and loved—and to praise God that He will make everything turn out for her good (Romans 8:28)</u>. The Bible tells us that the fear of man is a trap and that we cannot seek the approval of man and still serve God. Judah, the name of Leah's second son, means "praise." This implies that Leah had learned to worship and praise God for what He was doing in her life. The more the client relies on God; the less she will rely on and be influenced by what people think or say about her.

   Ge 29:35 And she conceived again, and bare a son: and she said, Now will I praise the LORD: therefore she called his name Judah; and left bearing.

   Pr 29:25 The fear of people bringeth a snare: but whoso putteth his trust in the LORD shall be safe.

   Ga 1:10 For do I now persuade men, or God? or do I seek to please men? for if I yet pleased men, I should not be the servant of Christ.

9. <u>A person who feels inferior will usually do whatever it takes to win the approval of others</u>. When Leah did not immediately have more children, she gave Zilpah, her servant, to Jacob as a wife. Although Leah was probably aware of the problems that this same strategy had caused Sarah, she was still so dominated by feelings of inferiority that she was willing to do almost anything to get Jacob's approval. This inner desperation makes the client appear to others to be needy and to have a problem.

   Ge 30:9 When Leah saw that she had left bearing, she took Zilpah her maid, and gave her Jacob to wife.

   10 And Zilpah Leah's maid bare Jacob a son.

10. <u>The client many times will verbally attack others when they do not feel accepted or blame others for being clickish or arrogant.</u> Leah named the second son by Zilpah, Gad, which means "to attack like a troop of soldiers."

    Ge 30:11 And Leah said, A troop cometh: and she called his name Gad.

11. <u>A person who feels inferior may waiver between feelings of happiness and depression depending on how she perceives she is being accepted by others.</u> I call this the emotional roller coaster. When a client's worth is based on the approval of others, she will live a life of emotional highs and lows and put herself at the mercy of other people's approval. Asher means "happiness." It comes from a root word that means "to advance or to make progress."

    Ge 30:12 And Zilpah Leah's maid bare Jacob a second son.

    13 And Leah said, Happy am I, for the daughters will call me blessed: and she called his name Asher.

12. <u>An important step in recovering from feelings of inferiority is to move beyond self-focus and begin again to care for others.</u> Mandrakes were known in that day as love apples and were supposed to excite sexual desire and favor procreation. Rachel at this time still did not have children, and Leah could have hoarded the mandrakes for herself. Instead, she gave some to Rachel in the hope that it would help them both have children. Of course, we can still clearly see Leah's bitterness in her answer to Rachel and desire to have another chance to conceive. Notwithstanding this, she did accept Rachel's offer, which worked in the best interests of both of them.

    Ge 30:14 And Reuben went in the days of wheat harvest, and found mandrakes in the field, and brought them unto his mother Leah. Then Rachel said to Leah, Give me, I pray thee, of thy son's mandrakes.

    15 And she said unto her, is it a small matter that thou hast taken my husband? and wouldest thou take away my son's mandrakes also? And Rachel said, Therefore he shall lie with thee to night for thy son's mandrakes.

13. <u>God honors those who care for others and will meet their needs.</u> The person who feels inferior usually becomes so self-centered that she will envy and compete with others instead of caring about them. The paradox of love is that, "Those who seek to be loved never find it, but those who give it liberally receive it back in abundance." God honored Leah's attempt to end the competition and work together with Rachel by giving Leah another son.

    Ge 30:16 And Jacob came out of the field in the evening, and Leah went out to meet him, and said, Thou must come in unto me; for surely I have hired thee with my son's mandrakes. And he lay with her that night.

    17 And God hearkened unto Leah, and she conceived, and bare Jacob the fifth son.

14. <u>When the client finally focuses on others, they learn by experience that "what goes around, comes around."</u> People like people who like and care about them, not those who compete against them. Issachar means, "there is recompense." I do not believe Leah was blessed because she gave her maiden to her husband, but because she quit competing with Rachel.

    Ge 30:18 And Leah said, God hath given me my hire, because I have given my maiden to my husband: and she called his name Issachar.

15. <u>The ultimate answer for overcoming feelings of inferiority is faith in God</u>. When the client finally believes that she is completely acceptable to God, she will be freed from her struggle to compete and compare herself to others. If she believes this, she will no longer feel so self-conscious. Zebulun means "exalted." By naming her next son "exalted," in her own words Leah was confessing her victory over her own feelings of inferiority. She had enough faith to declare to the world that she was okay and that she would eventually be exalted in the eyes of her husband and accepted by him. Although it should be sufficient for each of us that we are accepted and loved unconditionally by God, God understands that we still desire to be accepted by other people.

Ge 30:19 And Leah conceived again, and bare Jacob the sixth son.

20 And Leah said, God hath endued me with a good dowry; now will my husband dwell with me, because I have born him six sons: and she called his name Zebulun.

16. <u>When the client finally accepts herself, it is only a matter of time before she will be accepted by others</u>. Leah had a daughter named Dinah. Dinah means " judgment," based on a root meaning to "plead a cause." She had pleaded her cause or had presented evidence to the jury of her soul that she was not inferior, and she had received judgment that she was worthy of the acceptance of others.

Ge 30:21 And afterwards she bare a daughter, and called her name Dinah.

17. <u>Once the client finally is able to accept herself, her new view of herself will be challenged just as any belief based on God's truth will be challenged</u>. This is the "good fight of faith." Rachel now became pregnant and bore Joseph. Leah's envy could easily have been triggered by this event. Jacob proposed to move away from her father Laban and she had to decide if she was secure enough to follow Jacob, who still loved Rachel more than her, and yet expect a good life with him.

Ge 30:22 And God remembered Rachel, and God hearkened to her, and opened her womb.

23 And she conceived, and bare a son; and said, God hath taken away my reproach:

24 And she called his name Joseph; and said, The LORD shall add to me another son.

31:14 And Rachel and Leah answered and said unto him, Is there yet any portion or inheritance for us in our father's house?

15 Are we not counted of him strangers? for he hath sold us, and hath quite devoured also our money.

16 For all the riches which God hath taken from our father, that is ours, and our children's: now then, whatsoever God hath said unto thee, do.

18. <u>Even though she may now fully accept herself, a person who has previously struggled with feelings of inferiority must still deal with the perceptions of others, and trust God that He will eventually change their views</u>. When Laban went to search for his stolen idols, he searched Leah's tent before he searched Rachel's tent. And even after Jacob's wrestling match with God (when God changed his name to Israel), when Jacob feared an attack by Esau; he still put the two concubines and Leah and her children in front of Rachel and Joseph; clearly indicating that he still loved and wanted to protect Rachel more.

Ge 31:33 And Laban went into Jacob's tent, and into Leah's tent, and into the two maidservants' tents; but he found them not. Then went he out of Leah's tent, and entered into Rachel's tent.

Ge 33:1 And Jacob lifted up his eyes, and looked, and, behold, Esau came, and with him four hundred men. And he divided the children unto Leah, and unto Rachel, and unto the two handmaids.

2 And he put the handmaids and their children foremost, and Leah and her children after, and Rachel and Joseph hindermost.

19. <u>The greatest challenge to the faith of someone struggling with inferiority will come when the client's worth is directly confronted by an abusive person</u>. This can be a very difficult struggle. Leah's faith that she would eventually be "exalted" was challenged at the time when Dinah (exalted) was raped by Shechem, the son of Hamor. Shechem means "the back or shoulder" and Hamor means "he-ass." I believe that this suggests that the ultimate challenge of her faith was when she was confronted (daughter raped) by one who turned his back on her and acted like an "ass." She must avoid believing that the "rape" occurred because there was something wrong with her and must correctly perceive that the other person "had a problem" and needs help because of his rude and unacceptable behavior. Fortunately, Leah did not defend herself and attack Shechem. Unfortunately, her sons did. They killed Shechem, all the people of the town, and took all that they had.

Ge 34:1 And Dinah the daughter of Leah, which she bare unto Jacob, went out to see the daughters of the land.

2 And when Shechem the son of Hamor the Hivite, prince of the country, saw her, he took her, and lay with her, and defiled her.

26 And they slew Hamor and Shechem his son with the edge of the sword, and took Dinah out of Shechem's house, and went out.

27 The sons of Jacob came upon the slain, and spoiled the city, because they had defiled their sister.

20. <u>Eventually, through faith in God, the one who saw herself as inferior will be vindicated and find the acceptance that she always wanted</u>. Rachael died during the birth of her second son Benjamin and was buried near Bethlehem. Leah died in the land of Canaan before Jacob (now Israel) moved to Egypt. She was buried in the cave of Machpelah (double portion) that is in Mamre ("strength" or "fatness") along with Abraham, Sarah, Isaac, Rebekah, and eventually Jacob. Jacob, himself, gave the direction that he be buried along side of Leah, not Rachel; probably indicating a change of heart before his death. Her final victory, however, is this: **God chose Leah, through her son Judah, to be the progenitor of Christ; not Rachel! (Matthew 1:3)**

Ge 49:29 And he charged them, and said unto them, I am to be gathered unto my people: bury me with my fathers in the cave that is in the field of Ephron the Hittite,

30 In the cave that is in the field of Machpelah, which is before Mamre, in the land of Canaan, which Abraham bought with the field of Ephron the Hittite for a possession of a burying place.

31 There they buried Abraham and Sarah his wife; there they buried Isaac and Rebekah his wife; and there I buried Leah.

Overcoming Feelings of Inferiority

1. Realize that the root of the problem is a perception by the client that she is in someway inferior to those around her.

2. Because the client perceives herself as inferior, she becomes self-conscious and depressed, and excessively attempts to obtain the approval of others or withdraws to protect herself from rejection.

3. Her unnecessary attempts to obtain approval result in artificiality and an appearance of neediness that causes others to avoid her. Withdrawal makes others feel they are not liked or that the client is not friendly.

4. The client interprets this avoidance as rejection and further proof that she is indeed inferior or unacceptable in some way.

5. The client needs to find a place in life where she can become competent and excel in order to take her focus off the perceived areas of inferiority.

6. The client must accept God's evaluation of her and praise God that she is not inferior in God's eyes, is wonderfully made, and that God will work everything for the client's good.

7. The client must avoid the emotional swings caused by evaluating her worth based on her perceptions and the approval of others.

8. She must avoid self-consciousness and self-evaluation, focus on the needs of others, and refuse to compete with or envy others.

9. The client should expect that her faith in God that she is acceptable as a person will be challenged.

10. She must put her relationship with God first, believing that, as she reaches out to help others; God will eventually exalt her in the eyes of other people.

Chapter 6

Feelings of Abandonment
(Ishmael)

In many cases, low self-image is the direct result of feeling abandoned. Almost without exception, someone given up for adoption or physically or emotionally abandoned by their parents, develops low self-image. They ask themselves the question, "What was wrong with me that my parents did not want me?" Emotional abandonment or feeling unloved is also a root of rebellion among teenagers. Consequently, abandonment, which affects the self-image, can pervade the entire person and become a complex problem.

Michelle was the only child in a large family given up for adoption. Her parents gave her to an uncle who later abused her. Because she was so desperate for love, she became the victim of a series of authority figures who took advantage of her, and now she found herself struggling with an abusive and controlling husband. She did what she could to set boundaries in her marriage and her relationship improved. In Theophostic ministry, (see Smith, 1996) God revealed to her that He had and always would put someone in her life to take care of her. Although her new relationship with God helped to heal these deep wounds of abandonment, Michelle sometimes still struggles to feel worthwhile and to overcome fears of abandonment in her marriage.

We find our model for feelings of abandonment in the story of Ishmael beginning in Genesis Chapter 16:

1. <u>Abandonment is almost never due solely to the fault of the one abandoned</u>. Many times a conflict between parents or other problems cause the abandonment. Sarai gave Hagar (flight) to Abram in order to have children by her and then became angry when Hagar conceived and despised her. Sarai mistreated Hagar and she fled.

   Ge 16:1 Now Sarai Abram's wife bare him no children: and she had an handmaid, an Egyptian, whose name [was] Hagar.

   2 And Sarai said unto Abram, Behold now, the LORD hath restrained me from bearing: I pray thee, go in unto my maid; it may be that I may obtain children by her. And Abram hearkened to the voice of Sarai.

   3 And Sarai Abram's wife took Hagar her maid the Egyptian, after Abram had dwelt ten years in the land of Canaan, and gave her to her husband Abram to be his wife.

   4 And he went in unto Hagar, and she conceived: and when she saw that she had conceived, her mistress was despised in her eyes.

   5 And Sarai said unto Abram, My wrong [be] upon thee: I have given my maid into thy bosom; and when she saw that she had conceived, I was despised in her eyes: the LORD judge between me and thee.

   6 But Abram said unto Sarai, Behold, thy maid [is] in thy hand; do to her as it pleaseth thee. And when Sarai dealt hardly with her, she fled from her face.

2. <u>God cares about the abandoned person and wants the relationship to work</u>. God told Hagar to go back and submit to Sarai and He would bless her. The angel found her in the wilderness of Shur that means "wall." Abandonment or fleeing (Hagar means "flight") is usually a defense.

    Ge 16:7 And the angel of the LORD found her by a fountain of water in the wilderness, by the fountain in the way to Shur.

    8 And he said, Hagar, Sarai's maid, whence camest thou? and whither wilt thou go? And she said, I flee from the face of my mistress Sarai.

    9 And the angel of the LORD said unto her, Return to thy mistress, and submit thyself under her hands.

    10 And the angel of the LORD said unto her, I will multiply thy seed exceedingly, that it shall not be numbered for multitude.

3. <u>God told Hagar to name the child Ishmael, which means "the Lord has heard your affliction."</u> God hears the affliction of those who are abandoned and promises to take care of them. Psalms 27:10 states, "When my father and my mother forsake me, then the LORD will take me up." God promised that the descendents of Ishmael would be so numerous that they could not be counted. This truth has been manifested in two ways. The Arabs, the descendants of Ishmael, have grown in great numbers; and the numbers of abandoned children continue to increase to this day.

    Ge 16:11 And the angel of the LORD said unto her, Behold, thou [art] with child, and shalt bear a son, and shalt call his name Ishmael; because the LORD hath heard thy affliction.

4. <u>Abandonment by a father usually results in a life of rebellion against authority</u>. This is because an abandoned child perceives that either the parent does not have his best interests in mind or that there must be something wrong with him. If someone in authority does not really care about us, we rebel against that authority and if there is something wrong with us we will not be open to discipline.

    Ge 16:12 And he will be a wild man; his hand [will be] against every man, and every man's hand against him; and he shall dwell in the presence of all his brethren.

5. <u>What the abandoned person needs to realize is that God does see them and will look out for them</u>. Beer-lahai-roi means "well of the Living One seeing me."

    Ge 16:13 And she called the name of the LORD that spake unto her, Thou God seest me: for she said, Have I also here looked after him that seeth me?

    14 Wherefore the well was called Beerlahairoi; behold, [it is] between Kadesh and Bered.

6. <u>The abandoned person has great potential in God but has a tendency to live according to the flesh and not the Spirit, due to his hurt from abandonment</u>.

    Ge 16:15 And Hagar bare Abram a son: and Abram called his son's name, which Hagar bare, Ishmael.

    17:20 And as for Ishmael, I have heard thee: Behold, I have blessed him, and will make him fruitful, and will multiply him exceedingly; twelve princes shall he beget, and I will make him a great nation.

7. <u>The abandoned person needs to make a covenant to serve God and not the flesh</u>. Circumcision symbolized the cutting away of the flesh.

Ge 17:25 And Ishmael his son [was] thirteen years old, when he was circumcised in the flesh of his foreskin.

8. <u>Abandonment leads to contempt and contempt to further abandonment</u>. Most likely Ishmael realized that Isaac was the favored child and reacted out of anger and frustration.

Ge 21:9 And Sarah saw the son of Hagar the Egyptian, which she had born unto Abraham, mocking.

10 Wherefore she said unto Abraham, Cast out this bondwoman and her son: for the son of this bondwoman shall not be heir with my son, [even] with Isaac.

9. <u>In situations when a child is abandoned, the inheritance resulting from a good relationship with a good father is lost</u>. Even if the father really cares, time together is essential. Abraham did not want to abandon Ishmael but Sarah insisted.

Ge 21:11 And the thing was very grievous in Abraham's sight because of his son.

12 And God said unto Abraham, Let it not be grievous in thy sight because of the lad, and because of thy bondwoman; in all that Sarah hath said unto thee, hearken unto her voice; for in Isaac shall thy seed be called.

10. <u>People that have been rejected still have the potential to have a full productive life</u>.

Ge 21:13 And also of the son of the bondwoman will I make a nation, because he [is] thy seed.

11. <u>A child needs more than having his basic needs met to become a man. Bread stands for things that are profitable and useful and water stands for life</u>. Even if a child is provided the physical needs of life and emotional support in the care of his mother, it is usually not enough. He may still find himself wandering in the wilderness of life without a male role model, wondering what it is really like to be a man. Hagar, the single mother, is the one who must now carry the burden on her shoulder as she is sent away to wither and die emotionally.

Ge 21:14 And Abraham rose up early in the morning, and took bread, and a bottle of water, and gave [it] unto Hagar, putting [it] on her shoulder, and the child, and sent her away: and she departed, and wandered in the wilderness of Beersheba.

12. <u>There is nothing a mother can do to fully make up for the loss of a man in the lives of her children</u>. Of course, mentoring can help to some degree. Here Hagar chose to abandon her son again rather than to see him die. Some mothers choose emotionally to abandon their teenagers when they realize that there is nothing more that they can do for them.

Ge 21:15 And the water was spent in the bottle, and she cast the child under one of the shrubs.

16 And she went, and sat her down over against [him] a good way off, as it were a bowshot: for she said, Let me not see the death of the child. And she sat over against [him], and lift up her voice, and wept.

13. <u>But God will not abandon those who have been abandoned. God will hear their voice if they will call to Him</u>. Mothers are not to give up on their teens but lead them to the father that will "never leave them or forsake them."

    Ge 21:17 And God heard the voice of the lad; and the angel of God called to Hagar out of heaven, and said unto her, What aileth thee, Hagar? fear not; for God hath heard the voice of the lad where he [is].

14. <u>God has a plan to make the abandoned great if they will turn to Him</u>. She was told to lift up the lad (encourage him) and to hold him in her hand (provide emotional support).

    Ge 21:18 Arise, lift up the lad, and hold him in thine hand; for I will make him a great nation.

15. <u>It is the mother's job to allow God to open her eyes (of faith), and take of the well of water that the angel showed her (the Word of God) and give the water (life) to the lad</u>.

    Ge 21:19 And God opened her eyes, and she saw a well of water; and she went, and filled the bottle with water, and gave the lad drink.

16. <u>We must help the abandoned person to find this calling and place in life where he can thrive and find fulfillment even though he may still be struggling as God brings healing in his emotional wilderness</u>.

    Ge 21:20 And God was with the lad; and he grew, and dwelt in the wilderness, and became an archer.

17. <u>Even though they may be relying on God, the abandoned person still has to go through all the normal struggles of life in order to build his faith</u>. *Paran* means "a place of caverns" (a safe but dark dwelling place). This was the exact same wilderness that the children of Israel passed through on the way to the Promised Land.

    Ge 21:21 And he dwelt in the wilderness of Paran: and his mother took him a wife out of the land of Egypt.

18. <u>The abandoned person needs to be cautious of who he marries so that he does not again set up the abandonment issues in his family of origin</u>. In the verse above, Hagar, who was an Egyptian, took a wife from Egypt for Ishmael. This was not wise since Egypt stands for the world and all it offers.

19. <u>Even though the abandoned person now has God as a father, he still must deal with his feeling of abandonment by his natural father</u>. Ishmael joined Isaac in burying Abraham in the cave of Machpelah (double portion) in the field of Ephron (fawn-like) the son of Zohar (Tawny) the Hittite (fear), which [is] before Mamre; (Strength or fatness). This verse suggests that by burying his father at Mamre he also shared in the double portion of the life and strength that his father enjoyed.

    Ge 25:9 And his sons Isaac and Ishmael buried him in the cave of Machpelah, in the field of Ephron the son of Zohar the Hittite, which [is] before Mamre;

20. <u>The positive outcome from the emotional pain of abandonment takes time, but victory through God is possible</u>. We see this healing develop slowly in the names of his children that in ancient times were

chosen to describe life's conditions. He progressed through a dark struggle to become someone who finally accepted himself as he was; an original, one of a kind, human being that is loved and will never be abandoned again by his true Father—God.

Ge 25:13 And these [are] the names of the sons of Ishmael, by their names, according to their generations: the firstborn of Ishmael, Nebajoth (heights); and Kedar (dark), and Adbeel (chastened of God), and Mibsam (sweet odor),

14 And Mishma (a hearing), and Dumah (silence), and Massa (burden),

15 Hadar (honor), and Tema (desert), Jetur (enclosed), Naphish (refreshment), and Kedemah (original):

21. <u>The abandoned person can enjoy a full and long life similar to that found in the garden of Eden if he successfully works through the issues of his abandonment and makes God his true Father</u>. Havilah is the area near the original garden of Eden.

Ge 25:17 And these [are] the years of the life of Ishmael, an hundred and thirty and seven years: and he gave up the ghost and died; and was gathered unto his people.

18 And they dwelt from Havilah unto Shur, that [is] before Egypt, as thou goest toward Assyria: [and] he died in the presence of all his brethren.

Overcoming Feelings of Abandonment

1. Physical or emotional abandonment most often results in low self-image, because we ask what was wrong with us that other persons, especially our parents, did not want a relationship with us.

2. If our fathers have abandoned us, we will usually rebel against the authority figures in our lives because we feel that we cannot trust anyone except ourselves.

3. Once we have experienced abandonment, we may expect that others might also abandon us since we feel unworthy of their love.

4. Because the emotional pain of feeling worthless is so great, we will many times abandon or show contempt for others who we are afraid will abandon us. This results in additional experiences of abandonment.

5. Establishing a close, intimate relationship with God is the answer for overcoming abandonment, because He alone can be trusted completely to look out for us and never leave or forsake us. We must make a covenant with Him.

6. If possible, we must work through our issues of low self-image and our feelings of abandonment with those who have abandoned us in order to be completely free from the fear of more rejection and abandonment.

7. If we will do this, we can be set free from this trap and go on to experience a long and full life.

PART IV

The Perizzite Giants Boundary Problems

Chapter 7

A Chaotic Life
Lack of Boundaries
(Nehemiah)

When people grow up attempting to cope with alcoholic, dysfunctional, abusive, or emotionally distant families, they usually develop a low self-image and fail to establish healthy personal boundaries. This lack of boundaries results in a chaotic lifestyle. This is easy to understand when you consider what would happen in a city if no one knew who owned any of the property or the location of any of the property boundaries. The name Perizzite means "belonging to a village." In Bible times, villages were small, not very important, and lacked the walls necessary for their defense. Therefore, this biblical type implies that where the person lives is small or not very important (low self-image) and that the place has no walls and adequate defenses (lack of personal boundaries).

Establishing Boundaries

One of the universal results of dysfunctional or abusive relationships is the violation of personal boundaries. Personal boundaries are critical in the development and maintenance of healthy relationships. Personal boundaries are similar to physical boundaries. They tell us who owns the land, who is responsible for it, and where the property begins and ends. Personal boundaries tell us what is mine and what is not mine, what I am responsible for, and what I am not responsible for, what choices are mine, and what I am free to control. They help a person to keep the good in and the bad out. Compliants or codependent dependents allow the bad in. Avoidants or codependent avoidants keep the good out. Controllers or codependent independents disrespect other's boundaries and rarely maintain healthy boundaries themselves. (Cloud, 1992)

Laws are clear examples of boundaries. There are three specific steps in setting boundaries: 1. Agree on exactly what or where the boundary line will be. As an example, the law states that everyone must drive at or below the posted speed limit. 2. Agree on the consequences for violating the boundary. Again, in this example, the consequence for violating the law or boundary would be to pay a specific fine if caught breaking the law. 3. Make it clear that each person may drive above the speed limit if they are willing to pay the fine when they are caught. Of course, the idea of having a boundary is that it not be violated. In order for this to occur, the consequence must be significant enough to deter the violation of the boundary. The more important boundary violations require greater consequences. The true objective in setting boundaries is to ensure that the person who violates the boundary receives the consequences of his choice so that he can learn from the experience.

Larry and Gretchen both came from very dysfunctional families. He had been brought up in institutions and foster care all of his life and she had an extremely abusive and controlling father. Because both lacked any type of self-discipline, their children were out of control and their life consisted of a constant stream of repossessions, evictions and utility disconnections. They were investigated numerous times by social services for child neglect and abuse. They would not accept any type of help because they might feel controlled by the person helping them. They only seemed to function in a legalistic, condemning, and controlling church environment where clear external boundaries were provided for them. They are a good example of a family without boundaries.

When boundaries do not exist or when they are confused, a person's life becomes unmanageable. In Bible times, this problem was like a city where the walls had been destroyed and the gates burned. Such a town was utterly defenseless. The city of Jerusalem in the book of Nehemiah, following its destruction by the Babylonians, was without walls or gates. It symbolically represents the state of the person scarred by sin and abuse. After the temple (of the Spirit) was restored in 458 BC (a type of our initial salvation experience and the development or rebuilding of our spiritual life), it was now time for the walls of the city (the soul) to be rebuilt in 444 BC. Without the walls and gates of effective personal boundaries, the person's spirit will continually be affected by outside influences, which will try to control the soul (the city of Jerusalem). Jerusalem means "city of peace." Symbolically, without effective boundaries we can never have peace in our soul.

1. <u>The restoration of personal boundaries requires the establishment of an identity and good personal choices</u>. The identity is represented by the fixed boundaries of the walls, and the gates represent personal choices (which are based on values and principles). The doors stand for our will, and it is our choice whether we will open or shut the gate to particular influences or events. It should be noted that a codependent lacks an identity and consistently makes poor choices. He is such a people-pleaser that he changes his identity to fit in wherever he goes. What color is a chameleon? It has no color identity, just as a codependent has no personal identity. He tries to obtain an identity from those he associates with. He constantly wants others to make choices for him, so that he does not have to take responsibility for those choices and face rejection or failure. Because of this, sometimes he seems almost passive except when action is required to insure that his selfish needs are met.

2. <u>Each person will have problems with particular boundaries depending on his life experiences</u>. In Nehemiah, the gates help us identify the most usual problem areas. The gates define the selective or complex boundaries, which determine what we will allow into or prohibit from our souls. (For a more detailed explanation of these gates, see my book *Revelations That Will Set You Free*.) Here is the symbolism as I best understand it:

Valley gate	Low experiences of life and failures
Fountain gate	Spiritual experiences of life
Sheep gate	Relationships with people
Fish gate	Worldly physical and psychological nourishment
Old gate	Past experiences, traditions, and ways of doing things
Dung gate	Guilt and shameful experiences
Water gate	Those things that bring physical and spiritual life
Horse gate	Capabilities relied on to accomplish things
East gate	Expectations of the future, dreams, visions, and hopes
Miphkad gate	Influence of other people in life
Ephraim gate	Fruitfulness and productivity in life
Prison gate	Bondages, habits, lusts, and addictions

3. <u>It is the Holy Spirit's job, with the help of God's grace, to bring restoration</u>. Nehemiah means "Jehovah comforts" or the comforter, which is another name for the Holy Spirit. His father's name, Hachaliah means "whom Jehovah enlightens" which is one of the functions of the Holy Spirit. The news that Jerusalem's walls and gates were broken down was brought to Nehemiah by his brother, Hanani, which means "gracious," one of the main characteristics of the Holy Spirit.

4. <u>Sin is the root cause of a lack of boundaries which brings great affliction</u>. Hanani describes the situation in Nehemiah 1:3 as "The remnant that are left of the captivity there in the province [are] in great

affliction and reproach: the wall of Jerusalem also [is] broken down, and the gates thereof are burned with fire." In his prayer, Nehemiah makes it clear that the destruction of Jerusalem, the captivity of the Israelites, and their affliction were the direct result of sin. Sometimes the sin or dysfunction involved can go back several generations.

5. <u>The Holy Spirit is greatly distressed by the chaotic life of the abused person</u>. Nehemiah (the Holy Spirit) says in Nehemiah 1:4, "And it came to pass, when I heard these words, that I sat down and wept, and mourned [certain] days, and fasted, and prayed before the God of heaven..."

6. <u>The first step is confessing the sins which resulted in the lack of personal boundaries</u>. The first thing Nehemiah did was to pray and confess the sins of the people. (Nehemiah 1:6-7)

7. <u>Rebuilding of the boundaries begins with faith</u>. Hanani came to Nehemiah in the month Chisleu which means "His confidence" or "faith." Nehemiah also expressed his faith in the promise of God that if the children of Israel would return to God, He would bring them back to Jerusalem (the city of peace) and restore the city. We must believe that God is willing and able to restore our personalities and personal boundaries.

8. <u>We need God's help to rebuild our personalities</u>. Even Nehemiah (the Holy Spirit) had to go to the king (God) and ask assistance to rebuild Jerusalem. In the same way, without God the Father's help, we will not succeed because if we do not trust Him, our flesh will prevail. Our flesh allowed the boundaries (or walls) to be pulled down in the first place.

9. <u>Rebuilding boundaries will be resisted and sometimes mocked</u>. Sanballat (strong or Satan), the Horonite (Moabite or lust) and Tobiah the Ammonite (selfish desires) were exceedingly grieved and did everything they could to resist the rebuilding of the walls. Initially they even laughed at the idea that the city could be rebuilt. (Nehemiah 4:2,3)

10. <u>It takes many people working together to restore the numerous boundary deficits</u>. A very large number of people from all occupations are named as working on the wall. It takes many people—pastors, friends, relatives, co-workers, counselors, and support groups—to eventually help establish healthy boundaries.

11. <u>The abused person usually feels overwhelmed by emotions at the immensity of the task, and how long it will take</u>. Sanballat was joined by the Arabians (mixed emotions), the Ammonites (selfish desires), and the Ashdodites (self-destructive feelings) in the resistance.

12. <u>The first requirement in establishing boundaries is that the abuse must be stopped</u>. Watchfulness and strong initial boundaries in the weakest areas are important to insure that the abuse does not continue. It is easy for the client to fall into the old way of doing things. The abused person must have a plan on how to handle the expected attacks. This usually takes assertiveness training. Trust must be maintained in the Lord. The abused person must be ever alert to lust and selfish desires that have tempted him in the past to forfeit his boundaries. Under Nehemiah, half of the people stood guard in preparation for an attack while the other half worked.

13. <u>One of the most important tools for establishing boundaries and developing an identity is preaching</u>. Nehemiah constantly kept the trumpet by him in order to sound the warning. I believe the trumpet stands for preaching which challenges the person lacking boundaries to set and maintain appropriate boundary values. This provides the material for developing a Christian identity.

14. <u>Identifying and joining with a solid, biblically-based local church is important</u>. Nehemiah asked everyone to lodge within Jerusalem day and night. A close, intimate relationship with other Christians is critical for spiritual growth. They were so involved in building the city and defending themselves that they did not even take off their clothes except to wash. In the same way, the abused person must learn to always "wear" Christ's character and the armor of God and not take them off.

15. <u>When establishing boundaries, respect for the boundaries of others is equally important</u>. Some of those building the walls had taken advantage of the other builders. Nehemiah immediately put a stop to this. Unfortunately, boundaries can be used selfishly. The Christian must be as careful not to violate other people's boundaries while he is defending his own. When clients learn about boundaries, many initially use them incorrectly as a method of control. A respect for all boundaries is the basis of what is today called assertiveness.

16. <u>The flesh will try to divert us into doing something else before the task is done. As the abused person begins to recover, he many times is tempted to get involved in other activities, since his life has become less chaotic</u>. Over-extending oneself is a self-boundary violation. Sanballat asked for a meeting. Nehemiah refused and said, "I [am] doing a great work, so that I cannot come down: why should the work cease, whilst I leave it, and come down to you?" (Nehemiah 6:3)

17. <u>Sometimes people are afraid that setting boundaries is selfish and prideful</u>. Sanballat sent a letter saying that Nehemiah was going to rebel against the King and had made himself king. This and many other boundary myths are just diversions. Although some people believe that boundaries are the means of controlling others, they do not control because they do not take away the person's free choice. Even Christians sometimes question if boundary setting is biblical. Jesus used good boundaries and much of the Sermon on the Mount deals with this. Possibly the best example in the Bible is Jesus' attempt to restore Judas at the Last Supper. He clearly stated that this betrayal by a disciple was wrong, that the consequences if a man chose to do this would be so bad that "it would be better if that man had not been born," and then directed Judas to do whatever he chose to do quickly. (Matthew 26, John 13)

18. <u>Emotional withdrawal due to fear must be overcome</u>. There is a temptation to withdraw from relationships rather than face boundary problems. Shemaiah suggested that Nehemiah would be slain, and that he should hide in the temple for protection. This represents emotional withdrawal. Nehemiah 8:13 even suggested that it would be a sin to withdraw from the work out of fear. When a person attempts to avoid what is feared, the fear increases.

19. <u>It takes a long time to finish the task</u>. It took Nehemiah 12 years! He charged nothing for his work. Similarly, the Holy Spirit gives to us freely.

20. <u>When a Christian has a true personality transformation and maintains healthy boundaries, it gives glory to God</u>. When the walls were finished, everyone realized that God had done it.

21. <u>Once boundaries are established, the new personality must rely on God's favor to meet all of its needs and yield control to the grace of God through faith</u>. Hanani (grace) and Hananiah (Jehovah has favored) were appointed rulers. (Nehemiah 7:2)

22. <u>When established, the new boundaries must be exercised to keep the good in and the bad out</u>. The gates were only opened in broad daylight and guarded when they were open. Some of the most important self-boundary areas to be controlled are mentioned in the final verses of this book: 1. Sin must be put out of lives through confession and fasting. 2. Lust (Moabites) and selfish desires (Ammonites) must be excluded forever. 3. Violators of God's Sabbath law (the flesh) must be excluded. 4. Friends and marriage partners should be believers. 5. God's Word was to be brought into the city (the souls). 6. Joy must be maintained because "the joy of the LORD is your strength." (Nehemiah 8:1) 7. God's blessings must be remembered (they celebrated the Feast of Booths). 8. The covenant with God must be re-established.

Recovery involves a day-to-day practical working out of boundary problems in the client's life. In order to teach boundaries, I use *Boundaries* (Cloud and Townsend) and the associated workbook. I also sometimes use these books as resources in our Codependency and Abuse Recovery Support Groups.

Overcoming a Chaotic Lifestyle

1. The root problem of a chaotic lifestyle is lack of effective personal boundaries due to codependency, abuse, a dysfunctional past, or a lack of training during childhood.

2. The client must realize that control, manipulation, and returning evil for evil does not work, and choose to learn to use boundaries effectively.

3. Past patterns of abuse, dysfunction, or codependency must be faced and dealt with so that the client will be strong enough to set boundaries and consistently carry out the consequences when boundaries are violated in his life.

4. The client must learn to assertively respond to boundary violations from others. He must avoid passive, passive-aggressive and aggressive reactions to these violations.

5. The client must learn to communicate what he expects in his relationships with other people and help them to understand the natural consequences of violating each boundary.

6. He must begin setting boundaries and consistently carry out the consequences in his relationships without going overboard and using boundaries to try to control others.

7. He must set others free to make their own choices and learn from their own consequences, trusting God to meet his own needs.

8. The client must respect other's boundaries, communicate boundaries in a loving manner and develop an assertive lifestyle.

Chapter 8

The "Good Girl" Complex
The Codependent Dependent Passive
(Sarah)

When our needs for love, security, worth, or significance are not met, we attempt to meet these needs through depending on ourselves, relying on others, trying to control others, or using substances or things to make us happy. Today, in the recovery movement, this is called codependency. This term was originally coined to refer to a person married to an addict who was somehow dependent on the addict continuing to drink or use drugs. However, this excessively dependent or independent pattern is now recognized to be much more widespread in our society and has been identified as the underlying cause of numerous other problems.

I remember Janet. She was dating a man named Tom and they were in a constant cycle of conflict and separation. She would daily call her pastor and, if he was not available, anyone else in the church that would listen to her latest problem. She would speak for hours on the phone desperately attempting to feel good about herself. If someone listened to her and did not give her advice, she would feel unconditionally accepted and feel okay again. She would continue to call until the new confidant could no longer afford the loss of time and energy. At this point, she would call someone else and denounce her last supporter as unloving and rejecting. This went on until she had alienated almost everyone in her church. She finally found someone more codependent than herself in a support group to be her roommate. This lasted for a few days until, during an argument with her boyfriend; the woman took sides against her. The angry confrontation became so violent that the property owner evicted them. At this point, she decided that this church simply did not have any love and moved on to another church to repeat the process. Of course, not everyone is as codependent as Janet, but most churches have a number of people who cope with life in similarly dysfunctional ways.

Probably everyone in our society has a number of codependent characteristics, but for at least one-fourth or more of our population, these characteristics have become a predominant pattern of coping that results in dysfunctional relationships. In the United States and much of Europe, we teach codependent principles from the cradle up with nursery stories like Cinderella and Sleeping Beauty, romantic and Country Western music, and many popular movies. After discussing codependency, one pastor who primarily works with lower income families stated, "That's everyone in my congregation." Codependency makes up a large part of the psychological dysfunction that occupies a position between normal or healthy, and the mental disorders described in the Diagnostic and Statistical Manual of Mental Disorders (DSM IV).

It is difficult to produce a specific list of codependent characteristics because codependency includes a number of different styles for coping within the same basic problem. In fact, even the most well known books on this subject suggest widely differing traits and definitions. Part of this difficulty is because codependency includes both of the extremes of being too dependent or too independent on people or things. Therefore, a codependent may exhibit one extreme or the other extreme of a particular characteristic, or even oscillate frequently between both of these extremes. Notwithstanding these difficulties, in order to help the reader get a better understanding of this subject, I will present a list of the most common codependent characteristics based on my observations and experience in treating codependents.

1. <u>They are driven by compulsions to fill the void within them for love, security, worth, and/or significance</u>. Although they may initially deny it, codependents are selfishly attempting to meet their own needs, but will give to others in an attempt to get what they need back in return. They are also prone to addictions. According to *Love is a Choice*, the average codependent has at least two addictions. (Hemfelt, Minirth, and Meier, 1989)

2. <u>They are usually people pleasers</u>. This is because they are desperately trying to please others in order to get approval so that they can feel better about themselves. They fit in with and become like the people around them. Consequently, they have no set identity. On the other extreme, they may even declare that they do not care what others think about them as a defense against rejection.

3. <u>They have unresolved issues with their dysfunctional family of origin</u>. Many times they come from families that struggled with alcoholism, drug addictions, over-control, workaholism, or abuse. They may have been emotionally abandoned. Someone close to them in their family may have died or was severely handicapped. Their parents may have had numerous partners or may have married and divorced several times. They may have been adopted. It is even possible that they grew up in a codependent family and learned codependency as a way of functioning in life. Codependency is a problem that is propagated from generation to generation. In many cases, the codependent may actually recreate the original situation in new relationships in a vicarious attempt to resolve the original problem. This is why children from alcoholic or abusive families most often marry someone with similar problems. Since codependents tend to marry at approximately equivalent levels of codependency, they usually end up in dysfunctional relationships themselves.

4. <u>They are driven to accomplish and may become perfectionists as an attempt to compensate for their feelings of inadequacy</u>. They usually have a hard time admitting they are wrong, react strongly to criticism, and blame others for their feelings of rejection. They may also be critical and judgmental of others in order to make themselves feel more important or acceptable. They usually believe that if they could just fix their mate everything would be all right.

5. <u>Their relationships are based on conditional love and usually result in ongoing conflict typified by a series of fights, separations, and making up again</u>. Demands for love drive the other person away. Unfortunately, codependents have little to give emotionally to their mate; since they are so empty themselves. Usually one mate that cannot be alone marries another who is a "loner." Consequently, one of the spouses feels smothered and the other deprived.

6. <u>They have problems dealing with anger</u>. Either they stuff their anger and eventually blow up, or they react in rage when others do not meet their needs in the way they want them to be met. Their anger level is excessive because they are so insecure that they view the negative events of life as catastrophic. They easily feel rejected or are offended. They tend to take everything personally.

7. <u>They are emotionally over or under-connected with others</u>. They may believe they are responsible for the happiness of others. They cannot be happy if others are not happy. If one codependent falls into the emotional ditch, the other will fall too. They tend to feel guilty for what others have done, for how they have been treated, or if someone is not pleased with them.

8. <u>They are on an emotional roller coaster</u>. Because they are so insecure, their emotions rise and fall according to the circumstances and what others say or do. Although they may suppress or cover up their feelings, they will usually admit that inside they are in constant emotional turmoil.

9. <u>They want to be rescued or enabled, or they tend to rescue or enable others</u>. They will do for others what the other person can do for himself or herself, or they will expect others to fix them or do for them what they themselves are capable of doing.

10. <u>They are controlling, manipulating, or passive-aggressive</u>. Although they may deny it, they will do whatever it takes to get others to meet their needs. They will either control or abuse others to get their needs met or; if they are in a controlling relationship themselves, they will manipulate or act in passive-aggressive ways.

In order to understand better the confusing array of symptoms that typify codependency, I have identified three basic types and six subtypes of codependency in order to address this subject more clearly. Each of them has a distinct example and an in-depth model for recovery in the Bible. Each subtype will be covered in more depth later in this book.

1. <u>The codependent dependent,</u> which is the most obvious to the untrained observer, is better understood as the result of a deep hunger for love, a product of abusive relationships, and a lack of boundaries. Codependent dependents are usually women, but this is not always the case. The basic underlying characteristic is that she is overly insecure and dependent on others to meet her needs. She is the damsel in distress.

2. <u>The codependent independent</u> is the knight in ego-protective armor, who deals with his feelings of inadequacy through denial, performance, people pleasing, and rescuing. His external characteristics will differ significantly depending on his apparent worldly success or failure.

3. <u>The codependent avoidant</u> is a person controlled by fears. This type may avoid failure by engaging only in activities in which he knows he can succeed. He may find a mate to take responsibility for him in order to insulate himself against failure or he may withdraw from society and take on the role of a victim. Many times he or she is strongly attached to a number of pets or animals. The ultimate expression of the codependent avoidant is found in the homeless street person looking for a handout.

In addition to determining whether a person is codependent, it is important to determine the particular subtype of codependency since the different styles of coping require specific methods for recovery. Consequently, at Word of Life Institute, we have developed a Codependent Inventory to help us determine each specific subtype. This inventory can be found in the appendix of this book.

Codependent Dependence

Inevitably, those coming from alcoholic, dysfunctional, controlling, abusive, or codependent families of origin learn to cope with life in a codependent way. The codependent dependent is the most commonly identified type of codependency. Codependent dependence approximates a milder form of the Personality Dependence Disorder in DSM IV. It is seen clearest in a Cinderella looking for a prince to rescue her or in the over-responsible wife enabling the alcoholic husband to continue his alcoholism. From a boundary standpoint, this is the person who allows others to violate her personal boundaries, wants others to carry her load of personal responsibility, or who attempts to carry another's load in order to please them. Galatians Chapter 6 distinguishes between helping others who cannot help themselves and enabling others by taking responsibility for them in areas that they should shoulder themselves. This distinction is clear in Young's Literal Translation:

Ga 6:2 Bear one another's (unbearable) burdens, and so you will fulfill the law of Christ.

5 For each one will bear [his] own load. (Life's responsibilities) (YLT)

The Codependent Dependent Passive

As we have studied the problem of codependent dependence in more depth in our Christian counseling practice and the classes that we teach at Word of Life Institute, there appears to be two subtypes within this type of codependency. The first I call the Codependent Dependent Passive because she is attempting to meet her needs by being a "good girl" and doing what everyone wants her to do. She allows others to violate her boundaries so that her needs will be met. She is the damsel looking for a rescuer who will kill the dragon of life that is holding her captive and takes them both off to the castle to "live happily ever after." Unfortunately, in many cases these rescuers turn out to be codependent independents who are over-controlling, abusive, or, at least, boundary violators.

Carey was married to a wonderful guy named Bob. They reminded me of the ideal Barbie and Ken models. He owned his own business and made good money, but his business consumed most of his time. Both were focused primarily on the acquisition of material things and enjoying life. She watched his every move for signs of approval and was afraid to confront him on any issue for fear he might get angry and disapprove. It seemed that she could never measure up to his expectations, was anxious about almost everything, and seemed to "walk on egg shells" trying to maintain her "good girl" image. He, on the other hand, was insecure, wondering what would happen with his business and if their marriage would last. Sometimes he felt like he was her father and wondered if she would ever grow up so that he could truly rely on her. He was free to do almost anything he wanted to do if he was willing to put up with her keeping tabs on him and her pleas for more time together. Many times, he felt smothered by her excessive "neediness."

The most extensive biblical example of this subtype is found in the story of Sarah, the wife of Abraham. Some might object that they have been taught that Sarah is an example of what a Christian woman should be. Like most of the people in the Bible, Sarah did not begin life as a heroine of faith. She progressed step-by-step through faith in her recovery from codependency until she became a definite model of Christian womanhood. Unfortunately, some churches today make the mistake of applauding some of Sarah's dysfunctional traits as those typifying the ideal Christian woman. If we examine Sarah's life, I believe that the reader will be able to clearly identify her codependent dependent passive traits. Her story begins in Genesis Chapter 11.

1. The codependent dependent passive woman is seeking to live out the classical story of Cinderella in her life. This is suggested by the meaning of her name and that of her husband (before they were changed by God) in the original Hebrew language. Abram means "exalted father" and Sarai means "my princess." He was to be her exalted father figure or prince to meet all her needs, and she was to be his princess to be taken away to the castle to "live happily ever after."

2. Shame and feelings of inadequacy are the basis of codependent dependence. Sarai was barren without children. This was a great disgrace during the time in which she lived.

3. Low self-image is a prime characteristic of all types of codependency. Abram's family lived in Ur of the Chaldees, a region known for false religion and soothsaying. Soothsaying is associated with witchcraft and the use of drugs, possibly suggesting the origin of their codependency. They went to the land of Canaan, which we have already identified as meaning "lowland" or low self-image.

4. The codependent allows her personal boundaries to be violated in order to have her needs met. She usually fears that her "prince" will get angry or might leave her if she offends him by saying no. Abram was afraid that the people of Egypt might kill him to get his beautiful wife, Sarai. He asked her to lie and say that she was his sister. Because she denied that she was married, she was taken into Pharaoh's harem! Abram was not willing to admit his mistake or make any attempt to rescue her. God, Himself, had to intervene. We are not told that she complained to Abram even once concerning this clear boundary violation.

5. Codependents try to manipulate their mates and their circumstances in order to get their needs met. When Sarai did not have any children, she blamed God by saying, "the LORD hath restrained me from bearing." (Genesis 16:2) She suggested that Abram should impregnate Hagar, her maid, and she would count the child as hers. In this way, her shame of being barren might not be so obvious to strangers.

6. Underline: Codependent dependent passive traits include wanting approval, angry outbursts, jealousy, blaming others, and passive-aggression. When Hagar did become pregnant, Sarai became jealous because Hagar was able to conceive and became angry when Hagar despised her. She blamed Abram even though it was her idea. Sarai treated Hagar so badly that she had to flee. God had to intervene to rescue Hagar from Sarai.

7. The first step to recovery is developing an intimate relationship with God. Without salvation, codependent traits die hard because they are the flesh's way of coping with life. When God made a covenant (Old Testament salvation) with Abram (and Sarai since she was his wife), God changed their names to Abraham, which means "father of multitudes," and Sarah, which means "princess of God" or noblewoman. Both were destined to be great, psychologically whole persons who relied on Him to meet their needs instead of being so dependent on each other. Through faith in God, their low self-image and inadequacy were to be transformed into complete wholeness.

8. Deliverance from shame, codependent traits, and the development of faith takes time. When God stated that he would take away Sarah's shame by giving her a son, she laughed; and when God Himself confronted her, she denied that she had laughed. Maybe one of the reasons God named the boy Isaac (which means "laughter") was because He knew that he would get the last laugh when He proved that nothing (not even infertility or codependency) was too difficult for Him. Again, Abraham asked Sarah to lie and say that she was not his wife. This time she ended up in Abimeleck's harem. Again, Abraham did nothing to rescue her and God had to step in to deliver her. Yet, she continued to put up with the abuse and seemed to say nothing. Codependency dies hard.

9. Underline: Deliverance from shame is a key element in recovery. When Sarah conceived, her whole attitude changed. In the same way, when codependents finally realize that God loves them just the way they are and will meet all their needs through faith, the fear of inadequacy leaves, and for the first time they become whole people. In Genesis 21:6, Sarah said, "God hath made me to laugh, [so that] all that hear will laugh with me." Laughter often indicates that we feel accepted, that we have accepted ourselves as we are, and that we are enjoying life.

10. Underline: The second key element for recovery is learning to recognize and use boundaries appropriately. When the son of Hagar mocked Sarah's son Isaac, she did not just put up with it or attack Hagar as she had previously done. She took the problem to Abraham for resolution. Abraham took the problem to God who directed that Hagar and her son should be sent away. Distance is an excellent boundary.

11. Underline: Blessings, spiritual strength, and healthy relationships are the final signs that an individual has recovered from codependency. Sarah died at 127 years old and was buried in a grave at Machpelah (double portion) in Mamre (strength and fatness), which is in Hebron (association or relationships). To me this indicates that her relationships were blessed, spiritually strong, and healthy prior to her death. We are told that Abraham wept for her when she died.

12. Victory over codependency is achieved when we overcome our insecurity and learn to meet our needs through faith. This is summed up in the verses below:

    1 Pe 3:6 Even as Sara obeyed Abraham, calling him lord: whose daughters ye are, as long as ye do well (act righteously), and are not afraid with any amazement (not insecure).

    Heb 11:11 Through faith also Sara herself received strength to conceive seed, and was delivered of a child when she was past age, because she judged him faithful who had promised.

This type of client is most easily detected by her excessive neediness and dependence on others. An in-depth study of the life of Sarah usually is sufficient to help the client begin to understand and accept her part in her dysfunctional relationships. Clearly, the most important part in recovery is helping her develop a close, trusting faith that God loves her and will meet all of her needs even in the most difficult circumstances.

She should also resolve any outstanding family of origin issues and establish her worth in Christ. If possible, she should attend a Christian Codependent Support Group to learn more from others who are in the process of recovery and to receive the emotional support that she needs. I believe that *Love is a Choice* (1989), and its associated workbook (1991), by Hemfelt, Minirth, and Meier are the most appropriate additional resources for helping the codependent dependent passive.

Overcoming Codependent Dependent Passivity

1. The client must understand that the root of the problem is over-dependence on people instead of God to meet personal needs.

2. The codependent is desperately seeking love and approval through people pleasing, trying to be and do what others want, and allowing others to violate her personal boundaries in order to get her needs met.

3. She is a "good girl" and will do for others what they should be doing for themselves and blame herself if she is taken advantage of, mistreated or abused.

4. She must realize that her true motivation is selfishness and trying to cope with her own feelings of inadequacy by being good, caring for other people, pleasing, and enabling them.

5. The client must repent of her selfish efforts to meet her needs through people and learn to meet her needs through a close personal relationship with God.

6. The codependent must overcome her low self-image and feelings of inadequacy by accepting her position in Christ and God's evaluation of her.

7. She must understand that overly depending on others is the sin of idolatry and learn to use personal boundaries to develop healthy balanced, interdependent relationships with others.

Chapter 9

The Rescuer or "Savior" Complex
The Codependent Dependent Rescuer
(Abigail)

The Codependent Dependent Rescuer

If the type of dependent passive relationship described in the previous chapter has failed in her life or in the lives of her parents, a client will many times adopt a performance coping strategy and become the rescuer of a dysfunctional mate or addict. This type, I call the Codependent Dependent Rescuer. She believes that if she can rescue another, he will be grateful to her and will meet her needs in return. Unfortunately, for the dependent rescuer, this almost never happens. Deep within, she still would rather have him be the leader and rescue her. Many codependent dependent rescuers are nurses or members of other helping professions. Helping people just comes naturally to them. Of course, most of the time they do not realize that they are doing too much to help others, and their efforts are actually enabling others to continue in their dysfunctional lifestyles.

Joy was a third generation nurse. She had been dating the same man for over 5 years. She stood by him even when he had an affair with another woman. He was insecure and afraid to make decisions. Committing to a marriage meant the possibility of a divorce and failure. Failure was something he always tried to avoid. Although they were not engaged, she wanted to know where he was all the time and be with him as much as possible. He enjoyed the security she provided. Friends wondered how long she would enable his indecision, but somehow she just could not break off the relationship. She needed him too much.

It was not until I read *The Way Out of the Wilderness* by Henslin that I understood the story of Abigail in the book of 1st Samuel as a model of a codependent dependent rescuer. Until then, I had seen her as a model of how to deal with difficult circumstances. This is how most codependent rescuers initially view themselves—as the heroine or rescuer in a bad situation. Both Abigail and her husband, Nabal, were codependents. Abigail was a codependent dependent rescuer. Nabal was an alcoholic and a codependent independent worldly failure (which will be discussed later in more detail.) Most codependents have at least two addictions. (Hemfelt, Minirth and Meier, 1989). The story begins in 1st Samuel 25:2.

1. <u>Codependent dependent rescuers almost always marry someone who is also codependent and dysfunctional in some way.</u> Unresolved issues from the family of origin result in a reparative drive (we naturally want to try to fix our past), which influences the selection of a mate to recreate the unresolved problems in the new marriage. As already discussed, every damsel (codependent dependent) needs a knight (codependent independent) to rescue her. If the knight fails in the task, many times the damsel ends up trying to fix her dysfunctional knight so that he will meet her needs. Abigail was married to Nabal. Her name means "my father is joy" indicating her desire in life is to be happy. Unfortunately, Nabal, whose name means "fool," was stubborn, severe, evil, wicked, disagreeable, and a drunk. His underlying problem was feeling worthless (he was from the house of Caleb, which means "dog").

2. <u>Most mates of codependent dependents are incompetent, controlling, or abusive in some way</u>. Initially the codependent dependent rescuer is the "perfect" mate to enable a dysfunctional, abusive, or controlling husband. In order to please him, she avoids dealing with offenses and buries her emotional pain. Many times, she has had abusive or alcoholic parents, has "chosen" a husband to work out unresolved issues from the family of origin, and has learned codependent ways in order to cope with her husband's behavior. We are told that Nabal, instead of appreciating what David and his men had done to protect his sheep, "railed on them" and directly insulted David as a servant who "broke away from his master." (1 Samuel 25:10)

3. <u>The codependent dependent usually becomes the family "rescuer" protecting the mate from the consequences of his actions</u>. The young men did not go to Nabal when they realized that they were in danger, but to Abigail because "a man cannot speak to him (Nabal)." Clearly, things like this had happened before, and she had stepped into the gap to rescue the family time and time again.

4. <u>She believes that her mate is the problem and that if she could just fix him everything would be fine</u>. Note that Abigail in no way defended her husband when the young man called him "a man of belial"—an extremely derogatory phrase. They all saw Nabal as the problem, but no one was willing to confront or help him with his problems.

5. <u>Rather than deal with the situation directly by expressing her feelings, codependents just fix the problem</u>. Without asking her husband, Abigail loaded up enough food for 400 men and left to meet David and his men.

6. <u>They see themselves as the real hero or savior of the family</u>. In the times recorded in the Bible, it was almost unbelievable that a woman would attempt to confront 400 armed men and even expect them to listen to her message. She had numerous other options. She at least could have sent one of the young men as a messenger with the food to apologize, but it appears that she saw herself as the only one competent enough to handle the situation. Clearly, she had to do something at this point; or her family would have been destroyed. However, it was because she had enabled Nabal for so many years, rather than allow him to face his consequences, that this problem occurred in the first place. Without her, he would have had to face numerous less-critical consequences on other occasions and possibly would have learned from them.

7. <u>The codependent tries to cope with life herself in her own strength in worldly ways</u>. Abigail took two (division) hundred loaves (human efforts), and two bottles of wine (a worldly way to have joy), five (human weakness and infirmity) sheep (our own foolish ways) ready dressed, five measures of parched corn (temporal, earthly prosperity) and a hundred clusters of raisins (dried up fruits of human life and thoughts), and two hundred cakes of figs (our human attempts at righteousness) and laid them on asses (our own capabilities).

   1 Sa 25:18 Then Abigail made haste, and took two hundred loaves, and two bottles of wine, and five sheep ready dressed, and five measures of parched corn, and an hundred clusters of raisins, and two hundred cakes of figs, and laid them on asses.

   19 And she said unto her servants, Go on before me; behold, I come after you. But she told not her husband Nabal.

8. <u>The codependent fails to communicate and resolve issues with her mate out of fear of rejection</u>. Abigail did not tell Nabal what she was doing. She even had the servants leave first in order to hide it from her husband. The codependent fears her husband's anger and disapproval. It is as if he becomes a "false God" to be feared.

9. <u>Trying to completely meet a codependent's needs will fail</u>. Because of the codependent's intense need-deficit, no amount of loving support will ever completely fill her needs. She will only turn on

others, not appreciate what others do, and demand more. Nabal was also codependent. David states, "Surely in vain have I kept all that this [fellow] (Nabal) hath in the wilderness." We are not told to what extent Nabal ever tried to meet Abigail's needs; but if he had tried, his efforts would probably never have been enough.

10. <u>The codependent either is under- or over-responsible for others</u>. When Abigail met David, she initially claimed complete responsibility for what happened, and then degrades her husband Nabal (calling him a man of Belial or worthless one) and puts all the responsibility on him; since she was not there when David's messengers came. She avoids the thought that she had never confronted Nabal about his actions and had enabled him to remain as he was.

    1 Sa 25:24 And fell at his feet, and said, Upon me, my lord, upon me let this iniquity be: and let thine handmaid, I pray thee, speak in thine audience, and hear the words of thine handmaid.

    25 Let not my lord, I pray thee, regard this man of Belial, even Nabal: for as his name is, so is he; Nabal is his name, and folly is with him: but I thine handmaid saw not the young men of my lord, whom thou didst send.

11. <u>God does not want the church to take vengeance on codependents even though many times they deserve it</u>. I believe that David, here, represents the church. Codependents cause much havoc in churches, demanding love and an excessive amount of the pastor's time, and spreading gossip when someone fails to meet their needs in the way they want them to do. Eventually they will attack the church and pastor as unloving, and move on to another church. The answer is not excluding, ignoring or putting them down. David did not degrade Abigail or even Nabal.

12. <u>The codependent is many times extremely critical and derogatory toward his or her mate</u>. Abigail cursed those who seek evil for David with the curse that they would all become as bad as her husband!

    1 Sa 25:26 Now therefore, my lord, as the LORD liveth, and as thy soul liveth, seeing the LORD hath withholden thee from coming to shed blood, and from avenging thyself with thine own hand, now let thine enemies, and they that seek evil to my lord, be as Nabal.

13. <u>The codependent thrives on people pleasing</u>. Much of her conversation with David was flattery. She told him that she knew he would be king and that his house would succeed. She said that she believed that God fought his battles and that Saul, his enemy, would be "slung out, [as out] of the middle of a sling." She even told him that she believed that he had been without evil all his days.

    1 Sa 25:28 I pray thee, forgive the trespass of thine handmaid: for the LORD will certainly make my lord a sure house; because my lord fighteth the battles of the LORD, and evil hath not been found in thee all thy days.

    29 Yet a man has risen to pursue thee, and to seek thy soul: but the soul of my lord shall be bound in the bundle of life with the LORD thy God; and the souls of thine enemies, them shall he sling out, as out of the middle of a sling.

    30 And it shall come to pass, when the LORD shall have done to my lord according to all the good that he hath spoken concerning thee, and shall have appointed thee ruler over Israel;

14. <u>In truth, the codependent is only interested in taking care of herself</u>. Although they profess to love and care for others, everything they do has the ultimate aim of taking care of themselves. Abigail tried to protect herself, her family and her prosperity from destruction by David and his men. When she asked for forgiveness, she only asked for herself and not for her husband. The last thing she requested was "when the LORD shall have dealt well with my lord, then remember thine handmaid."

1 Sa 25:31 That this shall be no grief unto thee, nor offence of heart unto my lord, either that thou hast shed blood causeless, or that my lord hath avenged himself: but when the LORD shall have dealt well with my lord, then remember thine handmaid.

15. <u>The church is to help the codependent by giving unconditional acceptance and love but not enable her so that she can learn from her own consequences</u>. David thanked Abigail for her advice that he should not take vengeance. He accepted what she had to offer and stated that he would accept her person, indicating that he unconditionally accepted her.

1 Sa 25:32 And David said to Abigail, Blessed be the LORD God of Israel, which sent thee this day to meet me:

33 And blessed be thy advice, and blessed be thou, which hast kept me this day from coming to shed blood, and from avenging myself with mine own hand.

35 So David received of her hand that which she had brought him, and said unto her, Go up in peace to thine house; see, I have hearkened to thy voice, and have accepted thy person.

16. <u>The codependent usually is also addicted in some way</u>. Nabal handled his emotional problems by feasting, drinking, and taking false pride in his achievements. The Bible says that he was "very drunken." Trying to fix inside feelings with outside means, leads to addiction. We are not told what addictions Abigail might have had. The most common addictions for women are eating and buying things.

1 Sa 25:36 And Abigail came to Nabal; and, behold, he held a feast in his house, like the feast of a king; and Nabal's heart was merry within him, for he was very drunken: wherefore she told him nothing, less or more, until the morning light.

17. <u>The codependent becomes skilled in manipulating people</u>. Abigail had learned not to try to deal with Nabal while he was drunk. She waited for the next morning to tell him of his folly and her rescue. As is usually the case, instead of taking responsibility for his deadly error, he withdrew inside of himself, and became "as a stone." I believe that the phrase "his heart died within him" indicates that he gave up on life—the internal pain of feeling worthless that he had desperately tried to hide had become too great.

1 Sa 25:37 But it came to pass in the morning, when the wine was gone out of Nabal, and his wife had told him these things, that his heart died within him, and he became as a stone.

18. <u>The codependent's enabling eventually leads to the mates continuing dysfunction and many times death, especially when an addiction is involved</u>. Because Nabal had been protected from the consequences of his actions by Abigail and others, he was never forced by those consequences to change his life. The codependent many times actually believes that she is doing the right thing, but in fact is only selfishly protecting herself. Henslin, in *Out of the Wilderness*, suggests that Nabal died of an alcoholic seizure, stroke or heart attack related to his alcoholism. (Wilderness, p. 55)

1 Sa 25:38 And it came to pass about ten days after, that the LORD smote Nabal, that he died.

19. <u>The problems of codependency do not go away just because she remarries</u>. Most codependents believe that if they could just get out of the current situation or marriage, then things would be better. Abigail was still codependently people-pleasing when summoned by David to be his wife. She states, "Behold, [let] thine handmaid [be] a servant to wash the feet of the servants of my lord." She took

five damsels with her. Five stands for the weakness of every human being. (Wilson's, p. 192) Even marrying David, a man after God's own heart, did not totally resolve Abigail's codependent problems. David also had some of these tendencies, as is clearly seen in the later part of his life. As I have stated before, codependents usually marry another codependent.

1 Sa 25:39 And when David heard that Nabal was dead, he said, Blessed be the LORD, that hath pleaded the cause of my reproach from the hand of Nabal, and hath kept his servant from evil: for the LORD hath returned the wickedness of Nabal upon his own head. And David sent and communed with Abigail, to take her to him to wife.

20. <u>Although it is only the first step, a personal relationship with Jesus Christ and His church is one of the most important steps to recovery</u>. Again, I believe that David, in this story, stands for the church. Abigail married David. The answer to codependency is a personal relationship with Christ; since He alone can heal the deep hurts within and provide the infinite supply of unconditional love needed by the codependent.

21. <u>Just because a codependent is saved and joins a church does not necessarily alleviate all the codependent's problems</u>. Salvation is the process of complete wholeness, but it helps only to the degree the codependent yields her flesh to the lordship of Jesus Christ. Abigail, due to David's error of trying to escape from Saul by joining the Philistines, was captured by the Amalekites (the flesh). Because the church many times has had almost no understanding of codependency; it has mishandled its relationship with many codependents, and, as a result, many of them have been overcome again by the flesh. Many codependents end up feeling rejected by the church and continue to have issues with church leaders and members.

1 Sa 30:3 So David and his men came to the city, and, behold, it was burned with fire; and their wives, and their sons, and their daughters, were taken captives.

4 Then David and the people that were with him lifted up their voice and wept, until they had no more power to weep.

5 And David's two wives were taken captives, Ahinoam the Jezreelitess, and Abigail the wife of Nabal the Carmelite.

22. <u>Each time the codependent relapses and is again controlled by the flesh, the church is to do what it can to help</u>. David strengthened himself again in the Lord, and rescued his wives and children from the Amalikites (the flesh). Codependent support groups in the church provide one of the best ways to assist the codependent through unconditional love, acceptance, and support. Care must be taken for the struggling members of the church just as David cared first for the 200 men who were too weary to continue.

1 Sa 30: 6 And David was greatly distressed; for the people spake of stoning him, because the soul of all the people was grieved, every man for his sons and for his daughters: but David encouraged himself in the LORD his God.

18 And David recovered all that the Amalekites had carried away: and David rescued his two wives.

19 And there was nothing lacking to them, neither small nor great, neither sons nor daughters, neither spoil, nor any thing that they had taken to them: David recovered all.

21 And David came to the two hundred men, which were so faint that they could not follow David, whom they had made also to abide at the brook Besor: and they went forth to meet David, and to meet the people that were with him: and when David came near to the people, he saluted them.

24 For who will hearken unto you in this matter? but as his part is that goeth down to the battle, so shall his part be that tarrieth by the stuff: they shall part alike.

23. <u>The codependent must eventually turn all judgment over to God, instead of judging themselves or allowing other people to judge them</u>. Codependents are devastated emotionally by their own judgments of themselves and their perceptions of the judgments of others. They need to learn to accept God's judgment of them; that they are very good and that there is nothing they can do to change that, good or bad. David and Abigail's son was named Daniel which means "God is my judge." It is critically important for codependents to turn from pleasing people to accepting God as the only judge of their worth.

24. <u>The codependent must deal with her own codependency or her children will also become codependent</u>. What we are is passed on to the next generation. We are not told why, but God and David chose Solomon over Chileab (Abigail's son), who was next in line to be king after the death of Amnon. Possibly Chileab was too codependent, or maybe Bathsheba convinced David to choose Solomon, and Abigail did not protest. We do not even have an indication that Abigail protested about David's adultery. Maybe, like many codependents, she felt too unworthy to be treated with respect; or she had so many boundary violations in her marriage with Nabal that she did not know how to assertively stand for her rights.

Recovery from codependency is a process that usually takes a significant period of time. One secular counselor has estimated that it takes a period of five to six years. With God's help and answers, we usually expect therapy to last at least six months and that the client should remain in a support group for one to two years. After helping the client understand what codependency is and identifying her particular type of codependency, I always encourage them to start attending church and support group meetings immediately. Learning from others who are recovering or have recovered from codependency builds hope that recovery is possible, and provides the relationships and a source of unconditional love to assist in the recovery process.

As a primary resource, I use *Conquering Codependency* (McGee and McCleskey, 1993). I believe it is more appropriate for the codependent dependent rescuer while *Love is a Choice* (Hemfelt, Minirth, and Meier, 1989) is more appropriate for the codependent dependent passive. I conduct Marriage and Family Therapy for couples, and sometime during the recovery process, I assign the book *Boundaries* (Cloud and Townsend, 1989) and its associated workbook (1995). These help the client develop healthy personal boundaries useful in correcting current relationships and developing new healthy ones.

Overcoming Codependent Dependent Rescuing

1. The root of the problem is over-dependence on people instead of God to meet personal needs.

2. The codependent is desperately seeking love and approval because of a low self-image. She will control, manipulate, rescue others or allow the violation of personal boundaries in order to get her needs met.

3. She will do for others what they should be doing for themselves, become overwhelmed with all she is attempting to do, and eventually become bitter when other people do not meet her needs in return.

4. She tries to overcome feelings of inadequacy by people pleasing, rescuing or enabling. She believes that if she could just fix her mate then he would meet all her needs.

5. The client must repent of her selfish efforts to meet her needs through people and learn to meet her needs through a close personal relationship with God.

6. The codependent must overcome her low self-image and feelings of inadequacy by accepting God's evaluation of her and her position in Christ.

7. She must understand that controlling others is sin and learn to use personal boundaries to develop healthy relationships with others.

Chapter 10

The Dysfunctional Family
(David)

Dysfunctional families are characterized by emotionally needy people and a lack of effective healthy boundaries. They are usually the result of negative experiences growing up in an abusive, codependent, addictive, or otherwise dysfunctional family of origin. Children from these families are usually insecure, codependent, and lack any understanding of healthy boundaries. Applying boundaries to dysfunctional family situations has become an important part of marriage and family counseling today. Boundaries are the very basis of healthy relationships, and the perceived violation of boundaries is the basis of all offenses. The improper handling of offenses leads to a root of bitterness that is a significant factor in the majority of marriage failures.

Marital Difficulties (Michal)

In a seminar that I was teaching I made the statement, "Marriage can be heaven or hell on this earth. It is your choice which it will be." Because of the high expectations and tremendous possibility for love and teamwork in a marriage, marriage also contains the potential for tremendous pain, disappointment and betrayal. If a couple reacts out of their pain, things can easily escalate out of control.

Tom and Margarette had been children's ministers in a small denominational church. She had been working on her degree in business management and had the opportunity to start a daycare center at their church. Although she was inexperienced at managing such a center, the pastor had high regard for her and gave her permission to proceed. This was the dream of her life, and she put all her time into it. Her husband began to complain that she was not spending enough time with her family. She responded by accusing him of having an affair. She had been taught that she had to submit to whatever he did, and she was fed up with it. The pastor tried to counsel them but when he suggested that they begin by clarifying the boundaries of their marriage, she refused saying that that would just make her vulnerable to more abuse. She found another pastor that agreed she had every right to divorce him. Tom began a campaign of accusations against his wife and the pastor that eventually resulted in a church split. Before this marriage finally ended, the center she was trying to begin failed, and the entire church was engulfed in hatred and revenge. They had come a long way from the love they once enjoyed when they were first married.

Beginning in 1ˢᵗ Samuel Chapter 18, we are told the story of David's marriage to Michal, King Saul's youngest daughter. Like most couples, they began their marriage romantically in love. Sadly, through a process of disaffection, their marriage ended in contempt and deep hurt. This story gives us a model of how marriages fail.

1. <u>God has a plan for our lives, and this plan usually includes a compatible mate and a successful marriage.</u> Many times, however, we have our own ideas of whom we want to marry. One of my supervisors once stated, "When God gave you a helpmate, He was not necessarily giving you someone to make you happy; but someone who will help you identify and face the problems in your life."

This definitely seemed to be the case with David. He was originally supposed to marry King Saul's elder daughter Merab. Merab means "to increase." She was given instead to Adriel (flock of God) from Mehol (of dancing). Had David married her, she may have proved in the end to be a greater blessing to him than Michal was.

2. <u>Satan has a plan to destroy you through your marriage</u>. Saul's actual intention was that David would die trying to obtain the dowry to win one of Saul's daughters, and that his daughter would lead to David's downfall. That is the intention of Satan. He wants to use our marriages to bring us down.

    1 Sa 18:21 And Saul said, I will give him her, that she may be a snare to him, and that the hand of the Philistines may be against him. Wherefore Saul said to David, Thou shalt this day be my son in law in the one of the twain.

3. <u>The perception of love is essential to marriage</u>. If a man feels respected and appreciated, he will do almost anything for his wife. At its most rudimentary level, love is "having the other's best interests in mind." This is almost a magical line in marriage. On one side, the couple is on the same team and friends; on the other they are enemies trying to protect themselves and get their own needs met. Although Saul asked for the foreskins of 100 Philistines, David risked his life killing 200 Philistines to obtain the dowry so that he could marry Michal. He was willing to do more than he was asked. A woman usually judges the love of her husband by what her husband is willing to sacrifice for her. In fact, almost every wife evaluates everything her husband does in their relationship based upon the answer to only one question, "Does he really love me?"

    1 Sa 18:25 And Saul said, Thus shall ye say to David, The king desireth not any dowry, but an hundred foreskins of the Philistines, to be avenged of the king's enemies. But Saul thought to make David fall by the hand of the Philistines.

    27 Wherefore David arose and went, he and his men, and slew of the Philistines two hundred men; and David brought their foreskins, and they gave them in full tale to the king, that he might be the king's son in law. And Saul gave him Michal his daughter to wife.

    28 And Saul saw and knew that the LORD was with David, and that Michal Saul's daughter loved him.

4. <u>If a woman feels loved she will do almost anything for her husband</u>. When Saul sent men to kill David, Michal risked her life to help him escape in spite of the fact she was well aware of her father's dangerous fits of rage. The use of the image or idol here suggests that, to her, David was even more important to her than her gods were. Unfortunately, as we have previously seen in the discussion of codependency, many wives try to make their husband into the God "who will meet all their needs according to his riches in glory." David clearly could not measure up to such a task, especially since it appears he had not previously insisted that all images of other gods be removed from their house.

    1 Sa 19:11 Saul also sent messengers unto David's house, to watch him, and to slay him in the morning: and Michal David's wife told him, saying, If thou save not thy life to night, to morrow thou shalt be slain.

    12 So Michal let David down through a window: and he went, and fled, and escaped.

    13 And Michal took an image, and laid it in the bed, and put a pillow of goats' hair for his bolster, and covered it with a cloth.

    14 And when Saul sent messengers to take David, she said, He is sick.

15 And Saul sent the messengers again to see David, saying, Bring him up to me in the bed, that I may slay him.

16 And when the messengers were come in, behold, there was an image in the bed, with a pillow of goats' hair for his bolster.

17 And Saul said unto Michal, Why hast thou deceived me so, and sent away mine enemy, that he is escaped? And Michal answered Saul, He said unto me, Let me go; why should I kill thee?

5. <u>Offenses will happen in any marriage</u>. Because poor communication is so prevalent between husbands and wives, many times more than half of all the offenses in a marriage were not intended by their mate. All offenses are caused by perceived boundary violations. In this case, while Saul was hunting David to kill him, he gave Michal to another man. Phalti, her second husband, means "my deliverance." He was from Laish, which means "lion" which was in Gallim meaning "spring." This implies that he was a strong man (lion) who delivered Michal from her father's dysfunctional house and brought her a new life (like a spring of water.)

1 Sa 25:44 But Saul had given Michal his daughter, David's wife, to Phalti the son of Laish, which was of Gallim.

6. <u>The offenses continue to pile up</u>. After the death of Saul, David, as part of a peace treaty with Saul's son Ishbosheth, required that Michal be returned to him. Her second husband Phalti thought so much of Michal that he followed along crying until he was ordered by Abner, the commander of the army, to return home. David never asked her if she wanted to come back to him. Any time another person's free will is violated, a personal boundary violation has occurred. We can only guess how Michal felt about this, since by this time David had a number of other wives. Each offense erodes the belief that the other person has our best interest in mind. To a woman, each offense makes her question whether her mate truly loves her.

2 Sa 3:14 And David sent messengers to Ishbosheth Saul's son, saying, Deliver me my wife Michal, which I espoused to me for an hundred foreskins of the Philistines.

15 And Ishbosheth sent, and took her from her husband, even from Phaltiel the son of Laish.

16 And her husband went with her along weeping behind her to Bahurim. Then said Abner unto him, Go, return. And he returned.

7. <u>Unresolved offenses result in bitterness which eventually turns into contempt</u>. When David finally succeeded in bringing the Ark of God back to Jerusalem, Michal was offended by his open exuberance for the Lord. Possibly, she was jealous that he was happy when she was not. When a woman feels distance in a relationship, she many times assumes it is because her husband is interested in other women. She accused him of shameful behavior, another boundary violation. I suggest that this was a reaction to the previous offense.

2 Sa 6:16 And as the ark of the LORD came into the city of David, Michal Saul's daughter looked through a window, and saw king David leaping and dancing before the LORD; and <u>she despised him in her heart</u>.

20 Then David returned to bless his household. And Michal the daughter of Saul came out to meet David, and said, How glorious was the king of Israel to day, who uncovered himself to day in the eyes of the handmaids of his servants, as one of the vain fellows shamelessly uncovereth himself!

8. <u>Many times a husband will fail to probe for the underlying reason for his wife's displeasure and excuse his behavior, not realizing that he does not understand the real issue</u>. Instead of trying to understand Michal's emotional reaction, David reacted in anger, put down her father Saul and said he would continue doing what she disliked. It is not unusual for a husband to violate his wife's boundaries by discounting her feelings.

    2 Sa 6:21 And David said unto Michal, It was before the LORD, which <u>chose me before thy father, and before all his house,</u> to appoint me ruler over the people of the LORD, over Israel: <u>therefore will I play before the LORD</u>.

9. <u>The conflict may eventually result in the ending of intimacy in the marriage</u>. Who wants to make love with their enemy?

    2 Sa 6:23 Therefore Michal the daughter of Saul had no child unto the day of her death.

10. <u>When love has left a marriage it results in unmet needs that can lead to an affair</u>. Approximately ten years later, from his rooftop, David saw Bathsheba taking a bath. They slept together that night, she became pregnant, and David subsequently had Uriah, her husband, killed in order to cover up the affair. David later took Bathsheba as another of his wives.

11. <u>The bitterness continues until both are fully convinced that the other no longer has their best interests in mind</u>. When this happens they both become defensive and critical, and lose their feelings for each other. When there was a famine in the land because of Saul's persecution of the Gibeonites, David offered up Michal's five adopted sons for execution. To make matters worse, he spared Jonathan's son. Clearly, he valued his past relationship with Jonathan more than his relationship with Michal. I believe Michal would have seen what David did as a personal attack and a gross betrayal of their marriage. There was probably nothing worse that a husband could do to hurt his wife than to kill her children (even if they had been adopted). Unfortunately, there seems to be no limit to the terrible things that mates will do to hurt each other in an estranged marriage. It is ironic that Michal's five adopted children were hung during the days of harvest, a time normally associated with joy and abundance. Possibly this suggests that their marriage did not have to turn out this way, but could have been a wonderful blessing.

    2 Sa 21:7 But the king spared Mephibosheth, the son of Jonathan the son of Saul, because of the LORD'S oath that was between them, between David and Jonathan the son of Saul.

    8 But the king took the two sons of Rizpah the daughter of Aiah, whom she bare unto Saul, Armoni and Mephibosheth; and <u>the five sons of Michal the daughter of Saul,</u> whom she brought up for Adriel the son of Barzillai the Meholathite:

    9 And he delivered them into the hands of the Gibeonites, and they hanged them in the hill before the LORD: and they fell all seven together, and were put to death in the days of harvest, in the first days, in the beginning of barley harvest.

Unfortunately, in our society and churches today, over half of our marriages have followed a similar pattern that ends in divorce. Couples who were originally very much in love have ended their relationships in deep hurt and bitterness. It might even be hard to believe that many marriages from highly dysfunctional families can ever succeed. However, as we review the failures in David and Michal's marriage; we can see where simple communication skills and the application of effective boundaries could have changed the entire situation.

1. <u>The very basis of a marriage is a commitment to have the other's best interests in mind even when it may require sacrifice on our part</u>. The first major offense was when David used his political power to get Michal back. It is true he had every right to do so, especially in that time in history. But we have to ask the question if David was truly acting in Michal's best interest? He had a number of other wives at this time. He might have thought that what he was doing was best for everyone, but it appears he never asked her. Having the other's best interest in mind is basic to making the other person feel loved. Without it, a couple feels no better off than living with an enemy in the same house. Each mate usually concludes that they have to watch out for themselves, they are usually critical of each other and very little grace and mercy is shown in the marriage.

2. <u>Issues need to be resolved with solutions where everyone wins</u>. Most dysfunctional families operate as David and Michal did, resolving problems with win-lose solutions. Consequently, the person who loses becomes bitter or expects that he or she should win the next time. Many times the winner is the one who yells the loudest or has the least to lose. Mutual win-win agreements must be reached and perceived boundary violations must be dealt with when they occur. Many couples do not want to talk things through because trying to do so usually ends in a fight. If they do not talk, the buried anger will eventually result in bitterness that will defile the marriage. If a man will not talk things through, most women feel that they are not loved. This is because most women use communication to establish closeness in a relationship. Most men use communication primarily to accomplish tasks.

3. <u>Husbands and wives need to learn how to understand each other and communicate at a deeper level</u>. When Michal attacked David for dancing before the Lord without his tunic on, she was expressing the emotional pain of her marriage. Most men react the way David did. Had he not discounted her pain, this could have been an opportunity to understand or at least ask forgiveness for previous offenses. Like David, most men have not yet learned that a woman sends a primarily emotional message; and men send technically accurate data. The Bible directs that we must learn to live with the opposite gender "according to knowledge." (1 Peter 3:7) Teaching communication is a large part of counseling couples.

4. <u>Once communication is established, the couple needs to establish mutually agreed-upon boundaries</u>. This is done by identifying areas of continuing conflict. Since all offenses are the result of perceived boundary violations, previous conflicts help identify what boundary agreements are required. Each boundary consists of a clear, agreed-upon action or restraint and the natural consequences that will follow if it is violated. Boundaries work through behavior modification. If a person violates an agreement and gets a negative result, he will do it less often. If he gets a positive result, he will be encouraged to do it more often. Consequently, mutual boundary agreements will not immediately stop all conflicts, but they will eventually improve the marriage. If either mate violates an agreed-upon boundary, he or she will not have any excuse for not accepting the consequences. The first boundary that is usually required is an "anger break." The couple needs to agree on what they will do to keep an argument from escalating into an abusive fight. Usually this requires that they separate for a period of time and cool down before they attempt again to resolve the issue.

5. <u>Past offenses must be dealt with in order to end the bitterness in the marriage</u>. I suggest dealing with the future, then the present, then the past. I do this because it is much easier to forgive something that will probably not happen again. Boundary agreements provide a framework for working together in the future. Established boundaries also allow for current cooperation. For past issues I suggest what I call Monday Morning Quarterbacking (MMQ). This method is based on the analogy of reviewing the videotapes from the previous Sunday's football game. Each person is to be totally honest about what they did, why they did it, and how they perceived what happened. No blaming is allowed. Each is expected to take responsibility for what they did and ask for forgiveness if what

they did was wrong. The objective is not to find fault but to plan how to avoid the same problem in the future and to obtain forgiveness and closure.

6. <u>Because no one is or will ever be perfect, each spouse must quit trying to fix or blame his or her mate</u>. As you will probably remember, codependency is excessive dependence or independence on someone or something to meet our needs. Usually mates try to "fix each other" so that their needs can be met. We are to rely primarily on God to meet our unmet needs. The Bible tells us that we are not to set ourselves up to judge or try to fix one-another. We are all God's servants, and He asks us, "Why do you judge another man's servant?" (Romans 14:4) We are to proactively take responsibility for our own actions and not excuse our own behavior based on what someone else has done. Each of us will stand before God for what we have done. What our mate did or did not do will not be an excuse!

7. <u>As much as possible, those who are affected by or will receive the consequences of a decision should have a say in that decision</u>. In an ideal world, we would only receive the consequences of our own personal choices. In life, this is not always possible. We are almost always offended when we get someone else's consequences. Much of the conflict in a marriage can be resolved by including those who will receive the consequences in the decision process. Even after we are married, there are certain decisions that do not affect our mates. In these situations, each mate should be allowed to make their own choices as long as each one is willing to take responsibility for them and learn from his or her own consequences. In this case, the person should say, "I have a problem." This indicates to the other mate that they are not involved and will not receive significant consequences from any decision that is made. In situations where both mates are affected, they need to agree on the decision since both of them will receive the consequences of that decision. In speaking about problems that affect both mates, they should say, "We have a problem, what are we going to do about it?" If a person says to his mate "you have a problem," he is admitting that he is violating the other mate's boundaries because he has no right to be involved in a decision in which he does not receive any of the consequences. Of course, if either one chooses, he or she may ask the mate for advice even when the decision does not primarily affect them. However, the final decision should still be made by the mate who will, in fact, get the consequences of that decision. No person ever has a right to force his view upon another adult.

8. <u>The overall goal of marriage counseling is to help the couple resolve their conflicts to such an extent that they again perceive that their mates actually do have their best interests in mind</u>. Once this perception is re-established, they will again be able to cooperate on at least a friendship level and work toward a better marriage and life. Until both mates truly believe that the other one does have their best interest in mind, working together as a team is almost impossible and the marriage will continue to struggle.

It is not unusual for couples coming for marriage counseling to be so disheartened that they believe there is only one solution—divorce. Many times one of the mates comes hoping the counselor will agree that in their special situation God would sanction divorce, especially when domestic violence and abuse has occurred. The Bible is very clear that divorce is allowed only in cases of adultery (Matthew 5:32), or if the other mate is unsaved and chooses to leave (1st Corinthians 7:15). Because divorce results in such deep emotional pain and significant consequences, God requires us to do everything possible to prevent it. Sometimes temporary separation is required to protect one spouse from further abuse. However, I have found that if one of the partners will learn to biblically deal with his or her own problems and set strong, effective boundaries, the other mate will have to change or will eventually choose to divorce them. If the mate that leaves commits adultery or remarries, the first spouse has grounds for remarriage (because the divorce now meets biblical criteria). Either the marriage will be restored or if not restored at least the client will know that he has done everything possible to save the marriage. In either case, the non-offending spouse is better off since divorce recovery is much easier without the guilt of feeling they gave up on the marriage too soon.

Problems with Children (David's Children)

When a couple is in a dysfunctional relationship or when a marriage is conflicted, the entire family will be affected. Discipline will usually be inconsistent or ineffective. Without both love and effective boundaries, family life becomes chaotic.

Bob and Mary had a blended family. Bob's children came from a very dysfunctional environment and were totally out of control. Mary was traumatized by all the things the children did, but Bob could not bring himself to follow through on his threatened discipline, because he knew that his children had been neglected earlier in life. He blamed himself for allowing things to be so chaotic for so long. When his teenage son, who lived with them, did anything that bothered Mary and Mary complained; he would take his son's side and try to justify what his son had done. Mary believed that this meant that Bob loved his son more than her. She demanded that either he discipline his son or they both move out. He would have to choose between them. It appeared that in order for this couple to find reconciliation, they would have to wait until the teenage son grew up and left home. They truly had no idea of how to resolve the chaos in their home as long as the son remained. Fortunately, they eventually decided to go to counseling where they learned how to establish effective fair family rules that all three of them could live with. Although it took a number of months, peace was finally restored to their marriage.

In the Bible, the continuing story of King David's family demonstrates how poor choices by the parents can dramatically affect their children. This story continues in 2nd Samuel Chapter 12.

1. <u>Family problems generally originate with the parents</u>. Children come into the world with certain inherited personality traits and a blank slate. How they are brought up depends on the environment provided by the parents. The Bible tells us that David's problems with his children go back to his affair with Bathsheba and the murder of Uriah. Even by today's standards David's family was dysfunctional. In addition to this secret affair and murder, every one of his male children were from a different wife; and they were competing for his favor and eventually the throne. The fact that he favored Solomon, the son of Bathsheba, over the rest probably did not help.

   2 Sa 12:10 Now therefore the sword shall never depart from thine house; because thou hast despised me, and hast taken the wife of Uriah the Hittite to be thy wife.

   11 Thus saith the LORD, Behold, I will raise up evil against thee out of thine own house, and I will take thy wives before thine eyes, and give them unto thy neighbour, and he shall lie with thy wives in the sight of this sun.

2. <u>The sins of the parents can provide the seed for the sins that are repeated in the next generation</u>. In 2nd Samuel Chapter 13, we are told that Amnon, the oldest son of David, loved his step-sister Tamar. He acted like he was sick, asked David to send her to minister to him in his sickness, and, when she came, he raped her. The sexual sin, which began through David's adultery with Bathsheba, was repeated in the next generation. Unfortunately, most of the time the children will even go beyond the sins of their parents.

3. <u>Because of their own sins or insecurity, many times parents feel they have no right to set or enforce effective boundaries with their children</u>. Because of their past failures, they feel they cannot really blame their children, and therefore, fail to discipline them effectively. This almost inevitably leads to an increasingly dysfunctional family. We are told that David was "very wroth" over what Amnon had done but took no action. (2 Samuel 13:21)

4. <u>Without action to enforce effective boundaries, the dysfunction will escalate</u>. After two years passed Absalom, Tamar's brother, decided to take justice into his own hands and assassinate Amnon. Children do not respond to words but to action. Absalom felt that someone had to do something

about Tamar's rape, and David had done nothing. If the parents will not act, the children may feel justified in taking revenge for them.

5. <u>The lack of effective discipline results in a disrespect for the parent</u>. The fact that David was blatantly manipulated to be part of both the rape and the murder shows the disdain that the children had for their father.

6. <u>Children need both love and appropriate boundaries</u>. Children that have no boundaries feel insecure and do not develop responsibility. Children who are over-controlled and never given a chance to make choices never learn self-discipline. David's children were given excessive liberty as indicated by the inclusion of Jonadab (liberty) in both plots. (2 Samuel 13:5, 32) When Absalom was brought back from exile through the manipulation of Joab, David refused to see him. Possibly David saw his coldness as his means of showing disapproval for what Absalom had done. Absalom most likely saw David's actions as rejection and a lack of love.

7. <u>Rules or boundaries without perceived love brings rebellion</u>. Absalom conspired to over-throw and kill his own father. The basis of this rebellion was clear. He accused his father of not being just to the people. Of course, it was Tamar, his sister, who had not received justice; and Absalom, himself, felt rejected for doing what David should have done. The basis of his rebellion can also be tied directly to David's adultery, since a co-conspirator with Absalom was David's past advisor, Ahithophel, the grandfather of Bathsheba. Absalom carried out exactly what the prophet Nathan had predicted; he slept with his Father's concubines on the roof of the palace. (2 Samuel 16:21-22)

8. <u>Really caring for your children is not enough</u>. They have to know that you love them enough to discipline them. After Absalom's death, David's real feelings were apparent when he said he would have rather died himself.

   2 Sa 18:33 And the king was much moved, and went up to the chamber over the gate, and wept: and as he went, thus he said, O my son Absalom, my son, my son Absalom! would God I had died for thee, O Absalom, my son, my son!

9. <u>A lack of effective discipline will eventually result in rebellion</u>. While over controlling children usually results in a lack of self-control when they grow older, a lack of discipline makes a child feel that they have to take care of themselves. After Absolom's death, his brother Adaonijah decided to make himself king. We are told that David had never "displeased him at any time." Possibly this was because David was still grieving the death of Absalom. I recommend that every family needs a set of family rules. These are a set of mutually agreed-upon boundaries, which specify expectations, and the consequences for any violation. These boundaries need to be enforced consistently and impartially. They provide a framework within which children can be taught responsibility, yet allowed to learn from their own choices and consequences, so that they also learn self-discipline.

   1 Ki 1:5 Then Adonijah the son of Haggith exalted himself, saying, I will be king: and he prepared him chariots and horsemen, and fifty men to run before him.

   6 <u>And his father had not displeased him at any time in saying, Why hast thou done so?</u> and he also was a very goodly man; and his mother bare him after Absalom.

Principles of a Healthy Family (Joseph and Mary)

David's family did not recover from its problems. Two generations later, these problems resulted in the division of the nation of Israel. Consequently, in order to illustrate what a healthy family is to be like, we need to find another biblical example. Not all families are so dysfunctional that they end in divorce or that the children need years to recover from the effects of growing up in their family of origin. Some marriages are entered into by two reasonably healthy people who have learned to use effective boundaries in their lives and who rely primarily on God to meet their needs. We find such a family in the New Testament story of Joseph and Mary, the mother of Jesus.

1. <u>Both marriage partners must be completely dedicated to God and desire the will of God in their lives</u>. Doing God's will should be even more important to them than becoming married to a particular person. Mary was so humble and dedicated to having the will of God carried out in her life that she risked her coming marriage to Joseph. When the angel came to Mary, she openly accepted the will of God even though she did not understand it. Becoming pregnant before she was married would probably bring her disgrace, emotional pain and an end to her engagement to Joseph.

   Lu 1:38 And Mary said, Behold the handmaid of the Lord; be it unto me according to thy word. And the angel departed from her.

   Joseph was also open to the will of God and took Mary to be his wife in spite of the fact that she was already pregnant. It must have been hard for him to believe that she was somehow pregnant without having a relationship with another man even after the angel of the Lord revealed this to him in a dream. It is doubtful that any of his friends or the people of Nazareth would have believed this "story."

   Mt 1:20 But while he thought on these things, behold, the angel of the Lord appeared unto him in a dream, saying, Joseph, thou son of David, fear not to take unto thee Mary thy wife: for that which is conceived in her is of the Holy Ghost.

2. <u>They must believe that God has their best interests in mind no matter what He asks them to do</u>. Elizabeth complimented Mary on her faith in God and declared that what was promised would happen.

   Lu 1:41 And it came to pass, that, when Elisabeth heard the salutation of Mary, the babe leaped in her womb; and Elisabeth was filled with the Holy Ghost:

   42 And she spake out with a loud voice, and said, Blessed art thou among women, and blessed is the fruit of thy womb.

   45 <u>And blessed is she that believed</u>: for there shall be a performance of those things which were told her from the Lord.

3. <u>They must be dedicated to working together as a team to do what God directs, in spite of what difficulties life might bring</u>. A joint vision is essential to a strong marriage. The fact that Mary accompanied Joseph all the way to Bethlehem to register for the census when she was about to give birth is amazing. This trip is more than 70 miles mostly on rough trails and must have taken a number of days! Later, when Joseph had a dream that Herod would try to destroy the child, they left immediately that night for Egypt. When Joseph received another dream, they returned to Israel. They were both submitted to the direction of God in their lives and to each other.

4. <u>They must learn to work together for the betterment of the family and not easily give up</u>. Joseph and Mary's unity and teamwork are clearly illustrated when Jesus was twelve years of age. He stayed behind in Jerusalem after the Passover celebration and somehow they were not aware of it. When they did not find Him immediately, they sought him among the relatives. When they did not locate Him, they both returned to Jerusalem and kept searching together for three whole days. They did not seem to blame each other. (Luke 2:43-50)

5. <u>The parents of a healthy family must demonstrate the healthy use of boundaries to resolve family disagreements</u>. When they finally found Jesus, they simply asked Him why He had stayed in

Jerusalem. Jesus' answer shows that His action was the result of a boundary disagreement. It should be understood that when, in the Hebrew tradition, a boy turned 12 years old, he was considered a man and capable of making his own decisions. They expected Jesus to follow them home because He was their son, but He felt that He needed to stay longer in Jerusalem to prepare for what His Father in heaven was calling Him to do. He expected them to understand this. Even though they probably did not really understand His point of view, they accepted it; and He returned home and was obedient to them. The result of their healthy handling of this boundary situation was that Jesus increased in wisdom and favor in His relationships.

Lu 2:48 And when they saw him, they were amazed: and his mother said unto him, Son, why hast thou thus dealt with us? behold, thy father and I have sought thee sorrowing.

49 And he said unto them, How is it that ye sought me? wist ye not that I must be about my Father's business?

50 And they understood not the saying which he spake unto them.

51 And he went down with them, and came to Nazareth, and was subject unto them: but his mother kept all these sayings in her heart.

52 And Jesus increased in wisdom and stature, and in favour with God and man.

6. <u>Effective and honoring communication skills are essential for a healthy family</u>. At the wedding in Canaan, they ran out of wine. Mary succinctly approached Jesus with care that appropriate boundaries be maintained between them. He made it clear that He was now a grown man, so she did not have the right to tell Him what to do. She honored Him by telling the servants to do whatever He said and did not even suggest what choice He should make. This showed faith that He would do the right thing.

Jo 2:3 And when they wanted wine, the mother of Jesus saith unto him, They have no wine.
4 Jesus saith unto her, Woman, what have I to do with thee? mine hour is not yet come.

5 His mother saith unto the servants, Whatsoever he saith unto you, do it.

7. <u>Doing the will of God must be even more important than the family itself</u>. When Jesus' mother and brothers came wanting to speak to Him; He clearly set a boundary concerning His priorities. As a grown man, he must do the will of God rather than the desires of His family.

Mr 3:31 There came then his brethren and his mother, and, standing without, sent unto him, calling him.

32 And the multitude sat about him, and they said unto him, Behold, thy mother and thy brethren without seek for thee.

33 And he answered them, saying, Who is my mother, or my brethren?

34 And he looked round about on them which sat about him, and said, Behold my mother and my brethren!

35 For whosoever shall do the will of God, the same is my brother, and my sister, and mother.

8. <u>When conflicts arise, healthy family members do not try to control the other members, do not put others down for their choices, and set the other members free to make their own decisions and live with the consequences of their decisions</u>. Jesus' brothers suggested that He should go up to the feast, so he could increase his public following. Jesus explained that it was not yet time for Him to do that. They went to the feast anyway. This clearly demonstrates a healthy level of separateness in this

family, even though they did not agree on everything. In fact, His brothers were not even convinced He was the Messiah.

9. <u>Love for each other (having the other's best interest in mind) must take priority (even under the most dire circumstances)</u>. Even when Jesus was hanging on the cross, He still showed concern for His mother. By that time, Joseph must have already died or he would have been there. Jesus directed John to provide for Mary's needs, since He would no longer be able to do so.

Jo 19:26 When Jesus therefore saw his mother, and the disciple standing by, whom he loved, he saith unto his mother, Woman, behold thy son!

27 Then saith he to the disciple, Behold thy mother! And from that hour that disciple took her unto his own home.

10. <u>The real test of a healthy family is how the members of the next generation function during the remainder of their lifetime</u>. Jesus, Mary's son, went to the cross for all of humanity. His mother and brothers were all in the upper room at Pentecost. Jesus' brother James became one of the main leaders in the church in Jerusalem along with Peter. In spite of all the difficulties that this family suffered, Joseph and Mary successfully passed on the torch of serving and obeying God to the next generation.

Someone might complain that using the family of Jesus as a model moves it out of the realm of human possibilities. I do not believe that this is a valid point because Joseph and Mary appeared healthy even before Jesus' birth. Just because one of the members of the family was perfect (Jesus), this did not necessarily insure that all the members would be healthy. David's family was led by a man after God's own heart and was very dysfunctional. We are all called to be conformed to the image of Jesus through faith. No matter where we might be today, God expects us to become more functional through the process of salvation. This is made possible by walking in faith each day until we become the glorious, whole, healthy individuals and family members that He created us to be. It is God's goal that all families be transformed in a similar manner.

When I counsel families, I sometimes use *Boundaries* (1992), the *Boundaries Workbook* (1995), *Boundaries in Marriage* (1998), and *Boundaries with Children* (1999) by Cloud and Townsend as resources. For communication and gender differences, I use *Hidden Keys of a Loving Lasting Marriage* (1988) by Gary Smalley. For families on the verge of divorce, I recommend *Before a Bad Goodbye* (1999) by Tim Clinton, and for families with older children who are out of control, I suggest *Parenting Teens with Love and Logic* (1992) by Cline and Faye. More recently I have found *Safe Haven Marriage* (Hart and Morris, 2003) and *Love and Respect* (Eggerichs, 2004) especially useful.

Healing Dysfunctional Families

1. The first and most important step is for all members of the family to accept Christ as their Savior and Lord, quit trying to direct their own lives, give control over to God, and become willing to be obedient to His word.

2. Help each member of the family take responsibility for their own actions no matter what other members do. God holds us accountable for what we do and how we react, not what our mate or children do. We must learn to respond with what is right instead of reacting out of our hurt.

3. Teach the family communication skills so that they can discuss and resolve issues without fighting.

4. Teach all members of the family how to use effective boundaries to resolve conflict and not to be excessively passive or aggressive when their personal boundaries are violated.

5. Help develop a set of boundaries or rules for the family that all agree are reasonable and fair. These boundaries may have to include how the family will deal with arguments and outbursts of anger. They must be consistently followed.

6. Help the family discuss, resolve and forgive past offenses.

7. Once the family believes that the other members do have their best interests in mind, help them reach out in love to develop healthy relationships, work together as a team for the betterment of every member, and do the will of God.

Chapter 11

Injustice
(Jotham)

It is difficult for us to deal with the issue of injustice. It is inherent in every relationship problem or dysfunctional family situation. Although it is a common problem, it can also become a complex one when it leaves scars on the soul and changes a person's view of the world. A client's life can be deeply damaged because of some perceived injustice, especially in cases of governmental abuse, imprisonment, torture, or war. Without help, he may never recover. Post Traumatic Stress Disorder can last for a lifetime. Injustice is always a boundary violation, since for an injustice to exist it must be perceived that either the boundary or law has not been fairly applied or that the one who made the decision is not the one who is getting the consequences. Injustice threatens a person's feelings of security. When injustice prevails, people feel powerless. Consequently, experiences of injustice can lead to problems that affect people for a lifetime if they are not resolved. A person naturally wants to strike back and correct the wrong. However, even though God expects people to do their part, personally taking vengeance is not usually God's way of dealing with the problem.

Jacob and June felt they had been treated unjustly by the social service system and the courts. Both Jacob and June's last husband had a history of domestic violence. When Jacob was again involved in a violent incident, June's children were taken from her. The social service worker suggested that in order to get her children back, she needed to divorce Jacob. Even after they were divorced, her children were not returned. The lawyer suggested that in order to get her children back as soon as possible, they should just accept the charges, most of which were untrue. Although Jacob was never evaluated, he was presumed to be a threat to the children. Inexplicably, the children were placed in the custody of her first, much more domestically violent husband; and she was given few rights of visitation. The social services and the courts used the unfounded charges that she had accepted as the basis for refusing to return her children to her custody.

After Jacob and June did all that they could do, the only effective recourse was to place the entire situation into the hands of God. God is just and will eventually bring justice to even the most unjust situation, if we will put it into His hands. If we choose to handle the situation ourselves (be our own God), God will usually not become involved until we are willing to yield the situation to Him.

In Judges Chapter 8, the Bible describes an extreme case of injustice and gives us a model for resolving these kinds of problems. We normally trust that our government was established to provide justice and sometimes we rely too much on our courts to insure that justice will be carried out. Unfortunately, this does not always happen.

1. <u>Governmental injustice is an issue of power and control</u>. We want people to be in charge of our government that we believe will insure that our needs are met. Because Gideon had saved the nation from the Midianites, they wanted him to be king.

   Jud 8:22 Then the men of Israel said unto Gideon, rule thou over us, both thou, and thy son, and thy son's son also: for thou hast delivered us from the hand of Midian.

2. <u>In order to have peace we must place our trust primarily in God, not in man</u>. No legal system can ever guarantee justice because most people involved in the system are motivated by their own self-interest or selfishness. Gideon rightly suggested that God should be their ruler.

Jud 8:23 And Gideon said unto them, I will not rule over you, neither shall my son rule over you: the LORD shall rule over you.

3. <u>The seeds of injustice are planted when we value other things more than God (have idols), and trust primarily in human laws</u>. Even the laws of our country can become idols to us if we excessively trust and rely on them to bring us justice.

Jud 8:33 And it came to pass, as soon as Gideon was dead, that the children of Israel turned again, and went a whoring after Baalim, and made Baalberith (God of covenant or human laws) their god.

4. <u>Because human laws are based on selfishness, they can never bring true justice</u>. Although all profess to want justice, most only really desire to meet their own needs. We do not really want justice when we are at fault.

Jud 9:1 And Abimelech, the son of Jerubbaal (by a concubine) went to Shechem unto his mother's brethren, and communed with them, and with all the family of the house of his mother's father, saying,

2 Speak, I pray you, in the ears of all the men of Shechem, Whether [is] better for you, either that all the sons of Jerubbaal, [which are] threescore and ten persons, reign over you, or that one reign over you? remember also that I [am] your bone and your flesh.

3 And his mother's brethren spake of him in the ears of all the men of Shechem all these words: and their hearts inclined to follow Abimelech; for they said, He [is] our brother. (and will give our selfish interests priority.)

5. <u>People select leaders and make laws that benefit them</u>. Democracy is the most just of any system of government, because, at least ideally, each person has some say in the laws that govern the legal process. However, even in a democracy, each person votes for those representatives that reflect their personal views and whom they believe will make laws that are in their best interest. Because the people were convinced that Abimelech, their relative, would be favorable to them; they supported him with money from the temple of Baalberith, the god of the Philistines, which means "the lord of covenant." People give money to support those that they want to be elected.

Jud 9:4 And they gave him threescore and ten [pieces] of silver out of the house of Baalberith (covenant of God or human laws), wherewith Abimelech hired vain and light persons, which followed him.

6. <u>The result of selfishness in government is injustice</u>. People are not concerned about insuring that others' needs are met—just their own. The laws in the United States that support and defend abortion are a clear example of this. They defend the rights of the mother (who can vote) over the rights of the unborn child (who cannot vote). The people of Shechem supported Abimelech so that they could get their needs met even after he killed 69 of Gideon's innocent sons in order to usurp power.

Jud 9:5 And he went unto his father's house at Ophrah, and slew his brethren the sons of Jerubbaal, [being] threescore and ten persons, upon one stone: notwithstanding yet Jotham (Jehovah is perfect) the youngest son of Jerubbaal was left; for he hid himself.

7. <u>Human leaders are chosen through a selfish power struggle for predominance</u>. The fact that these men came from Millo (which means "rampart or mound") suggests that they saw all of life as a struggle to win the battle of "king of the hill." Such competition is never fair or just for everyone. In fact, everyone eventually loses.

Jud 9:6 And all the men of Shechem gathered together, and all the house of Millo, and went, and made Abimelech king, by the plain of the pillar that [was] in Shechem.

8. <u>Injustice must be confronted</u>. Jotham's name means "Jehovah is perfect." Although he trusted God to be perfect and just, he still had an obligation to confront this clear injustice, just as we have an obligation to confront injustice such as abortion in our land. He confronted it from Mount Gerizin, the mountain from which the Israelites said the blessing over those who would obey the law when they entered into the Promised Land. I believe that this suggests that God has a special blessing for those who will confront injustice.

Jud 9:7 And when they told [it] to Jotham, he went and stood in the top of mount Gerizim (The Mountain of Blessing) and lifted up his voice, and cried, and said unto them, Hearken unto me, ye men of Shechem, that God may hearken unto you.

9. <u>Because human government is based on vested interest, most of those who are truly productive and would be a blessing will not compete for political power</u>. Gideon had refused to reign over Israel or let his sons be king, because he believed that God should be their king. Because of the constant competition, name-calling, and "dirty tricks" involved in politics, few Christians have been willing to participate in the electoral process. Unfortunately, this lack of participation has allowed many unjust laws to be enacted and injustice to prevail in our governmental system. Jothan's story suggests that, at least in his day, only rough people who wanted to strive for power (the bramble bush) would accept a position of political leadership.

Jud 9:8 The trees went forth [on a time] to anoint a king over them; and they said unto the olive tree (Israel from the religious standpoint), Reign thou over us.

9 But the olive tree said unto them, Should I leave my fatness, wherewith by me they honour God and man, and go to be promoted over the trees?

10 And the trees said to the fig tree (represents Israel from a political standpoint), Come thou, [and] reign over us.

11 But the fig tree said unto them, Should I forsake my sweetness, and my good fruit, and go to be promoted over the trees?

12 Then said the trees unto the vine (a type of the nation of Israel which brings forth good things), Come thou, [and] reign over us.

13 And the vine said unto them, Should I leave my wine, which cheereth God and man, and go to be promoted over the trees?

14 Then said all the trees unto the bramble, Come thou, [and] reign over us.

10. <u>How foolish it is to put our trust in people who have a vested interest in being leaders, because their selfishness will inevitably bring injustice</u>. These verses suggest that if we are naïve enough to believe

that selfish, competitive people are going to be a blessing to us, we will be burned. Unfortunately, because we allow the bramble bushes of life to lead us our collective Christian life is devoured.

Jud 9:15 And the bramble (the thorn tree represents disagreeable life filled with antagonism, criticism, and hatred) said unto the trees, If in truth ye anoint me king over you, [then] come [and] put your trust in my shadow: and if not, let fire come out of the bramble, and devour the cedars (the collective Christian life) of Lebanon.

11. <u>How can a government, which is based on injustice or power struggles, ever bring justice?</u> The fact is that no matter how much effort we put into a governmental system, it can never bring the complete justice that God wants to provide. Jotham, in his speech, clearly expressed the injustice done to his family and suggested that those who do injustice will eventually reap what they sow.

Jud 9:16 Now therefore, if ye have done truly and sincerely, in that ye have made Abimelech king, and if ye have dealt well with Jerubbaal and his house, and have done unto him according to the deserving of his hands;

17 (For my father fought for you, and adventured his life far, and delivered you out of the hand of Midian:

18 And ye are risen up against my father's house this day, and have slain his sons, threescore and ten persons, upon one stone, and have made Abimelech, the son of his maidservant, king over the men of Shechem, because he [is] your brother;)

19 If ye then have dealt truly and sincerely with Jerubbaal and with his house this day, [then] rejoice ye in Abimelech, and let him also rejoice in you:

12. <u>Injustice will eventually consume itself if, through forgiveness, we give up our rights to God for vengeance.</u> Those who act unjustly come under a curse that results from their own selfishness. They may feel that they will get away with it—and for a season it may appear that they do—but eventually all those who do injustice will be consumed by it.

Jud 9:20 But if not, let fire come out from Abimelech, and devour the men of Shechem (human reliance), and the house of Millo (rampart – king of the hill or struggles for power); and let fire come out from the men of Shechem, and from the house of Millo, and devour Abimelech.

13. <u>After releasing our rights to God, we need to trust in Him for life.</u> After doing everything that we can to confront injustice, we need to turn the entire situation over to God and go on with our lives.

Jud 9:21 And Jotham ran away, and fled, and went to Beer (a well, an oasis in the desert), and dwelt there, for fear of Abimelech his brother.

14. <u>It usually takes time for God's justice to prevail, because God gives time for all men to repent.</u> Because in biblical times a successful king reigned forty years, the time that elapsed before Abimelech began to reap his consequences was not very long. Of course, people who have been victimized always want justice to occur immediately. It took three years before God began to deal with Abimelech.

Jud 9:22 When Abimelech had reigned three years over Israel,

23 Then God sent an evil spirit between Abimelech and the men of Shechem; and the men of Shechem dealt treacherously with Abimelech:

15. <u>God knows how to take vengeance and how to avenge injustice</u>. God works behind the scenes and is in control even when it does not appear that He is. Just as Abimelech had dealt treacherously with the sons of Gideon, so the people of Shechem who had supported him, eventually turned on him. In the same way, Abimelech turned on them and destroyed them.

Jud 9:23 Then God sent an evil spirit between Abimelech and the men of Shechem; and the men of Shechem dealt treacherously with Abimelech:

24 That the cruelty [done] to the threescore and ten sons of Jerubbaal might come, and their blood be laid upon Abimelech their brother, which slew them; and upon the men of Shechem, which aided him in the killing of his brethren.

45 And Abimelech fought against the city all that day; and he took the city (of Shechem), and slew the people that [was] therein, and beat down the city, and sowed it with salt.

16. <u>Human covenants and laws will not protect unjust people</u>. Those who support a political candidate expect that candidate to protect them from injustice. This is seldom the case in the end. The people of Shechem tried to escape into the house of their god (government), but Abimelech used trees to burn them to death. Trees many times represent positions of power or people. Those who have achieved power will often use others who are in power to carry out whatever they want to do. Relying on government instead of God is definitely not a sure way to protect oneself from injustice.

Jud 9:46 And when all the men of the tower of Shechem heard [that], they entered into an hold of the house of the god Berith (god of covenants or human government).

47 And it was told Abimelech, that all the men of the tower of Shechem were gathered together.

48 And Abimelech gat him up to mount Zalmon, he and all the people that [were] with him; and Abimelech took an axe in his hand, and cut down a bough from the trees, and took it, and laid [it] on his shoulder, and said unto the people that [were] with him, What ye have seen me do, make haste, [and] do as I [have done].

49 And all the people likewise cut down every man his bough, and followed Abimelech, and put [them] to the hold, and set the hold on fire upon them; so that all the men of the tower of Shechem died also, about a thousand men and women.

17. <u>Even though unjust people may achieve notoriety, their end will be shame</u>. All those who desire to be powerful, and use injustice to obtain power, will eventually be destroyed in their attempt to maintain it. The town of Thebez means "conspicuous" based on a root word, which means "to bleach white." All injustice will eventually be brought to justice. This is absolutely true since, if justice has not occurred prior to the end of time, all men will be judged according to their works on the Day of Judgment. Instead of becoming someone of importance, those that do injustice will find that it leads to shame and humiliation. In biblical times, to be killed by a woman was one of the most shameful things that could happen to a man. God has a way of putting those who do injustice in their place. A person who thinks he can do injustice and get away with it should realize that it will eventually destroy him. Abimelech's skull (thinking) was crushed.

Jud 9:50 Then went Abimelech to Thebez (conspicuous), and encamped against Thebez, and took it.

51 But there was a strong tower within the city, and thither fled all the men and women, and all they of the city, and shut [it] to them, and gat them up to the top of the tower.

52 And Abimelech came unto the tower, and fought against it, and went hard unto the door of the tower to burn it with fire.

53 And a certain woman cast a piece of a millstone upon Abimelech's head, and all to brake his skull.

18. <u>Suicide and destruction will be the eventual end of evil men</u>. In his shame, Abimelech had his armor bearer kill him. Trusting in injustice is a form of committing suicide. It can only bring more injustice, shame, and disaster into one's life.

Jud 9:54 Then he called hastily unto the young man his armourbearer, and said unto him, Draw thy sword, and slay me, that men say not of me, A woman slew him. And his young man thrust him through, and he died.

19. <u>When we trust God, He always brings justice in the end</u>. Although we might not see it as clearly as it is described in this story; when we turn an injustice over to God, He works behind the scenes to bring justice. Eventually justice will prevail, and the workers of injustice will receive the vengeance that they deserve. God is a God of justice, and the success of His entire creation depends on it. Those that violate it are cursed.

Jud 9:56 Thus God rendered the wickedness of Abimelech, which he did unto his father, in slaying his seventy brethren:

57 And all the evil of the men of Shechem did God render upon their heads: and upon them came the curse of Jotham the son of Jerubbaal.

Overcoming Injustice

1. We must trust in God to lead and direct our lives.

2. Human governments based on selfishness can never guarantee true justice.

3. Selfishness and struggles for power are the seeds of injustice.

4. We are to confront injustice when it occurs.

5. If we are treated unjustly, we are to turn our situation over to God by forgiving the offender and rely primarily on Him to bring us justice and peace.

6. It takes time, but justice will eventually prevail.

7. The seeds of injustice will consume those who do injustice and will eventually result in judgment against those who do evil.

PART V

The Amorite Giants Pursuing Prominence

Chapter 12

Chronic Failure
The Codependent Independent
Worldly Failure
(Saul)

The pursuit of prominence is a problem that pervades our entire society. As I have become more experienced in the area of codependency, I have identified this form of striving for prominence as codependent independence. This person copes with feelings of low self-worth and inadequacy through performance, people pleasing, over-achievement, and rescuing. He is or wants to be the proverbial "knight in shining armor" looking for a damsel (the codependent dependent), corporation, or cause to rescue. As a general (but almost absolute) rule, a codependent usually marries another codependent. Every damsel needs a knight to rescue her from the dragon of life, and every knight needs a damsel to rescue. As already discussed, the Amorite tribe represents problems with prominence. The Bible warns us about this problem when it asks in Mark 8:36, "For what shall it profit a man, if he shall gain the whole world, and lose his own soul?"

The codependent independent's performance, accomplishments and achievements are his attempt to heal his low self-worth and feelings of inadequacy. I divide the codependent independent psychological complex into two basic types: worldly failure and worldly success. Of course, a client will most likely fall somewhere between these two extremes and show some symptoms of each. King David might be an example of this combination, especially after his adultery with Bathsheba.

Codependent Independent Worldly Failure

In a competitive world, all will eventually fail. As long as a person succeeds, they will be promoted to more difficult tasks and greater responsibility. Even those who have reached the very top of their field will eventually have to step down due to age or circumstances. However, when failure becomes chronic it is usually due to significant underlying problems. Sometimes it is difficult to determine whether the client should be considered a worldly success or failure because of the extensive facades developed by both. Extreme anger and jealousy are usually the tip-off. Both may be equally competitive and aggressive, but the real difference is how they view themselves. Sometimes they view themselves a success in one area and a failure in another.

Rodney was a huge success to outside observers. He had built his small automobile sales business into a multi-million dollar corporation. Only those close to him knew a different side of him. His almost daily eruptions of rage at his co-workers, wife, and family were symptoms of the tremendous insecurity that lay within him. He was almost totally unable to take responsibility for his decisions and blamed everyone else involved when things went wrong. For those that could weather his emotional storms, the lax supervision, good wages and excellent benefits made employment tolerable. Because his father died when he was young and he grew up in a one-parent family, his greatest insecurities concerned his role as a husband and a father of his five children. After 15 years, he suddenly divorced his wife. He decided to "cut his losses" and devote his full energy to his business where he could succeed. To Rodney, this was the only logical thing to do!

In looking for a biblical model, King Saul is a clear example of a codependent independent worldly failure. (He was the first codependent that the Lord personally identified to me.) Codependent traits are more subtle and harder to detect in the independent type of codependency. This is because they usually develop strong ego-defenses and an elaborate facade to cover any signs of inadequacy. Only by carefully watching their actions and observing their defenses can we see between the cracks in their carefully built suit of armor. It is usually even harder to see this problem in Christians, because they may have correct Christian beliefs, be walking to some degree in the Spirit (which masks codependent symptoms) and be using the church and religion as their area of accomplishment. Therefore, counselors inexperienced with codependency may not even recognize a problem. At its root is pride in being overly independent and a façade of outward confidence in order to cover up feelings of deep inadequacy. The codependent independent is attempting to become his own god and meet all of his own needs. It is usually very difficult to convince the codependent independent that he has a problem.

Let us investigate what the Bible tells us about this problem beginning in 1st Samuel Chapter 9:

1. The root problem is an attempt to deal with feelings of inadequacy through performance. These feelings of inadequacy many times come from a child's inability to measure up to his parent's expectations, the result of a family dysfunction, or "learning" how to cope with life from a codependent parent. Saul's father's name, Kish, means " to bend," which I interpret to mean that he was flexible in his relationships or a people pleaser—one of the main traits of codependency. Kish's father's name was Abiel (God is my father) and Abiel's father was Zeror (bundle or complex). Saul means "to ask, inquire, or demand," which is a list of the ways a codependent meets his needs. The asses of Saul's father were lost, and he was sent to find them. Asses or donkeys symbolize capability to do work. Therefore, Saul's father sent him on a quest to prove himself capable or useful to his father. Not being able to live up to a father's expectations is a precursor to codependency. Although this may seem to be reading too much into this situation, I believe that these events, at a minimum, show Saul's feelings of inadequacy and his attempt to meet these needs through performance—the very basis of his problem. Without any question, he was being taught to be a rescuer.

2. The codependent independent looks very good on the outside to compensate for the emptiness within. In his appearance, Saul was a head taller that everyone else. Saul looked good on the outside, which is another possible indication of codependent independence.

3. Many codependent independents become an over-achiever to compensate for how they feel inside. Many times in stories, the Bible uses the locations where the person travels to indicate something about the person himself. Consequently, I believe these verses give us a list of some of Saul's codependent characteristics and ways that he tried to meet his needs. Saul and his servant passed Mount Ephraim, which means "double ash-heap" which many times stands for shame; possibly indicating how he felt inside. They then traveled through the land of Shalisha which means "to do a third time" or possibly to be an over-achiever or perfectionist. Since they still did not find the asses, they proceeded to the land of Shalim, which means "foxes" possibly indicating that he tried to act as if he was smart. Next, they went through the land of the Benjamites, which means "son of the right hand." This may suggest that he was still trying to please his father. Following this, they journeyed to the land of Zuph, which means "honeycomb" and probably indicating that if all else failed he would just seek pleasure. Finally, after many failures, Saul began to worry about his dad's possible disapproval of his continuing fruitless search and suggested that they return home. For Saul, as with many codependents, continuing to try and fail seemed more emotionally damaging than just giving up.

4. The real answer for codependency is to seek God to meet the client's innermost needs. Saul's servant suggested that they inquire of God about the location of the asses. As with many codependents, Saul believed that he must do something to get the favor of God and the prophet (just as codependents try to please people to get their needs met) and, therefore, felt he needed to give money to the prophet. The prophet Samuel told him that his father's asses had been found (indicating that seeking God

will result in an answer to any problem). In fact, the ultimate answer to codependency is believing that God will meet all of our innermost needs.

5. <u>Every person is called by God to help others, but not to help them in a codependent manner.</u> God had told Samuel that he would send him someone who would "save my people out of the hand of the Philistines." Samuel told Saul that he would tell him "all that is in thine heart." Saul, as most codependent independents, truly wanted to be a rescuer and a hero.

6. <u>The codependent's fear of being inadequate conflicts with his desire to "be someone."</u> Even though it was his deepest desire to be king, Saul protested that he and his family were too insignificant for the task.

7. <u>The fastest most effective method for recovery from codependency is to walk in the Spirit.</u> Samuel anointed Saul's head with oil, which represents the anointing of the Holy Spirit. The codependent must take steps to acquire the power of the Holy Spirit, which are outlined in the verses that followed this event:

   a. Quit trying to meet his innermost needs himself. (The asses had been found)
   b. Obtain a revelation of God. He came to the plain of Tabor (location of the mountain of transfiguration)
   c. Appropriate the sacrifice of Jesus (the kid goats)
   d. Appropriate the body of Christ (the bread)
   e. Accept the forgiveness of sins (the bottle of wine)
   f. Obtain a double portion of these (they gave him two loaves)
   g. Acquire the ability to speak for God (the Spirit of prophecy)

1 Sa 10:1 Then Samuel took a vial of oil, and poured *it* upon his head, and kissed him, and said, *Is it* not because the LORD hath anointed thee *to be* captain over his inheritance?

2 When thou art departed from me to day, then thou shalt find two men by Rachel's sepulchre in the border of Benjamin at Zelzah; and they will say unto thee, The asses which thou wentest to seek are found: and, lo, thy father hath left the care of the asses, and sorroweth for you, saying, What shall I do for my son?

3 Then shalt thou go on forward from thence, and thou shalt come to the plain of Tabor, and there shall meet thee three men going up to God to Bethel, one carrying three kids, and another carrying three loaves of bread, and another carrying a bottle of wine:

4 And they will salute thee, and give thee two *loaves* of bread; which thou shalt receive of their hands.

5 After that thou shalt come to the hill of God, where *is* the garrison of the Philistines: and it shall come to pass, when thou art come thither to the city, that thou shalt meet a company of prophets coming down from the high place with a psaltery, and a tabret, and a pipe, and a harp, before them; and they shall prophesy:

6 And the Spirit of the LORD will come upon thee, and thou shalt prophesy with them, and shalt be turned into another man.

From this time on until the Spirit departed from Saul because of his disobedience, Saul became a fairly good king and avoided most of his codependent tendencies. Even after he was rejected by some Israelites at his coronation, he did not take revenge but held his peace.

8. <u>The codependent needs to learn to listen to spiritual leadership instead of trying to do what he wants.</u> Saul was directed to go down to Gilgal (the church) and await direction from Samuel.

9. <u>The underlying feelings of inadequacy cause the codependent to oscillate between overconfidence (pride) and a fear of failure</u>. Saul hid in the baggage when he was to be crowned king. This is a clear indication of his inner feelings of inadequacy. God, Himself, had to reveal where he was hiding. Although God understands the codependent's emotional problems, He many times chooses to use him anyway. Saul's prideful ways became apparent later.

10. <u>Codependency is actually idolatry</u>. At its heart, codependency is an attempt by a person to be his own god and rely on himself to meet his own needs in his own strength. Therefore, it is a rejection of God. At Mizpeh, Samuel accused the Israelites of rejecting God because they wanted their own earthly king. This is exactly what the codependent does. The choice is between serving the vain things of this world or God. Samuel said in 1st Samuel 12: 20-21, "...turn not aside from following the LORD, but serve the LORD with all your heart; And turn ye not aside: for [then should ye go] after vain [things], which cannot profit nor deliver; for they [are] vain."

11. <u>Codependents usually refuse to acknowledge their ever-present fear of failure</u>. This is clear from the actions of the people when the Philistines pitched at Michmash (hidden), eastward from Bethaven (house of hollowness). All the people "followed him trembling." The leader sets the mood for his followers. (1 Samuel 13:7)

12. <u>When God does not do things in the way a codependent desires, the codependent will usually make it happen himself</u>. Because Samuel was late and the people were deserting him, Saul decided to offer the sacrifice himself. The codependent has an inner tendency to want to do it himself so he can get the credit and feel good about himself. The tendency of the codependent is to use God to meet his needs rather than to serve God. Most codependents try to use God as their genie.

13. <u>They tend to blame others for their mistakes</u>. Saul blamed the people and circumstances for "forcing" him to violate Samuel's directions. In Chapter 14, when Saul put a foolish curse on anyone who ate food before they killed all the enemy soldiers, he was willing to kill his own son Jonathan (who had not heard the curse and ate something) rather than admit he had made a mistake. Only the people kept him from killing the very person who had brought the victory.

14. <u>The children of the codependent will be like him</u>. The names of Saul's children hint at codependent traits: Jonathan (Jehovah has given—sees God as Someone Who is to give to him), Ishui (he resembles me—pride), Melchishua (my God is wealth—relying on riches), Merab (increase—what he is striving for) and Michal (who is like God—what he wants to be). Codependency is a sin that passes from one generation to the next.

15. <u>The codependent avoids crucifying the flesh and his pride</u>. When called to utterly destroy the Amalekites and all they had, he left all the good livestock and King Agag (pride) alive. Amalek stands for the flesh where the very root of codependency resides. Pride is usually a defense mechanism for low self worth. Saul did not want to completely destroy the flesh, just as the codependent has a very hard time "crucifying his flesh."

16. <u>People-pleasing is one of the most prominent traits of codependency</u>. Saul tried to deny his failure by saying it was the people who did it, and that they had taken the sheep and oxen for a sacrifice to the Lord. Samuel then got to the heart of the issue: "Saul had rejected the Word of the Lord." (1 Samuel 15:23) Saul finally admitted that he did it "because I feared the people, and obeyed their voice." (v. 24) Even after he was told that because of his rebellion, God was going to take away the kingdom; he wanted Samuel to go with him to worship so that the people would not realize that anything was wrong.

17. <u>Without the moderating Spirit of God, the underlying codependency will take control of the person's life</u>. When the Spirit of God departed from Saul, an evil spirit took over (codependency). Because codependency is a work of the flesh, the absence of the power of the Holy Spirit allows it to dominate

the soul. Galatians 5:16 makes the issue clear: "… Walk in the Spirit, and ye shall not fulfill the lust of the flesh." This power of the Spirit is so important in treating codependency that I have called this verse the "Band-aid of codependency." By simply giving or rededicating their lives to Christ, I have seen almost unbelievable changes in codependent clients. However, this help only continues as long as the client maintains a close relationship with God. Unfortunately, most codependents, like Saul, have so many problems in their relationship with God that they find walking in obedience to God's Spirit extremely difficult.

18. Extreme jealousy and domestic violence are many times manifestations of codependent independence. In 1st Samuel Chapter 18, David was given more credit for victory in the songs of the women than Saul. Saul became so jealous that he threw a javelin at David and did what he could to kill him even though he was Saul's son-in-law. He even threw a javelin at Jonathan, his own son, because he thought that Jonathan had sided with David. In 1st Samuel Chapter 22, he killed Ahimelech, the priest and all of his relatives including the women and children of Nob; because he thought they had supported David.

19. Underneath his facade, the codependent feels less than others. When in 1st Samuel 24:7, David spared Saul's life in a cave, Saul said, "Thou [art] more righteous than I: for thou hast rewarded me good, whereas I have rewarded thee evil."

20. Many times the codependent believes God is against him and blames God or others for his failures. In verse 18, Saul said that he believed that God had delivered him into David's hand.

21. The codependent quickly forgets his insights into his own feelings of inadequacy and his promises to change. In 1st Samuel 26:21, Saul again tried to kill David, and David again spared him. This time Saul said, "I have sinned: return, my son David: for I will no more do thee harm, because my soul was precious in thine eyes this day: behold, I have played the fool, and have erred exceedingly." Saul finally quit pursuing David when David escaped to the land of the Philistines. **Distance must sometimes be used as a boundary against codependent behavior.**

22. The real issue is righteousness—making unbiased, just decisions and being able to carry them out. Righteousness, especially in this case, included having the right amount of dependence or independence from each person or thing. A similar term used in the recovery movement is "interdependence." David responded to Saul in 1st Samuel 26:23, "The LORD render to every man his righteousness and his faithfulness."

23. Either faith in God will overcome our codependency or the codependency will overcome our faith in God. Saul got to the point where he could no longer hear from God at all. His trust in God had turned to fear. He finally went to the witch of Endor to learn his future (1 Samuel 28:18-25). Saul had previously ordered all witches to be executed.

24. The key issue in codependency is a battle with the flesh. Saul was told by Samuel (or a familiar spirit impersonating him) that he and his sons would die in battle the next day. This occurred, "Because thou obeyedst not the voice of the LORD, nor executedst his fierce wrath upon Amalek, therefore hath the LORD done this thing unto thee this day." (1 Samuel 28:18) Saul's ultimate downfall was because he had refused to decisively deal with the dominance of the flesh (Amalek) in his life.

25. Codependent Independent Worldly Failure will eventually result in self-destruction. In spite of the prophecy that he and his sons would be killed in battle the next day, he chose to go into battle anyway in order to save face. After being wounded, he asked his armor-bearer to kill him and when the armor-bearer would not, he fell on his own sword. Many codependent independent worldly failures eventually resort to self-destructive behaviors like alcohol, drugs or suicide.

26. <u>Often the codependent's family is also destroyed by his behavior</u>. Codependency is a generational sin. All of Saul's sons died in battle with him even though at least Jonathan had not gone along with many of his actions.

Codependent independent worldly failures are difficult clients to counsel. They usually come to counseling only after a major failure or when their family is threatening to leave them. They have a difficult time admitting their mistakes, are usually very angry, and quit counseling as soon as they get a minimum level of relief or are not required to come any longer. Pride is a major barrier and their strong desire to perform makes them want to fix themselves. Many times domestic violence or verbal abuse is involved. They must stop this behavior before other issues can be addressed. A model for helping abusers will be discussed in detail later in this book. Because of their strong desire to control others, I believe that *Conquering Codependency* (Springle, 1993) is the best resource to deal with codependent independent clients.

Overcoming Codependent Independent Worldly Failure

1. The root problem is attempting to meet feelings of inadequacy without God through personal accomplishments and failing in the attempt.

2. Usually he is an angry controller who blames others for his problems and failures because of his feelings of inadequacy.

3. The client builds an external facade, tries to force others to meet his needs rather than deal with his own problems, buries his emotions and hides his insecurity. He is dependent on his performance and other's opinions for evaluating his worth. He is defensive, takes criticism personally and reacts angrily.

4. The client must realize that he is trying to be his own God, repent of his efforts to direct his own life, and take responsibility for his own actions, instead of blaming others. He must learn to manage his anger and trust God to meet his needs.

5. He must understand that controlling others is sin, set others free to make their own choices, deal with his own emotional problems and trust God in his relationships.

6. The client must overcome his low self-image, feelings of inadequacy, and defense mechanism of pride by accepting God's evaluation of him and his position in Christ.

7. He must actively reject the lie that his successes make him more worthwhile and that failures make him worthless. He must accept his worth in Christ and the unconditional love that God has for him.

Chapter 13

Workaholism
The Codependent Independent
Worldly Success
(Solomon)

Codependent Independent Worldly Success

Today our society is driven primarily by a desire for success. Consequently, probably the hardest type of client to convince of his problem is the codependent independent worldly success. He is a workaholic. Even when he realizes that he has a problem, the codependent independent worldly success is even less likely to remain in therapy for an extended period of time than the worldly failure. Because everything goes his way, this over-achiever climbs to the top of his profession, receives all the acclaim that the world offers, but eventually finds out that all he has done is empty and meaningless. His inner pain and feelings of inadequacy remain. In the end, many times he has sacrificed his family and all that is dear to him for what turns out to be nothing at all.

Mark was an extremely successful aeronautical engineer. He was self-taught and had brilliantly worked himself up to the position of senior engineer in his company even though he did not have a college degree. His daughter was my identified patient. She had attempted suicide, because she was not selected as a national merit scholar. This might be hard for some of us to understand, but in this family, unless you were the best you were "trash." She aspired to be a surgeon and feared that without becoming a national merit scholar she would not get the scholarships she would need to succeed. If she failed, the rejection she anticipated from her father would make life not worth living. Her older brother, who also could not live up to his father's expectations, had been sent off to a military school so that he could learn discipline. Mark's wife, Margie, was the typical "good girl" who tried to smooth everything over, helped make things work for her husband, and lived in fear of Mark's disapproval. As we shall see, usually the children pay the price of the codependent independent's drive to succeed at all costs.

The best and most well known biblical type of this significant, seldom identified, psychological problem is King Solomon. We find this story in 1st Kings Chapter 2-11.

1. <u>They may come from what seems like a great Christian heritage and have everything going for them</u>. Solomon, on the surface, had absolutely everything going for him. To understand at all how he could be codependent, we have to look at the dark secrets of David's dysfunctional family: David's affair with Bathsheba, his murder of Uriah, the rape of Tamar, the murder of Amnon, Absolom's rebellion, David's refusal to discipline his children, and David's ability to act as if nothing was wrong. Solomon admitted his feelings of inadequacy in the words, "I am but a little child," (1 Kings 3:7) when he requested wisdom to rule from God. On the other hand, David may have actually spent more time with Solomon than the rest of his sons (Proverbs 4). David had commanded Solomon to follow God with all his heart, in order that one of his descendants would sit on the throne of Israel forever. (1 Kings 2:3, 4)

2. <u>God wants to bless the codependent independent, but the more he is blessed the greater danger that he will try to run his own life</u>. God offered Solomon any wish, but he chose wisdom to rule and

judge between good and evil. Because he chose this, God blessed him with riches and honor, which are sometimes also the result of wisdom. These became part of his downfall.

3. <u>Close observation is sometimes required to see the signs of codependency</u>. In Solomon's case, we first see these signs of his codependency when he married Pharaoh's daughter and later sacrificed in the pagan high places to please his wives. Israelites were not to marry anyone outside of Israel, and they were prohibited from sacrificing in the high places. In fact, they were supposed to tear the high places down. Solomon's marriage to Pharaoh's daughter suggests an alliance with the things of the world (Egypt), and his sacrifices in the high places suggest worshiping his own intellect or wisdom.

4. <u>The codependent independent struggles with being too independent</u>. Although he was told that everything in his future was contingent on his obedience to God, his actions showed that he was convinced that he could do a better job of running his own life. Many times the codependent actually is unaware that he is running his own life instead of yielding to God. Some codependents even believe that whatever they think or want to do is what God is telling them to do. God clearly warned Solomon, but the warnings went unheeded.

5. <u>The underlying issue is trying to meet their needs themselves, even if it is at the expense of others</u>. In the story of the two harlots in 1st Kings Chapter 3, one of the prostitutes accidentally rolled over on her baby while she slept during the night; and the baby died. This tragedy represents the inner loss and hurt that has been experienced by the codependent. Instead of accepting and dealing with the loss, the first prostitute took the other's child and said that the child was hers. In the same way, the codependent independent uses what others have (their baby) to meet his need for worth and significance. He plays "king of the hill" in the "rat race" of life so that he can be "successful" and feel good about himself but he does not really care about other people. Codependents are more interested in their success than the needs of the people that work for them or even the members of their own families. In this story, Solomon was able to determine which prostitute really loved the baby when he threatened to have the child cut in half. The true mother loved the child and had the child's best interest in mind, even ahead of her own interests. The codependent independent only wants something to meet his needs and would rather destroy it than to let another have it! This is the "toxic," selfish "love" of codependency. King Solomon gave himself the answer to his own problem of codependency: The King (God) will give responsibility and real success (the live baby) to those who care more for other people than for their own vested interests.

1 Ki 3:16 Then came there two women, that were harlots, unto the king, and stood before him.

17 And the one woman said, O my lord, I and this woman dwell in one house; and I was delivered of a child with her in the house.

18 And it came to pass the third day after that I was delivered, that this woman was delivered also: and we were together; there was no stranger with us in the house, save we two in the house.

19 And this woman's child died in the night; because she overlaid it.

20 And she arose at midnight, and took my son from beside me, while thine handmaid slept, and laid it in her bosom, and laid her dead child in my bosom.

21 And when I rose in the morning to give my child suck, behold, it was dead: but when I had considered it in the morning, behold, it was not my son, which I did bear.

22 And the other woman said, Nay; but the living is my son, and the dead is thy son. And this said, No; but the dead is thy son, and the living is my son. Thus they spake before the king.

23 Then said the king, The one saith, This is my son that liveth, and thy son is the dead: and the other saith, Nay; but thy son is the dead, and my son is the living.

24 And the king said, Bring me a sword. And they brought a sword before the king.

25 And the king said, Divide the living child in two, and give half to the one, and half to the other.

26 Then spake the woman whose the living child was unto the king, for her bowels yearned upon her son, and she said, O my lord, give her the living child, and in no wise slay it. But the other said, Let it be neither mine nor thine, but divide it.

27 Then the king answered and said, Give her the living child, and in no wise slay it: she is the mother thereof.

6. <u>In order to recover from codependency we must experience God's unconditional love and learn to trust Him</u>. Solomon gave the child to the real mother. This child needed the love of its real mother. As she loved and cared for him, the child would learn to trust her to meet all of his needs. In the same way, the codependent needs to feel loved by God so that he can learn to trust God for his worth, significance, love and security. He must face the pain of his own emptiness and turn to God for help, or he will continue to attempt to be his own god and try to meet his own needs.

7. <u>Natural wisdom, talent, approval and accomplishment are never enough</u>. Solomon exceeded all the wise men of his time. He was one of the most learned men. He studied science, wrote 3000 proverbs, and 1005 songs. A large number of people including kings and queens came to hear him. He had all the approval any man could ever have, but it was never enough. He had to do more. This is the problem with trying to use external accomplishments to fix how a person feels about himself internally. The external "solution" develops into a lust or addiction that can never be satisfied.

8. <u>Even great religious accomplishments can be motivated wrongly by codependency and legalism</u>. The temple symbolizes Solomon's heart. We are told that "he loved God." He started with all the best intentions to accomplish something for God. He wanted to please God, just like he wanted to please everyone else; so he performed well at the task of building the temple. Solomon built the majestic temple for God, but when the Ark of the Covenant was brought into it, it contained only the tablets of the law (which stand for legalism and our attempts to please God in our own strength). I counseled a pastor who had fallen into this same trap. Only after a great failure was he able to see his codependent independent motivation. He had always performed in order to please his father, and now he finally understood that he had been driven to do the same for God.

9. <u>Overly independent people are not known for their love for the Word of God, their desire to submit to authority, or their admission of sin</u>. Noticeably missing from the Ark when it was brought into the temple was the manna (God's Word), Aaron's rod that budded (God's authority), and the gold hemorrhoids given by the Philistines when the Ark was taken in Samuel's time (a sacrifice for sin). (1 Kings 8:9) However, this is not always the case. Sometimes a codependent might read the Bible, submit to authority, and confess his sins if he thinks that these actions will accomplish his goals.

10. <u>A codependent is unable to maintain appropriate priorities</u>. Because of his drivenness and perfectionism, he is unable to keep his life in balance. Selfishness, accomplishments and people pleasing overshadow everything else. Solomon's priorities can be clearly seen in the fact that it took him seven years to build God's house and thirteen years to build his own. (1 Kings 6:38, 7:1)

11. <u>God wants to fill the codependent's heart and meet his needs</u>. When Solomon dedicated the temple, even though the Ark of the Covenant contained only the stone tablets of legalism, God filled the temple (Solomon's heart) with the cloud of glory. Solomon's excessive attempts to please God are clearly seen again in the 22,000 oxen (work) and 120,000 sheep (sin atonement) that he sacrificed.

12. <u>Complete submission to the will of God is required in order for the codependent independent to recover</u>. To God obedience and relationship are more important than performance (sacrifices). This

is exactly what God said to King Saul after he failed to completely destroy the Amalekites (the flesh). (1 Samuel 15:22) In 1ˢᵗ Kings Chapter 9, we are told that God again appeared to Solomon and promised that if he would obey (surrender control of his life) he would be blessed. We can understand why God emphasized this point every time he appeared to Solomon.

13. <u>If the codependent refuses to truly submit to God's direction, destruction will follow</u>. God put it this way:

1 Kings 9:4 And if thou wilt walk before me, as David thy father walked, in integrity of heart, and in uprightness, to do according to all that I have commanded thee, [and] wilt keep my statutes and my judgments:

5 Then I will establish the throne of thy kingdom upon Israel for ever, as I promised to David thy father, saying, There shall not fail thee a man upon the throne of Israel.

6 [But] if ye shall at all turn from following me, ye or your children, and will not keep my commandments [and] my statutes which I have set before you, but go and serve other gods, and worship them:

7 Then will I cut off Israel out of the land which I have given them; and this house, which I have hallowed for my name, will I cast out of my sight; and Israel shall be a proverb and a byword among all people:

14. <u>The codependent independent brings on his own destruction by using and abusing other people and things in an attempt to meet his needs</u>. We see this beginning to happen when Solomon gave Hiram substandard cities in payment for cedar and fir trees. Instead of destroying the remaining Amorites, Hittites, Perizzites, Hivites and Jebusites, he put them to forced labor. As has already been stated, these tribes stand for psychological problems of prominence, fear, lack of boundaries, addictions and abuse. Instead of dealing with his problems, he tried to use them for his service. Like Saul, Solomon refused to deal with the problems of his flesh and this led to his downfall.

15. <u>The praise of others only stimulates the desire for greater accomplishments—overachievers hang together and validate each other</u>. The Queen of Sheba fed Solomon's ego, and he gave her anything she wanted.

16. <u>The codependent independent, who originally oscillates between pride and feelings of inadequacy, easily becomes victim to his own defense of pride</u>. Solomon made 200 targets of gold (goals) and 300 shields of gold (defenses), an ivory throne with six steps (man's sufficiency) and 24 lions (strength) of gold (deity). The Bible warns us that God resists the proud and that pride comes before the fall. (James 4:6, Proverbs 16:18)

17. <u>A codependent will eventually be overcome by the things that he worships</u>. Solomon bought more and more horses and chariots (worldly means) and eventually took 1000 women to meet his needs. He had so much gold and silver that silver was not even counted as valuable during his reign. Relationship addiction, sexual addiction, and possibly alcoholism seem to have predominated in his later life. From various writings of his in the Old Testament, we learn that his accomplishments proved hollow. (especially Ecclesiastes) God specifically prohibited kings from accumulating large amounts of gold, having many horses, or many wives, but Solomon seems to have felt that he was exempt from these laws. He chose to follow his lust rather than God's law, and eventually, these things (especially the women) led him astray.

De 17:15 Thou shalt in any wise set him king over thee, whom the LORD thy God shall choose: one from among thy brethren shalt thou set king over thee: thou mayest not set a stranger over thee, which is not thy brother.

16 But he shall not multiply horses to himself, nor cause the people to return to Egypt, to the end that he should multiply horses: forasmuch as the LORD hath said unto you, Ye shall henceforth return no more that way.

17 Neither shall he multiply wives to himself, that his heart turn not away: neither shall he greatly multiply to himself silver and gold.

18. <u>The lusts and addictions of the flesh will eventually overcome all resistance</u>. Solomon's wives were Moabites (lust), Ammonites (selfish desire), Edomites (earthly), Zidonians (getting things), and Hittites (fear). In 1st Kings 11:2, it tells us that "Solomon clave (to cling strongly) unto these in love (human love or sex)." His 700 wives and 300 concubines demonstrate the level of his addiction. These turned his heart from the Lord. As we will clearly see when we study addictions in depth, either the addict's faith will overcome his addictions, or his addictions will overcome his faith.

19. <u>Lust and addictions will corrupt the codependents morals and lead him to do what he said he would never do</u>. In 1st Kings 11: 5, it states that Solomon went after Ashtoreth the goddess of the Zidonians (sex), and after Milcom, the abomination of the Ammonites (selfish desires). These all led him away from God.

20. <u>A codependent will go so far as to sacrifice his family to meet his needs</u>. Solomon built a high place of worship for Chemosh (which means "subduer," a god which required human sacrifice), the abomination of Moab (lust), Molech (the god for which first born children were burned alive on the altar) and the abomination of the children of Ammon (selfish desires). I believe this symbolizes that the codependent worldly success will sacrifice his family for achievement and lust, through neglecting and abusing them.

    1 Kings 11:7 Then did Solomon build an high place for Chemosh, the abomination of Moab, in the hill that is before Jerusalem, and for Molech, the abomination of the children of Ammon.

21. <u>His addictions and his abuse of others will lead to more and more trouble for the codependent</u>. The world (Egypt) and the people around him will eventually oppose the codependent when they are tired of being used by him. Solomon overtaxed the country so much to meet his insatiable thirst for accomplishment that the people rose up to demand relief of this burden from his son Reheboam. Because Reheboam stated that he would even accomplish more than his father, the people rebelled and made Jeroboam the king over ten tribes. Jeroboam means "the people will contend." (1 Kings 4: 4-16)

22. <u>All of his accomplishments and addictions will eventually prove hollow</u>. Solomon wrote many proverbs to warn others not to go the way he did. The entire book of Ecclesiastes is Solomon's final answer to life. He tells us "that all is vanity (worthlessness)." (Ecclesiastes 1:14) This is the final realization of the codependent independent.

23. <u>The codependent independent many times has to learn things the hard way</u>. In Proverbs 4:3, Solomon tells of the importance of listening to your father; and in verse 23 he warns, "Keep thy heart with all diligence; for out of it [are] the issues of life." In Proverbs 5:3-5, he warns, "For the lips of a strange woman drop [as] an honeycomb, and her mouth [is] smoother than oil: But her end is bitter as wormwood, sharp as a two-edged sword. Her feet go down to death; her steps take hold on hell." In Proverbs 20:1, he warns against alcoholism, "Wine [is] a mocker, strong drink [is] raging: and whosoever is deceived thereby is not wise."

24. <u>He may eventually understand his error and realize that he has been trying to be his own god</u>. Although authorities disagree on whether Solomon returned to God at the end of his life, it does appear that he at least understood his error in disobeying God. In Ecclesiastes 12:13, he gives us his advice

concerning how to escape from codependent independence: "Let us hear the conclusion of the whole matter: Fear God, and keep his commandments: for this [is] the whole [duty] of man."

25. <u>The ultimate consequences will fall on the next generation</u>. Reheboam, reflecting the pride of his father, lost 10 of the 12 tribes of Israel; because he would not turn from his father's way of using others. Adoram (pride), his tax collector, was stoned to death; and Reheboam barely escaped alive, when they attempted to collect the taxes. Codependent independence works only for a limited time until the consequences of using others destroys all that has been built.

In treating the codependent independent worldly success, I start by challenging them with three questions: 1. What is it that you have accomplished so far in your life that will still be worth something 200 years from now? 2. What is going to happen to you tomorrow? 3. What is the mission that God has assigned you on this earth? Of course, there is almost nothing that we can do that will last 200 years; we cannot even predict what will happen tomorrow, and without God we have no idea what our mission on earth is supposed to be. I conclude, that if this is so, how do they think they can control and direct their lives? All the rats in the rat race of life are just running around in circles and the faster ones who are lapping the others still have no idea where they are going. Of course, this is the message of the book of Ecclesiastes, which I then ask them to read. As another resource, I suggest they read *We Are Driven* (1991) by Hemfelt, Minirth, and Meier which addresses this problem in a more general yet revealing way. As an overall program for recovery, I have found that codependent independents seem to relate better to *Conquering Codependency* (1993) by Pat Springle, rather than other programs, because it is more concrete and action-oriented. In addition, many times it is necessary to help the client deal with anger, abusive behavior, and addictions. These issues will be dealt with extensively in subsequent chapters.

Overcoming Codependent Independent Worldly Success

1. The root problem is trying to meet feelings of inadequacy through personal accomplishments without God.

2. He is excessively driven to be an overachiever, controller, rescuer and enabler in his relationships because of his insecurity.

3. The client builds an external facade, buries his emotions, and hides his insecurity.

4. He is overly dependent on his performance and other's opinions in evaluating his worth.

5. The client must realize that he is trying to be his own god. He must repent of his efforts to direct his own life and meet his own needs through excessive accomplishment, and trust God to meet them.

6. He must understand that controlling others is sin. He must set others free to make their own choices and trust God in his relationships.

7. The client must overcome his low self-image, feelings of inadequacy, and defense mechanism of pride by accepting God's evaluation of him and his position in Christ.

8. He must actively reject the lie that his successes make him more worthwhile and realize that all his accomplishments are vanity.

PART VI

The Hittite Giants
Avoiding Fear

Chapter 14

Irresponsibility and Procrastination The Codependent Responsibility Avoidant
(Jonah)

Codependent Avoidance

In conquering the land of Canaan, it was not just the City of Jericho (fear) that had to be overcome but the entire Hittite tribe or complex of fear. In the story of the conquering of Jericho, we learned the basic principles: that it is faith working through love that overcomes fear, and that fear must be confronted or it will increase. At that time, I briefly discussed the simpler problems of anxiety attacks, worry, phobias, panic attacks, and obsessive-compulsivity. As I have already stated, faith combined with systematic desensitization is a very effective means of dealing with most simple fears. In this section, I intend to concentrate on the more difficult, complicated problems related to fear.

I have defined codependency as "excessive dependence or independence on people or things." I have identified three basic types of codependency. Those who try to meet their needs by being over-dependent on others (dependent), those who try to meet their needs through performance and rescuing others (independent), and those who try to meet their needs through avoiding responsibility and relationships (avoidant). In this part, I will elaborate on the problems of the codependent avoidant whose primary characteristic is an attempt to avoid fear.

For those familiar with DSM IV, the problem of codependent avoidance is a milder form of what is called Avoidant Personality Disorder. When fear of responsibility and relationships becomes a primary part of a client's personality, it affects almost every area of his life. It is typified by the overly dependent person who has experienced ongoing hurt and failure to such an extent that the fear of responsibility or relationships has all but immobilized them. They have given up trying to meet higher-level needs. They are satisfied just to be "safe" and might typically be labeled neurotic. A productive and abundant life is out of the question. Defenses have taken over. Many times these are ingrained welfare recipients, people-users, the chronically unemployed or homeless vagrants.

Codependent Responsibility Avoidance

The codependent responsibility avoidant uses a strategy for life that minimizes failure at all costs. If he only does what he knows he can succeed at, he will be a success. Of course, for this strategy to succeed he needs someone else who will do whatever tasks he wishes to avoid. For this job, he usually enlists a codependent dependent rescuer either in the form of a mate, a parent or a friend.

Dan was a laid-back type of person that nothing seemed to bother. Deep inside he had a fear of failure that kept him focused on his job, a place where he could be successful. He had never been married before. When he met June, she impressed him as one of those people who has it all together. A perfectionist at heart, she had been bringing up three girls by herself until she met Dan. June's previous husband had been controlling, abusive, and an alcoholic. Due to her fear of being controlled, she demanded that she have her way. He felt that nothing he did or any of the decisions he made were ever good enough for her. The more Dan felt alienated from the family, the less he did. The less he did, the more she felt she had to do. They now had a typical over-under responsible marriage. He had a vested interest in avoiding responsibility, and she felt superior because of her competence. Deep inside, however, Dan felt like a failure for not being the leader of the family, and June resented the fact that he was not the responsible leader she wanted him to be.

In order to understanding this problem from a biblical perspective and learn how to assist clients with this problem, let us examine the familiar story of Jonah in the Book of Jonah.

1. <u>The codependent avoidant sees himself as powerless, defenseless and overwhelmed by life</u>. Jonah's name means "dove." Doves are weak, powerless, and defenseless against anything that might attack them. Their only hope is to escape by flying away.

2. <u>He does not see the untapped potential in his life</u>. Jonah was the son of Amittai which means "faithful, right, sure, and truthful." This was the untapped potential that was in Jonah.

3. <u>He has a victim mentality based on all the hurt he has experienced</u>. In 2nd Kings 14:25, we find out that Jonah was from Gathhepher, which means "winepress of digging." I interpret this to mean that just as it takes work to dig a winepress and as grapes are crushed in a winepress, he had worked hard only to have a crushing experience. This verse also suggests that one of his prophecies did not take place until the time of the kings of Israel. Possibly, when his prophecy was not immediately fulfilled, he came under sharp criticism.

   2 Ki 14:25 He restored the coast of Israel from the entering of Hamath unto the sea of the plain, according to the word of the LORD God of Israel, which he spake by the hand of his servant Jonah, the son of Amittai, the prophet, which [was] of Gathhepher.

4. <u>A codependent sees the challenges of life as overwhelming</u>. Jonah was called to go to Ninevah, the capital of Assyria, whose god corresponded to Hercules—a man-god of great size and strength. The codependent avoidant feels like a dove asked to take on Hercules. Life just requires too much to bear. The avoidant usually feels inadequate to do almost anything.

5. <u>The avoidant many times attempts to escape into fantasy (Tarshish means "contemplation") or seeks the pleasures of life to get away from God, who he believes required too much from him</u>. The avoidant is usually angry with God because he believes that God expects too much of him and that God should have made things work out the way he wanted them to be. Consequently, Jonah ran from God to try to find a nicer, easier, protected life (Joppa means "bright, beauty, fair") and, in doing so, he cut himself off from the very thing he needed—faith and trust in God.

6. <u>The codependent avoidant will try to get others to meet his needs</u>. Ships usually stand for the capability to accomplish things. Jonah tried to use someone else's capability (a hired ship) to escape from what he saw as the overwhelming demands of life. He expected someone else to take care of him.

7. <u>The avoidant is overwhelmed by the problems of life, many of which he has created through his attempt to escape his fears</u>. Jonah was the one who chose the ship for his attempt to escape from God. Even though the tempest was life threatening, Jonah was asleep, trying to ignore his problems. He was awakened by others (usually the codependent's relatives and friends) who saw the destruction coming on all of their lives. Because the codependent does not carry his own weight in life, his problems affect and threaten everyone involved.

8. <u>He will frustrate all the attempts of others to really help him</u>. The last thing he wants to do is call on God, Whom he blames for the overwhelming demands of life. Others, especially relatives or friends who unsuccessfully try to help him, eventually realize that it is the codependent avoidant (Jonah) who is the root of their problems.

9. <u>When all attempts to help fail, he will eventually be abandoned by family and friends</u>. When the sailors were finally forced to throw Jonah overboard the seas became calm. In the same way, those who finally give up trying to help the codependent avoidant find their lives return to normal. When they finally quit trying to help, the family and friends may feel guilty because they have abandoned the codependent avoidant (just as the sailors of Jonah's ship did).

10. <u>The underlying problem is that he expects others to do for him what he is capable of (but afraid of) doing for himself</u>. The codependent's extreme neediness, combined with fear, results in dysfunctional ways of coping with life, which result in further rejection and hurt.

11. <u>The underlying cause is that the codependent avoidant feels unloved and unworthy</u>. To understand this, we must turn to the end of the story of Jonah. Jonah was exceedingly angry with God, because God did not destroy Nineveh when its people repented of their sin. The codependent avoidant becomes very angry because he perceives that others are more blessed than he is. He sees this "mistreatment" as a sign that God must love others more. This triggers feelings of being unloved, worthless and inadequate, which most codependents have experienced in past relationships, especially in their families of origin.

12. <u>A predominant trait is that he is overly concerned about what people think about him</u>. If God spared the Ninevites, others might think of Jonah as a false prophet because he prophesied that in 40 days the city would be destroyed. He did not care as much for the 120,000 people of Ninevah as he did for his own reputation.

13. <u>He sees himself as a victim and is totally focused on his own problems</u>. The codependent avoidant is in a perpetual pity-party. He believes that the world owes him a living because of all that "God" and others have done to him. It is almost as if he is challenging God to prove that He loves him, just as other types of codependents attempt to manipulate others around them into showing love in order to meet their needs.

14. <u>The codependent avoidant sees everything as catastrophic</u>. Jonah was so mad at God for being so kind to the Ninevites by sparing them, that he asked God to kill him. He felt it was better for him to die than for his prophecy not to come true, or for others to be blessed instead of him.

15. <u>The codependent avoidant is really codependent on God</u>. We find this final insight into the problem in the episode about the gourd. The sun was hot. This represents the difficulties of life. The codependent avoidant sees himself as a victim because of all the problems in life that have happened to him. God made a gourd grow which protected Jonah from the sun. When a worm killed the gourd, Jonah became "angry enough to die," and said that he felt justified in his anger. Jonah expected God to do for him what he is capable of doing for himself. God makes it plain that He will not do this. An example of this would be a 15-year-old who still wants his mother to tie his shoelaces because he is afraid he might do it wrong. God expects us to do our part and take responsibility for our own life, just as any healthy parent expects his own child to do what he can to meet his own needs.

The Biblical Solution

1. <u>Helping the codependent avoidant begins with refusing to do for him what he can do for himself</u>. This is based on a correct Greek translation of Galatians 6:2, 5 (see the earlier chapter on boundaries) which tell us that, as Christians, we should assist other people with "mountains that are about to crush them," but that we are to "let everyone carry their own backpack." As long as "helpers" enable the codependent so that he does not have to face his own consequences, he will not be motivated to face his fears and deal with his problems.

2. <u>The codependent avoidant must repent!</u> After being cast overboard, God prepared a fish to swallow Jonah. I believe that the fish stands for the problems of this world that seem to engulf but are unable

to digest the codependent avoidant. He must get so sick of his pity-party and victim mentality that he loses any hope of ever getting his needs met through his dysfunctional manipulations. Only then will he turn in desperation to God for help.

3. <u>He must recognize that dying to his selfishness and trusting Jesus is the answer</u>. The Bible tells us that Jonah's three days and three nights in the fish are a type of Jesus' death and resurrection. Matthew 12:40 states, "For as Jonas (Jonah) was three days and three nights in the whale's belly; so shall the Son of man be three days and three nights in the heart of the earth." The client must learn to trust in God for his needs as Jesus did and be willing to die to himself (delay gratification). His fears will dissipate only as he relies on Christ's provision for him instead of relying on his ability to manipulate others.

4. <u>The client must choose to call out to God for help</u>. Most clients will not cry out to God for help until they are absolutely overwhelmed by their circumstances. Jonah finally cried out to God for help when he had run out of options:

   Jonah 2:1 Then Jonah prayed unto the LORD his God out of the fish's belly,

   2 And said, I cried by reason of MINE AFFLICTION unto the LORD, and he heard me; out of the belly of hell cried I, [and] thou heardest my voice.

   3 For thou hadst cast me into the deep, in the midst of the seas; and the floods compassed me about: all thy billows and thy waves passed over me.

   4 Then I said, I am cast out of thy sight; yet I will look again toward thy holy temple.

   5 The waters compassed me about, [even] to the soul: the depth closed me round about, the weeds were wrapped about my head.

   6 I went down to the bottoms of the mountains (problems); the earth with her bars [was] about me for ever: yet hast thou brought up my life from corruption, O LORD my God.

   7 When my soul fainted within me I remembered the LORD: and my prayer came in unto thee, into thine holy temple.

5. <u>The codependent avoidant must realize that, without God, his own attempts are futile</u>. Until he is willing to do his part and trust God, God will not have mercy on him and deliver him from his codependency. This is clear from Jonah 2:8: "They that observe vanities (fruitless attempts to deal with his problems themselves) forsake their own mercy."

6. <u>He must believe that God is on his side, be thankful for all God has done for him, and be willing to obey God</u>. Unless a person is willing to obey, God cannot help him because God will not override an individual's free will. When Jonah repented, the fish vomited him out onto dry land. I believe the dry land stands for the security that the client will have when he chooses to trust God to meet his needs through faith.

7. <u>The client must do what God directs in spite of his fears</u>. Jonah had to go back to Ninevah and do exactly what God had directed him to do. In the same way, the codependent avoidant must go back to face the same fears he has tried to avoid and, this time, do as God directs. Forty (days) stands for testing in human life. This usually includes the process of overcoming fear through progressively trusting God to deal with those fears, as discussed in the conquest of Jericho. A slow, systematic desensitization process is required for reentering life as faith and trust in God grow. It took Jonah three days to cross the city. Three stands for completeness. The codependent avoidant is not done until he has faced all of his fears and has overcome them in the real world. The people of Ninevah repented. The very people, and even the leaders, that Jonah feared so much, heeded his prophecy. In the same way, the fears that have bound the codependent avoidant have to yield to God's wonderful Word of deliverance when the codependent avoidant trusts God and faces them.

8. <u>He must speak what God tells him to speak</u>. The client must learn to speak faith about his future (prophesy) and to not speak anything God does not say (negative self-talk). Speaking what God says about our future builds faith.

9. <u>The client must start doing what he can do for himself</u>. Jonah built a booth to shadow himself from the sun. God responded by preparing the gourd to show that he did love him and would respond when Jonah did his part. Jonah was "exceedingly glad." The codependent's emotions are very much tied to his circumstances. Jonah had made some progress, but he was not yet completely recovered. God prepared a worm (which stands for degraded men) and it destroyed the gourd (God's provision). Men and circumstances in life will attempt to destroy the client's blessings. Jonah was able to function in good circumstances, but reverted to codependent behavior when circumstances became unfavorable.

10. <u>The codependent avoidant must learn to face even negative circumstances without a victim mentality</u>. A very hot wind came up and made Jonah almost faint. Codependent avoidants usually see any reversals of circumstances as a sign that God does not really love them. Jonah again wished to die. The final victory will come only when the client realizes that he is not a victim, and that God loves everybody equally, treats everyone with mercy, and loves His children unconditionally no matter whether they succeed or fail. The codependent avoidant should also understand that the mercy of God does eventually end if we continue to refuse to repent. The people of Ninevah later returned to their sin and the city was destroyed and never rebuilt again. (Nahum 3)

Because codependent responsibility avoidants fear failure and believe that life is too difficult for them, their relationship and trust in God needs to be rebuilt. *Experiencing God : Knowing and Doing the Will of God* (1990) by Henry Blackaby and Claude King, is an excellent resource. Through the use of boundaries, clients need to be forced to take more and more responsibility for their own lives. This should be done slowly, starting with areas where success is more probable. In the case of an over-under responsible marriage, boundaries are also required for the dependent rescuer to stop her from trying to require him to meet her perfectionistic standards and from being overly critical of her mate. Many times the mate will have to refuse to enable the avoidant in a particular area. He or she must be willing to suffer whatever consequences result before the responsibility avoidant realizes that if he does not do it, he will fail. This realization is key to motivating him to take on the responsibilities that he wishes to avoid.

Overcoming Codependent Responsibility Avoidance

1. The overall problem is a fear of failure, which causes the client to avoid situations in which he might fail or not perform as successfully as he wishes.

2. He must take responsibility for his own life and others must refuse to do for him what he can do for himself.

3. The client must repent of his desire to protect himself at all costs by refusing to do things that might result in failure.

4. The client must quit blaming others and trust God to meet his needs.

5. He must realize that his attempts to manipulate others to meet his needs are futile and that, without God, he is powerless to meet them.

6. The client must cry out to God for help to make him adequate for the tasks he is called to do.

7. The client must understand that God is on his side, be thankful to God for what he has done, and be willing to obey God.

8. The client must do what God directs in spite of his fears.

9. He must speak to himself only what God tells him to speak.

10. The client must start doing what he can do for himself and trust God to make him adequate for every task.

Chapter 15

Victim Mentality
The Codependent Relationship
Avoidant
(Tamar)

Codependent Relationship Avoidance

The codependent relationship avoidant many times begins life in her family of origin as the "lost child," and has been so badly hurt in intimate relationships that she avoids them, and spends the rest of her life as a victim looking for society or someone else to vindicate her or take revenge on her perceived abusers.

It seemed that Linda had been abused all of her life. After being abandoned by her father, she had gone from one father figure to another. Each had taken advantage of her sexually. Her last sexual relationship had been with her youth pastor and had lasted over four years. She was bitter and wanted this pastor punished. Although she was able to maintain a job at a large company by changing jobs after each conflict with bosses and co-workers, she lived isolated in a small house with five animals. They were her best friends. From time to time, she tried to get help from people at her church and from a series of pastors and counselors. She was looking for someone to defend and protect her. When each "rescuer" either set relationship boundaries or refused to get involved in her attempts to redress her wrongs, she would break off the relationship. Under pressure, the youth pastor who abused her confessed and resigned from the ministry. Because both were adults, no disciplinary action was ever taken.

The problem of Codependent Relationship Avoidance is best described in the story of Tamar, the daughter of King David. Her story begins in 2nd Samuel Chapter 13.

1. <u>God's plan for codependent avoidants is that they have a victorious life even under difficult circumstances</u>. Instead, they see themselves as an oppressed, emotionally broken victim. Sometimes they develop a proud, defiant attitude. Tamar's name means "palm tree" which in the Bible typifies victory under adverse circumstances. (Wilson, 1957) She is the daughter of Maacah which means "oppression," who was the granddaughter of Talmai which means "furrowed or broken up." Talmai was the king of Greshur, which means "proud beholder."

2. <u>Because of extremely negative experiences, usually by people they trusted who have taken advantage or excessive liberty with them, they withdraw in fear from relationships</u>. David's firstborn son, Amnon, wanted to have sex with Tamar, his half-sister. His friend Jonadab suggested a plan. Jonadab means "liberty." King David was unknowingly brought into the plot. I believe that this suggests that David's sexual sin with Bathsheba was being repeated in the next generation. David even directed Tamar to go to Amnon's house.

3. <u>Many times they start out as naive "good girls" who are set up to be hurt</u>. Tamar naively went to Amnon's house, fixed food for him, and even went into his bedroom without suspecting anything.

4. <u>They want to do what is right but are ashamed about the abuse they have suffered</u>. They allow the abuse to affect their self-image. Tamar complained in 2nd Samuel 13:13, "And I, whither shall I cause my shame to go?" She even suggests that David might allow them to marry.

5. <u>Sometimes the abuser will even despise the codependent, because they seem so weak and passive</u>. In 2nd Samuel 13:15, it states that "Amnon hated her exceedingly; so that the hatred wherewith he hated her [was] greater than the love wherewith he had loved her." Subsequently, Amnon threw her out.

6. <u>They are usually abused again and again</u>. She made it clear that the evil of sending her away was greater than the rape itself. Statistics suggest that women who have been raped once have a 200% greater chance of being raped again than another woman who never has been raped before.

7. <u>Because they allow the shame to affect how they perceive themselves, it goes deep within their character, and they become desolate and withdraw from close relationships</u>. Tamar ripped the garment she was wearing (her character), put ashes on her head (shame for the past), laid her hand on her head (actions based on how she feels). She took the shame for the injustice perpetrated on her. Her brother Absalom suggested that she hide what happened and took her into his home. When shame is hidden, it turns to toxic shame—I am a bad person. In 2nd Samuel 13:20, it states that, "Tamar remained desolate in her brother Absalom's house."

8. <u>Through a victim mentality and pity-party, they seek someone to take up their cause</u>. King David, who should have defended her as her father, was angry but did nothing. I believe that she recruited her brother Absalom who became her avenger and killed Amnon two years later. Again, David was unwittingly used in the plot (suggesting a generational tie to his sin with Bathsheba), and Jonadab (liberty) had a hand in it.

9. <u>The consequences fall on the avenger and all who try to help the codependent relationship avoidant</u>. Although it was Tamar who was originally abused and sought vengeance, Absalom was blamed for killing Amnon and had to flee for his life.

10. <u>The codependent relationship avoidant will help from behind the scenes but only as part of an alliance</u>. Tamar's part in this plot is clear when we realize that Absalom escaped to stay with Talmai, Tamar's grandfather. Absalom also named his daughter Tamar.

11. <u>Her anger and desire for vengeance will eventually be turned on those who she perceives failed to protect or bring justice for her</u>. After Amnon's death, Tamar's anger turned against David. I believe she instigated Absalom's rebellion against their father, King David. He barely escaped with his life. Absalom's complaint against King David was that he failed to carry out justice. He felt he could do better himself. (2 Samuel 15:4) **It is interesting to note that victims of abuse are usually angrier with the person who should have protected them than they are at the abuser himself.**

12. <u>The codependent relationship avoidant views the entire matter as an attempt to seek justice; but, in fact, she is seeking to justify herself and to get revenge on her abusers</u>. Many others are destroyed in the process of gaining revenge. Absalom brought Ahithophel, David's advisor, into the conspiracy. Ahithophel was also seeking revenge. He was Bathsheba's grandfather. David had committed adultery with Bathsheba and had killed her husband Uriah to cover up his sin. When Ahithophel realized that his vengeance against David would not succeed because Absalom would not follow his advice, he committed suicide.

13. <u>Because he believes he has been recruited into a "just" cause, even the objectivity of the rescuer is distorted. Instead of listening to Ahithophel, Absalom listened to Hushai the Archite, one of David's best friends</u>. Absalom probably also justified what he was doing because in biblical times it was the brother's duty to protect his sisters. Somehow, he seems to have forgotten that he was also to honor his father. He even had sex with his Father's concubines on the roof of the palace.

14. <u>The "rescuer" ends up paying the price for his attempt to obtain vengeance for the codependent avoidant</u>. When Absalom lost the battle to David's men, his head and hair (pride) became caught in

an oak tree (which stands for "bitter sorrow"). Joab thrust three darts through his heart and killed him. Usually it is the rescuer who pays the price for the bitterness of the victim.

15. <u>The rescuer will only be remembered as being a monument to the "fruitlessness" of doing for others what they should have done for themselves</u>. In 2nd Samuel 18:18, we are told, "Now Absalom in his lifetime had taken and reared up for himself a pillar, which [is] in the king's dale: for he said, I have no son to keep my name in remembrance: and he called the pillar after his own name: and it is called unto this day, Absalom's place."

Healing the Relationship Avoidant

Unfortunately, as far as we know, Tamar never recovered from her codependency. In order to find the solution for the codependent relationship avoidant client, we must turn to the New Testament and the ministry of Jesus. First, let us review in John Chapter 5 the problem that we find at the Pool of Bethesda and then observe how Jesus handled it.

1. <u>The underlying factor in codependent relationship avoidance is an extreme level of human neediness</u>. We are told that at the pool of Bethesda there were five porches. Five stands for the weakness of every human being. Bethesda means "house of mercy."

2. <u>Codependent relationship avoidants are waiting for a miracle because they see themselves in an impossible situation</u>. Relationship avoidants are afraid that if they get emotionally close to healthy people they will be rejected and hurt again. They know that they need relationships, but because they do not want to be hurt again, they will only relate to those with problems like their own. At the Pool of Bethesda, there were only other dysfunctional needy people. They all believed that somehow an angel was going to come, stir up the water, and heal them. Relationship avoidants are usually mad at God for not doing a miracle and healing them in the manner that they want to be healed. Deep down, however, they really do not believe that it will happen. They are too worthless for God to want to help them. To them, this is obvious because if He loved them; He would have already healed them a long time ago.

3. <u>If relationship avoidants are not looking for vengeance, they are consumed with a "pity party," spending their years hopelessly complaining</u>. The man in this story had been crippled for 38 years and was just sitting around with other people with handicaps (probably complaining).

4. <u>The first question to be answered is whether they really want to be whole. Pity loves company, and commiseration has its benefits</u>. In John 5:6, Jesus asked him, "Wilt thou be made whole?" Many homeless people begin to "enjoy" their role as a victim and their "freedom" from responsibility and close relationships. It all feels so safe. If they became healthy, they would be expected to be responsible and have healthy relationships, the very things they fear the most.

5. <u>Codependent avoidants have an excuse for everything</u>. The lame man answered Jesus that the reason he was not healed was because no one helped him so that he could be the first one into the water to be healed. He saw the problem as a lack of help, not a lack of initiative. (If he really believed he would be healed, He could have sat at the edge of the pool and fell in when the water was stirred.) Avoidants see everything as somebody else's fault; never their own.

6. <u>Jesus has the power and the desire to make them whole if they are willing</u>. Jesus told him that if he wanted to be healed, he would have to do his part by first acting according to his faith. When He believed and took up his bed, he was able to walk. When codependent avoidants are willing to face their fears and do their part, healing will quickly follow.

7. <u>Codependent avoidants are looking for someone to tell them what to do; so that if it fails, they can blame the other person and avoid responsibility</u>. The Jews complained that Jesus had healed and had

told the man to carry his bed (which they considered work) on the Sabbath Day. The man blamed Jesus.

8. <u>They become angry when confronted with the fact that what they are doing is sin</u>. Jesus later found him in the temple and warned him to quit sinning. He responded by telling the Jews that it was Jesus who was to be blamed for telling him to work (take up his bed) on the Sabbath day. Confronting and helping codependent avoidants should be done with caution.

It is usually a clear indication that your client is a codependent relationship avoidant when they want you to take responsibility for directly fixing their problem or guaranteeing their safety. The counselor must be extremely careful that they do not allow the client to become overly dependent on them. If this occurs, and the counselor does not do what they ask, all the pent up rage from the past abuse may become displaced on the counselor. Since the real issue is fear of rejection caused by abuse or injustice, the client needs to be helped to address the abuse and then to progressively take action to face the fear. If appropriate, the avoidant can seek redress of his wrongs himself, according to biblical principles. In many cases, the client will have to forgive and grieve the past losses before he is able to put his past behind him. He needs to learn to give up his perceived right for vengeance, trust God, and put his situation into God's hands. Only God is able to bring true justice. As resources, I use *The Wounded Heart* (1990) by Allender and an appropriate codependent workbook.

Summing Up Codependency

Now that we have discussed all six subtypes of codependency, let me summarize what we have learned. It is clear that this problem is caused by an attempt to meet our deepest needs without God. This is what the Bible calls idolatry. However, our new idols are ourselves, others, our accomplishments or the things of this world. The codependent dependent passive tries to make someone else into her savior. The codependent dependent rescuer tries to get her needs met by saving a dysfunctional man. The codependent independent is trying to become his own god. If he succeeds, he becomes addicted to his own work or accomplishments. If he fails, he looks for a codependent dependent rescuer to help and support him. The responsibility avoidant tries to avoid failure by finding someone to do the things he feels inadequate to do. The relationship avoidant is trying to get others to care for, avenge, and save him. These strategies lead directly to becoming overly dependent on what they believe will meet their needs. Beginning with Luke 12:27, the scriptures make the error of this approach to life elegantly clear:

> Lu 12:27 Consider the lilies how they grow: they toil not, they spin not; and yet I say unto you, that Solomon in all his glory was not arrayed like one of these.

> 28 If then God so clothe the grass, which is to day in the field, and to morrow is cast into the oven; how much more [will he clothe] you, O ye of little faith?

> 29 And seek not ye what ye shall eat, or what ye shall drink, neither be ye of doubtful mind.

> 30 For all these things do the nations of the world seek after: and your Father knoweth that ye have need of these things.

> 31 But rather seek ye the kingdom of God; and all these things shall be added unto you.

Overcoming Codependent Relationship Avoidance

1. The overall problem is a fear of rejection causing the client to avoid situations in which he might be rejected or to find someone to help him get revenge for past rejections or abuse.

2. He must take responsibility for his own life. Others must refuse to do for him what he can do for himself, especially taking responsibility for redressing his wrongs.

3. The client must repent from his desire to protect himself at all costs and quit blaming others for not protecting or meeting his needs.

4. He must realize that he is powerless without God to meet his own needs or bring true justice to his situation.

5. He must repent of his own sin, low self-image, defensiveness, reliance on others, and desire for getting personal revenge.

6. The client must cry out to God for justice, become willing to forgive past hurts, take responsibly for his part in the rejections or abuse and, if the offender repents, be willing to reconcile with the abuser or those who failed to protect him.

7. The client must see himself as God sees him—not as a victim, but through the help of God, as an overcomer—and be thankful to God, and willing to obey Him.

8. The client must start doing what he can do for himself to build healthy relationships, set healthy boundaries and trust God to make him adequate for every task.

PART VII

The Jebusite Giants
Abusive Behavior

Chapter 16

Abusiveness
(Jacob)

Perhaps one of the most significant problems in our society today is that of personal abuse. Physical, emotional, verbal and sexual abuse is the precipitating event that underlies many psychological problems, including most subtypes of codependency. These types of abuse have become so prevalent in our society that they have become a significant part of most counselors' caseloads. Fortunately, the Bible gives us excellent models for dealing with the abuser. As already discussed, the Perizzite tribe represents the problems of people without personal boundaries who put up with the abuse, and the Jebusite tribe represents the problems of the abuser. Jebus means "threshing place" or a place where grain is beaten to remove its husks. The abuser verbally, emotionally, sexually, or physically abuses others to get his needs met.

Although I have counseled many abusers over the years of my ministry, James stands out as a typical example of how resistant classical domestic violence perpetrators are to change. Initially, he was not at all open to any form of counseling, and he intensely denied the significant effect his verbal abuse and violence was having on his family. He had been a career Marine and had served during the war in Vietnam. To James, the world was a very threatening and insecure place where he could not trust anyone. He would become very controlling and aggressive when threatened. He perceived his family problems as disrespect toward himself and the product of the insidious manipulation of women. Typically, after an explosive episode, he would be repentant. We would work on establishing boundaries, which would last until his tension cycle would reach a point where he again felt his wife was against him. At that point, he would refuse to abide by the boundaries and would even tear up the contract. As one child after another became angry and rebellious, he became more aware of the damage that this abusive cycle was having on his family. As his wife became more confident of herself, she demanded separation until his problem could be resolved. Although the physical violence and verbal abuse became less frequent, social services and police intervention continued until his wife filed for divorce.

Although the Bible, like life, gives us many varied examples of abusive behavior, the most comprehensive model of this psychological problem is found in the account of Jacob and his children. Abuse, like codependency, is a generational sin. In Genesis Chapter 25, we find the story of Jacob, an abuser. In the following chapter, we will study the story of Joseph, his son, who was abused by his brothers, as a model for abuse recovery.

Understanding Abusive Relationships

1. <u>Most abusive relationships have their origin in past abuse and power struggles</u>. Unfortunately, an abused person usually becomes an abuser. Crossing another's boundaries seems to give a feeling of power. The victim feels powerless and, consequently, learns to gain power through becoming an abuser himself. Isaac grew up in the middle of an ongoing power struggle with Ishmael. His wife Rebekah's name means "ensnarer." Her father's name was Bethuel (God destroys), and he was from Syria (exalted) possibly indicating a pride problem. Self-enlargement or pride, which is many times

an indication of low self-worth, is a root problem in power struggles. Rebekah's brother was Laban who later abused Jacob. Both Isaac and Rebekah were, at least somewhat responsible for the power struggle between Jacob and Esau by favoring one child over another. However, Jacob and Esau even struggled in the womb. I believe this is clear symbology that the competition had been passed on from previous generations.

2. At the most fundamental level, abuse results from an attempt to get needs met at the expense of another person. Sibling rivalry between children is usually a competition for the love and attention of the parents and for a superior position in the family. Jacob and Esau chose different methods of trying to meet their own needs. Jacob looked to the Spirit, and Esau tried to meet his needs through the flesh. When Isaac favored Esau and Rebekah favored Jacob, the conflict intensified.

3. Needy people who want others to meet their needs become victims of abuse. People who are overly needy make themselves vulnerable to abuse because they allow their boundaries to be violated in order to get their needs met. Almost invariably, an abuser marries a mate who feels inadequate. Esau was extremely hungry when he came in from the field and wanted some of Jacob's pottage. In spite of the fact that pottage is clearly not as valuable as a birthright, Esau accepted Jacob's offer of an exchange due to his hunger. The flesh wants its needs met now and has little regard for the cost. Very needy people, who want what others have in order to meet their needs, invite abuse, focus on short-term needs, and tend not to heed long-term consequences.

4. Abuse is a learned behavior. One of the best indicators of whether someone will be abusive is whether they have been abused or have witnessed ongoing abuse. Abraham had twice abused Sarah by asking her to deny that she was his wife in a misguided effort to protect himself. Isaac did exactly the same thing to Rebekah in Gerar, with similar results (Genesis 26:7). Esau gave up his birthright for some pottage in order to get his immediate need met, just as Sarah and Rebekah had lied to please their husbands. (Genesis 25:34)

5. Envy is one of the underlying causes of abuse. Jacob wanted the blessing from his father, which was rightly Esau's. With the help of Rebekah, he stole Esau's blessing by pretending to be Esau. He may have justified what he did by saying to himself that they were twins or that his brother did not deserve the blessing, because he did not value the things of God, or because it had been prophesied that the elder would serve the younger.

6. Abuse leads victims to desire revenge. Aggression, that is the desire to cross another's boundaries because our boundaries have been violated, is one of the most common responses to abuse. The other most common response is to become passive and do nothing. This leads to anger which leads to bitterness. When abuse has not been rectified, long-term damage is inevitably done to the relationship. Esau hated Jacob and planned to kill him after Isaac died.

7. The abuser will eventually be abused. The Bible tells us that what we sow we will reap. Jacob escaped to Laban only to find himself on the receiving end of abuse. As recorded in Genesis Chapter 29, he served Laban for Rachel and was given Leah. After serving another seven years, he finally was allowed to marry Rachel. In the years that followed, Laban changed the wage agreements with Jacob many times in order to take advantage of him.

8. Unresolved issues from the family of origin will recur in the following generation. The abuse of the previous generation will be repeated again and again. Jacob favored Rachel over Leah, setting up a competition for his love that would ultimately result in the abuse of Joseph. Even the children of the family were named according to the current status of the power struggle between Leah and Rachel!

9. God is on the side of the abused. Through a dream, Jacob was given a strategy from God, which resulted in Jacob obtaining most of Laban's wealth reversing the effect of the abuse. No matter how

hard the abuser tries unfairly to get his needs met, in the end abuse always results in a loss for the abuser.

10. <u>It is God's will that abusive relationships be appropriately resolved, but many times a time of separation is required as part of the resolution.</u> After Jacob noticed that Laban had turned against him, God directed him to leave. In this case, he was leaving one abusive relationship to resolve his abusive relationship with Esau.

11. <u>Separation is designed to help resolve the relationship, not avoid it.</u> Jacob's separtion from Laban forced Laban to deal with the problem. Many times, the abuser will simply escalate the abuse in order to get the victim to return. Here God intervened in a dream warning Laban not to abuse Jacob again. Unfortunately, many times a victim will then respond by becoming an abuser. Rachel paid her father back by stealing his gods (Genesis 31:19).

12. <u>Appropriate boundaries are the answer for resolving abusive relationships.</u> After both Laban and Jacob communicated their respective perceptions of the situation, they established a boundary covenant. (Genesis 31:44-55) We see here the three parts of a boundary: 1. A clear line that they agree not to cross. They agreed not to pass the monument at Mizpah to do the other person harm. Jacob also agreed that he would not harm Laban's daughters or take any other wives. 2. Specific consequences for violating the boundary (in this case that God would judge them). 3. A normalization of the relationship (they ate together) with the understanding that the other would not violate the boundary.

Treatment of the Abuser

In Genesis Chapter 32, the Bible gives us a model for the recovery of the abuser as we continue the story of Jacob's life.

1. <u>The first step for assisting the abuser is to help him break through his denial and face the fact that he is an abuser.</u> Sometimes this starts when he is confronted by the victim. This is one of the hardest steps for the abuser, because he must face the shame he feels and his fear of retribution. Jacob sent messengers to Esau asking for favor. The abuser should take the first step as a means of demonstrating repentance.

2. <u>Even after a long time, abuse does not resolve itself without facing the abused person's anger.</u> The messengers returned with the news that Esau was coming with 400 armed men. If not resolved, bitterness over abuse can last a lifetime.

3. <u>The abuser needs to carefully take responsibility for what he has done.</u> He must realize that he deserves nothing but abuse in return. Jacob separated his herds and family in case Esau retaliated.

4. <u>The abuser needs God's help in the reconciliation.</u> He needs to realize that God owes him nothing. Jacob appealed mentioning the fact that God had directed him to return home. He needed God to give him favor and to change him, so that he would no longer try to meet his needs at another's expense. He had to learn to trust God to meet his needs.

5. <u>The abuser needs to offer restitution.</u> In this case, Jacob prepared an elaborate present for Esau. The abused will be looking for signs that real repentance has occurred. Jacob hoped to appease Esau with a present.

6. <u>Most of all, the abuser must face himself!</u> He has selfishly tried to force others to meet his needs. He has violated others. Jacob wrestled with the angel all night. The result was that the angel put his thigh out of joint. The thigh stands for strength. The abuser must wrestle with God until God convinces him to quit trying to do things in his own strength and look to God to be his strength and his provision for life. Only when we believe that our needs will be met by God will we be set

free from the temptation to meet our needs at the expense of others. The abuser must learn to want to respect other's boundaries just as he desires others to respect his boundaries. This event resulted in the transformation of Jacob (supplanter or abuser). Because of this transformation, Jacob was renamed Israel (one who prevails with God). **It is faith in God to meet his needs that changes the abuser into one who wants what is best for the other person and leads to the mutual respect of personal boundaries.**

7. <u>True repentance by the abuser is the answer to reconciling abusive relationships</u>. Without it, the abuse will recur. True repentance is demonstrated by actions. Jacob truly sought his brother's forgiveness through humility, gifts and a plea for mercy. Even when given the chance to keep the present, he insisted on giving it. Restitution is important, not just to the abused but also for the healing of the abuser.

8. <u>Even when true repentance has occurred, it is still wise to keep a safe distance between the abused and the abuser</u>. Trust takes time to develop and must be based on a lengthy history of non-abuse. Jacob discretely chose to not have Esau directly accompany him lest some other conflict occur that might disrupt the frail re-established relationship. (Genesis 33:15)

The underlying cause of abuse is clear. People abuse others in order to get their needs met at the expense of the other person. This is also true of power struggles. The underlying fear that needs will not be met leads the abuser to try to force others to meet those needs. Faith is the fundamental answer for the abuser. If he can actually trust God to meet his needs, the underlying cause of the abuse—fear that his needs will not be met—will be overcome through faith in God's provision. In actual practice, physical, emotional, and verbal abusers need additional help learning how to manage their anger, get in touch with their innermost feelings, understand boundaries, deal with the root problems in their families of origin, remove their facades and respect other's right to be in charge of their own lives. Sexual abusers, especially pedophiles, need very significant help in breaking down their denial, dealing with the lusts that they have developed, unlearning their sexual myths, and developing biblically healthy sexual interactions. In fact, denial and lying to cover up their abuse of children is so prevalent that therapy should not be attempted for pedophiles without the aid of a lie detector or other means of detecting deception.

As additional resources when dealing with physical abuse and anger, I use *Change is the Third Path* (1996) by Lindsey, McBride, and Platt and *The Anger Workbook* (1995) by Carter and Minirth. Additional references on abuse include *Violent No More* (1993) by Paymar, *Verbal Abuse: Healing the Hidden Wound* (1992) by Ketterman, *Anger is a Choice* (1982) by LaHaye, *Battered into Submission* (1989) by Alsdurf and Alsdurf, *In the Name of Submission* (1986) by Strom, *What's He So Angry About* (1995) by Stoop, and *Treating Child Sex Offenders and Victims* (1988) by Salter.

Steps for the Recovery of Abusers

1. Abuse is an attempt to alleviate fears that the client's needs will not be met through forcing, controlling or manipulating others to meet those needs.

2. All abuse or offense is a violation of the personal boundaries of the abused.

3. Although many abusers have been abused themselves, this fact can never justify abuse because assertive options always exist.

4. The abuser must break through his denial, take responsibility for his actions and face the fact that he is an abuser.

5. He must learn that his attempts to control other people or his circumstances will fail. These attempts are at the root of his anger cycle and violence. He must turn control of his life over to God believing that God will provide for all his needs.

6. He must repent, face those he has abused, ask forgiveness and make restitution when possible.

7. He must agree to establish and respect healthy mutual boundaries in order to prevent continued abuse. True repentance always results in changed behavior.

Chapter 17

Abuse Recovery
(Joseph)

Codependency and a lack of boundaries provide fertile ground for abuse and victimization. This is because all of us are selfish at least to some extent and may even inadvertently take advantage of others who do not express how they feel and do not stand up for themselves. Of course, abusers will do whatever it takes to get their needs met at the expense of others. Even after developing a basic understanding of the methods for establishing healthy boundaries and for recovering from codependency (as discussed in previous chapters), we still need a comprehensive model for recovering from abuse and for the reconciliation of relationships.

Many times the abused person will remain in an abusive relationship out of fear and intimidation. Jackie is a good example of this. She attended our Codependency Support Group for at least a year. She had been in a verbally and sometimes physically abusive marriage for over twenty years. She just did not seem to have the strength to do anything about it. After each episode of abuse, she would just forgive her husband and try harder to not offend him again. This never worked for long. She may have confused the biblical command to forgive with the direction to reconcile, which is only required if the other person demonstrates true repentance. (Matthew 18) In one particular group I attended, we were discussing how a codependent dependent will put up with abuse and allow her boundaries to be violated again and again; because she fears that her own needs will not be met. She finally realized that her reluctance to confront the abuse was due to her own selfishness and that she was allowing her children to be damaged by it. The following week she told her husband that the next time he touched her or the children in anger she would call the police. By setting a long needed personal boundary, she began the process of healing in her family.

Possibly, one of the most dramatic accounts of recovering from abuse is found in the story of Joseph, beginning in Genesis Chapter 30.

1. <u>Even if the abused person is guilty of provocation, there is never an excuse for abusing someone</u>. Jacob blatantly favored Joseph over his brothers by making him a coat of many colors. Joseph unwisely shared his dreams with his brothers further agitating their envy, but this did not justify their desire to kill him or to kidnap and sell him as a slave! The abused person must realize that he did not "deserve" the abuse. Abusers many times try to convince the abused person that he "caused" the abuse. Sometimes, the victim believes that the abuser is right. The victim needs to understand that this is never true. Abuse, whether it is physical, emotional, verbal or sexual, is a major boundary violation and is never justified by anything another person does. The Bible makes it very clear that we are not to take revenge on those that wrong us. Assertive options always exist.

2. <u>The abused person should not automatically leave the relationship but do everything possible to remain in the relationship while setting boundaries to provide protection from the abuse</u>. Joseph did not run away from his brothers although they were verbally abusive to him. In spite of their comments, he obeyed his father and went to see if they were doing well. The Bible directs that a wife should not leave her husband. (1 Corinthians 7:10b) I believe God gave that admonition because a

high percentage of women who leave their husbands eventually divorce. If they separate, the victim will, in most cases, experience relief from the continuing struggles in the marriage. Consequently, there is a great temptation to just divorce rather than renew the efforts to improve the marriage. In cases of physical or sexual abuse, calling the police or obtaining a restraining order may be required to reinforce boundaries, but God's plan is that they work out their differences, if possible. In cases of long-term severe abuse, separation, testing of repentance and a slow reconciliation is almost always required. If the victim maintains good boundaries, the abuser will eventually leave or divorce her if he is not willing to work to improve the relationship. My experience is that most women who choose to leave rather than work out a relationship with a mate who is willing to change, end up losing in the long run, both financially and in their relationships with their children

3. <u>The abused person must resist seeing himself as worthless</u>. Because of the way he is being treated, an abused person many times accepts the fact that there must be something wrong with him. This is especially true of young children because they see themselves as the cause of all that happens around them (due to childhood egocentrism). I sometimes ask my clients what the victims of the Oklahoma City Federal Building bombing did to make themselves so worthless? Of course, the answer is that just because they were victims of a bombing did not mean that they were, in some way, less worthwhile than other people. Low self-image perpetuates abuse because a person usually feels unworthy of fair treatment or lashes out because of the deep emotional pain caused by feeling worthless. Although his brothers had valued Joseph only as a child slave (They sold him for 20 pieces of silver), Joseph did not allow himself to have a pity-party or devalue himself. I suggest that clients evaluate similar situations by saying to themselves, "They have a problem. I will pray for them." This helps the abused person avoid the trap of taking things personally or feeling devalued.

4. <u>The abused person must forgive the past, never forget who he is in Christ, and keep a good attitude in spite of the abuse</u>. Abuse can make a person feel as if his life is not worth living and can result in bitterness. This kind of contempt is responsible for most of the long-term effects of the abuse. The self-contempt and other-contempt that is used as a defense against shame sets up additional abusive situations and limits the quality of life of the abused person. (Allender, 1990) Joseph was sold to the captain of the guard, who in those days was the chief executioner; but Joseph kept a good attitude and even excelled under these circumstances. In every situation, he chose to do his very best in spite of how he had been treated. Joseph's name means "increaser." Those who are careful to keep a good attitude increase in life rather than get run over by it. Joseph resisted choosing a lifestyle designed to solely protect himself from further abuse. He chose to take full responsibility for his part of every relationship and trusted God for his protection.

5. <u>The abused person must learn to do what is right and not enable the abuser</u>. The temptation for the abused is to go along with things in order to escape the anger of the abuser or to try to please the abuser hoping that this will lessen the abuse. Unfortunately, when this is done, the abuser's violation of boundaries is rewarded and the abusive behavior usually increases. There is no limit to the control that is desired by an abuser. Joseph refused to violate another's boundaries. He would not sleep with his master's wife even though this may have been the easiest way out. He may have even been able to justify it as an opportunity to gain favor with his master's wife, or because it had been requested by her.

6. <u>Maintaining appropriate boundaries sometimes initially results in increased abuse or unfair accusations</u>. When the abused person finally sets and maintains appropriate boundaries, the initial reaction is many times anger and further attempts to control and abuse. Because Joseph refused to sleep with his master's wife, she accused him of attempted rape, and he was imprisoned. (Genesis 39:12-20)

7. <u>The abuser needs to hold on to the fact that God will show him mercy and eventually bring deliverance</u>. It is easy for an abused person to lose heart and just give in to the abuse or leave. Joseph

again found favor in prison and became the head trustee of the prison, in spite of the unfairness of the situation.

8. <u>The abused person needs to continue to do what is loving, right and good without regard for the circumstances or reaction of the abuser</u>. When he can no longer blame the other person, the abuser is many times forced to deal with his own problems. This is the basis of non-violent resistance. Even though Joseph's dreams seemed far from fulfillment, he continued to minister to others by interpreting their dreams. This is what Dr. Allender (1990) calls bold love—when the abused refuses to become defensive, contemptuous, or bitter, and instead cares enough to boldly do what is best for others, including the abuser.

9. <u>Recovery from abuse usually takes a significant period of time</u>. Expecting that the abuser is going to make a miraculous change usually brings disappointment. One major pitfall is expecting that when an abuser shows evidence of repentance that it will last. In actuality, change, especially in the domestic violent perpetrator, usually progresses slowly through a series of repentances and regressions. As tension and anger rebuilds, so do defensiveness and control. A remorseful period usually follows an angry incident but is only part of the tension and anger cycle. As the problem gets worse, even these periods of remorse eventually fade. Joseph hoped that the end of his abuse was in sight when he correctly interpreted the dream of the butler. However, it was not until two years later that he was finally delivered.

10. <u>The victim must understand his position in Christ</u>. The low self-image of the abused person must be replaced with his position as "a child of the king." After being taken from prison, Joseph was elevated to second in the kingdom and given almost unlimited authority. In the same way, the abused person must understand his position as a joint-heir with Jesus and reassert this authority over his own life. He must accept the ring (authority), fine linen (imputed righteousness) and gold chain (self-worth) from the king. All the citizens of Egypt were required to bow, showing their respect for Joseph. The victim must realize that all God's resources are available to him and God will meet all his needs. He must also understand that he is worth as much as, but no more than the abuser, and he will always be unconditionally loved by God. These revelations do not usually occur until the end of the recovery process. If the victim is suddenly elevated too early in the process of recovery while he is still bitter, he may use his new position as an opportunity to leave the relationship or take vengeance on the perpetrators.

11. <u>The victim must understand that he is called to "save" his own world</u>. Only by the victim changing himself can his world be saved. Joseph was given the name Zaphnathpaaneah (Savior of the world— revealer of secrets). Abusive and codependent relationships continue because they are allowed to continue. I am not suggesting that the abused person is somehow responsible for the abuse, which is never justifiable, but that he has allowed it to continue due to fear, neediness, and, sometimes, a misunderstanding of biblical submission. Spiritual authority and submission are only valid to the extent that the authority follows the directions of his higher authority. The ultimate higher authority is God. Wives are to follow their husband's leadership as long as he is not in violation of the Bible. Abuse is always a violation of the scriptures. Submission means cooperation, which definitely does not include putting up with abuse.

12. <u>The abused person must learn not to focus on the abuse (or bitterness will result) but focus on doing what is best for the relationship</u>. One of my favorite phrases in counseling angry people is "attack the problem, not the person." The abused must give up his right to take vengeance and deal with the pain of the past, so that he can even-handedly accomplish the task set before him. Joseph had two sons born during the years of plenty. Manasseh means "causing forgetfulness" and Ephraim means "double ash-heap or shame." He put the past behind him, and he saw his past struggles as unimportant ashes and residue of the previous abuse. He attributed both accomplishments to God in Genesis

41:51-52, " For God, [said he], hath made me forget all my toil, and all my father's house…For God hath caused me to be fruitful in the land of my affliction."

13. <u>The abused person needs to be strengthened before beginning the reconciliation process</u>. Most abuse victims have been emotionally beaten down for years and have developed codependent, enabling ways of functioning. The victim is usually afraid of abandonment and the abuser's anger and is incapable of confronting or testing the abuser effectively. He must be strengthened through counseling or support group participation. Joseph had to gather in supplies for the time of famine to come. This building time is like a time of plenty. Its purpose is to strengthen the victim so that the abuse can be confronted and repentance tested.

14. <u>Effective boundary setting is essential and almost never pleasant</u>. Usually, only emotional famine will drive the abuser to meet the appropriate boundaries of the victim. The balance of power shifts, as the victim feels strong enough to suffer the loss of the abuser, if necessary. As the victim becomes less codependent, the abuser is forced to change and do his part in the relationship or he will starve emotionally. Joseph required the people of Egypt, who had also abused him as a slave and prisoner, to do what they could in exchange for food and did not give the food away free of charge. In the same way, the abuser is required to do his part in the relationship. Joseph, with his stored resources, eventually acquired all the land and resources of the people of Egypt for the king, but never violated the rights of the people in any way. The object of boundary setting is not a reversing of power in favor of the abused, but doing what is right and fair and what is in the best interest of each person involved.

15. <u>The abuser must repent and submit himself to God before reconciliation should be attempted</u>. Healthy boundaries will force the abuser to either leave or change. Abuse cannot continue in a healthy relationship. Effective, balanced boundaries, accompanied by true unconditional love and acceptance, become a powerful combination. God used the same combination in saving us. He sent his Son to demonstrate His love, but in order to receive Him we must repent. Note God, not Joseph, brought about the change in Joseph's brothers. The abused must be fully convinced that repentance has occurred before reconciliation should be attempted. If true repentance has not occurred, the abuse will reoccur. As I have stated above, Joseph did not freely give the grain to the Egyptians, but over a period of time acquired all their goods and each of them became slaves to Pharaoh. In the same way, the abuser and all he has must come into submission to God. The abuser must learn to trust God to meet his needs and give up control of his life to God. Without this, he will continue to try to meet his own needs at the expense of others and an ongoing power struggle will continue in the relationship.

God's Plan for Reconciliation

1. <u>God does not require the abused person to make themselves emotionally vulnerable to an unrepentant abuser to be abused again</u>. Joseph had the opportunity to be reconciled with his brothers as early as Genesis Chapter 42, but he did not attempt reconciliation until he could verify that his brothers had really changed. If he had immediately reconciled with his brothers and they had not changed, they could have done him significant political harm. The abusive husband, if he has not repented, is also in a position to do his wife significant damage. It is critical not to begin this process of testing repentance too early in the recovery process. If this happens, the wife will quickly perceive that the abusive husband has not changed as much as she would like, lose hope, and exit the relationship.

2. <u>The abused person is not under any obligation to maintain a special relationship with the abuser, if he has not repented</u>. Sometimes the abuser draws the abused back into the relationship through guilt or pity. Matthew 18 suggests that if another Christian refuses to repent they are to be treated as a publican and a sinner. Therefore, we should pray for them but not put ourselves in vulnerable

situations. Joseph chose to keep his emotional distance and formal boundaries until he was convinced that his brothers had repented. This is a wise strategy for the abused, since the abuser usually attempts to manipulate the victim into returning prematurely in order to meet his own needs.

3. <u>The abused has a right to test the sincerity of the abuser until he is reasonably satisfied that the abuser has changed</u>. Joseph suggested that his brothers might be spies and put them in prison for three days to see how they would react. I believe this symbolizes the first test to see if they would respect Joseph's boundaries. Many times, the abuser continues to pursue the abused person even after the victim requests more distance in the relationship. Sometimes this even involves stalking the victim.

4. <u>When the abused acts assertively and not aggressively, the abuser must deal with his own guilt</u>. Because Joseph did not attempt to take revenge on them, his brothers were forced to deal with their own guilt. They said in Genesis 42:21, "We [are] verily guilty concerning our brother, in that we saw the anguish of his soul, when he besought us, and we would not hear; therefore is this distress come upon us."

5. <u>Another effective test is to do something beyond what is expected to see if the abuser will take advantage of it</u>. This is the proverbial "hot coals on the head," or exchanging good for evil. (Proverbs 25:21-22, Romans 12:21) Joseph returned the money to them that they had paid for the corn. They responded, "What is this that God hath done unto us?" It is important that the abuser does not see this as a sign of premature reconciliation or weakness. This is a clear example of Joseph exercising bold love.

6. <u>The abuser hates confrontation and will avoid facing his abuse</u>. Often, this is accomplished through avoiding the person whom he has abused or by denying or minimizing what he did. Most of the time, the abuser will deal only with his past abuse if it is absolutely necessary in order to get his current needs met. Joseph's family returned only when they ran out of corn again, in spite of the fact that Simeon was in prison. Israel was afraid of losing Benjamin, and his brothers did not wish to face Joseph again (although they did not realize at this time that he was their brother).

7. <u>The abuser must be given no choice but to repent or starve emotionally</u>. Distance must be maintained until it is clear that true repentance has occurred. In most cases, only a lack of emotional need satisfaction will provide enough motivation to begin real change. The abuser usually "wants to have his cake and eat it too."

8. <u>The first signs of repentance are attempts to do things in a non-abusive manner</u>. Joseph's brothers took with them a present of the best they had and brought again the money that had been returned to them in case it was an oversight. In addition, they were prepared to accept whatever was about to happen. This is the mindset the abuser must have.

9. <u>The testing must continue until repentance has clearly been demonstrated</u>. Joseph continued testing them as he slowly allowed them to become a little closer emotionally. This time he invited them to his home. In the first test, at dinner, he gave Benjamin five times as much food as the other brothers to see if they would react jealously. In the second test, he accused them of stealing his silver cup. Silver stands for redemption. He questioned whether they were trying to manipulate their way back into the relationship instead of authentically repenting and accepting redemption. The final test came when Benjamin, the only one of his brothers with the same mother, was "caught" with the silver cup. Would his brothers abandon Benjamin or prove themselves to be loyal and trustworthy?

10. <u>Only after the abuser has proven that he has repented and that he is now trustworthy, should emotional closeness be restored</u>. When Judah offered to take Benjamin's place and all the brothers returned with Benjamin, Joseph was convinced that they had changed, and he revealed himself to them. However, caution still needed to be maintained because relapse is common once the

relationship has been restored. Adequate boundaries for protection must be left in place and slowly reduced over time. Joseph settled his brothers in the land of Goshen, some distance from the capital. He also warned his brothers not to fight on the way when they left to bring their father back to Egypt.

11. <u>After true repentance, the next step is forgiveness</u>. Joseph said in Genesis 45:5, "Now therefore be not grieved, nor angry with yourselves, that ye sold me hither: for God did send me before you to preserve life." Repentance and forgiveness are the foundation of true reconciliation.

12. <u>The ultimate question is whether the abuser remains primarily selfish in his dealings or does he have the best interest of the abused in mind</u>. This is the basis of a healthy relationship. Only time can tell this. We have no indication that Joseph's brothers ever abused him again. They remained afraid that after their father Israel's death, Joseph would still seek revenge, but he never did.

In summarizing what we have learned concerning codependent and abusive relationships, we should now realize that both the abuser and the victim play their respective roles in the abuse by attempting to selfishly meet their needs. This, of course, does not in any way justify the abuse or the abuser. All abuse and offense are violations of personal boundaries. Jesus warned, "offenses will come, but woe unto them that bring them." (Luke 17:1) We all face abusive relationships, at least to some extent. The question is, how will we handle them? The abuser crosses another's boundaries in order to get the victim to meet his needs. Many times, the victim allows the abuser to cross her own personal boundaries out of fear that the abuser will either leave or increase the abuse. This is especially true of the codependent dependent.

In dealing with domestic violence, emotional, or verbal abuse, I begin counseling each individual separately. In most cases, initially only the victim comes for therapy. After explaining God's plan for marriage and healthy relationships and the principles of abuse recovery as outlined above, I usually begin therapy with the victim by simultaneously teaching her (usually it is the wife who is abused) healthy boundaries and dealing with her codependency through either our Codependency or Women's Abuse Recovery support groups. The goal is to strengthen the victim enough so that she will be willing to take biblical action to stop the abuse. I use the books *Boundaries* (1992) by Cloud and Townsend and *Love is a Choice* (1989) by Hemfelt, Minirth, and Meyer with the victim. I sometimes also incorporate the chapters from *The Wounded Heart* (1990) by Allender that deal with contempt, defenses against abuse, and bold love. If the abuser refuses to cooperate in ending the abuse, then separation may be required until the abuser can be helped.

In some cases, the abuser will seek therapy after his wife begins setting and carrying out healthy boundaries. However, most abusers enter therapy at court direction after an arrest for domestic violence. I use *Change is the Third Path* (1996) by Lindsey, McBride and Platt in group therapy with domestic violence abusers. I try to stop the control and balance the power in the relationship through teaching him to respect his mate's opinions and feelings. Once the abuser has shown definite signs of repentance and there is no longer a danger of escalating the violence through what is revealed during therapy, I begin marital counseling. I attempt to have them set mutually agreed-upon boundaries with established consequences, especially in the area of anger management and abusive behavior. I then deal with the emotions from the past and attempt to defuse current conflict with "anger breaks" which tend to reduce the tension building, abusive cycle.

Reconciliation is worked out one step at a time. The next step is taken only when the current level of re-approach is successful (without any abusive behavior). Usually, this type of reconciliation requires a written boundary contract that applies to the whole family. I try to teach them to solve problems as a team. As more and more success is achieved over a significant period of time, trust is rebuilt and fear is slowly overcome. The overall plan is to fix the future, then the present, then the past. I find that true forgiveness is more easily accomplished once the chance of repeated abuse is almost nonexistent. However, the testing of repentance and restoring emotional vulnerability should not be attempted until the past has been forgiven. One of the most difficult obstacles to be overcome is the buried anger and bitterness the victim feels toward the abuser. Once fear of abuse is removed, many times this anger is unleashed on the abuser. If this is not processed and overcome, the relationship may end in divorce rather than reconciliation even if the abuser makes considerable improvement. The critical line of believing that the other person has their best interests in mind must be surpassed. Finally, when the intimate relationship is rebuilt and the couple can function reasonably well as a team, work can begin on the emotional long-term healing of the family as a whole. Boundaries can eventually be softened as healing occurs.

In dealing with sexual abuse, the first responsibility of the counselor is to prevent further abuse as well as report any current childhood sexual abuse to authorities. For moderate levels of sexual abuse, I recommend *Helping Victims of Sexual Abuse* (1989) by Heitritter and Vought. I use *The Wounded Heart* (1990) by Allender for heavier levels of abuse like rape and incest. Both books present clear biblical steps for recovery from this type of abuse.

The root problems underlying abusive behavior are the fear that personal needs will go unmet; and the belief that these needs will be met by controlling other people. Only God can completely satisfy these basic inner needs. Therefore, when the abuser and the victim truly turn to God in faith, problems resulting from abuse can permanently and completely be resolved. Consequently, if the counselor deals primarily with healing the damage from the abuse, he does a disservice to his clients. Faith must be built that God can be trusted to meet all of their needs. God has provided the total answer to this issue. Clients need to trust Him to meet all of their needs through faith, defend their boundaries and respect the boundaries of others.

Steps for the Recovery of Victims of Abuse

1. Abuse victims are many times codependent dependents without adequate boundaries.

2. The client must understand that her treatment by others does not make her less worthwhile or somehow responsible for the abuse.

3. The victim must deal with her underlying feelings of inadequacy and codependency in order to gain enough strength to confront the abuser.

4. The abused person must learn to do what is right in spite of fear, set appropriate boundaries and not enable the abuser.

5. The client must repent of her selfish efforts to protect herself at all costs and learn to meet her needs through God.

6. The client must confront the abuser with bold love and refuse reconciliation until true repentance has clearly occurred.

7. If the abuser repents, the victim should forgive him and reconcile the relationship, but maintain good boundaries to prevent a repetition of the abuse.

PART VIII

The Hivite Giants
Addictive Behavior

Chapter 18

Addictions
(Samson)

As I have already discussed, Gibeon was a Hivite city. Hivite means "life-giving" and stands for those desires and lusts that we see as assisting the quality of our lives and meeting our deepest needs. While the verbal, emotional, physical and sexual abuser tries to get his needs met at the expense of others, the addict attempts to get his needs met by killing his emotional pain through some form of activity or drug. Because the addict seldom quits his addictive behavior even when it is severely damaging to his life, he is actually abusing himself. Today, addictions are categorized either as substance addictions, like drugs and alcohol, or process addictions, like sex, eating, gambling or workaholism.

Ron was an extremely talented man who was criticized and put down at an early age. Although he was able to maintain a good job in spite of an addiction to methamphetamine drugs, his family suffered from his rage and psychotic episodes "when he had used too much" and his long periods of depression when he crashed. As is often the case, he married a dependent rescuer. When she discovered that he had used drugs again, she would viciously degrade his character in an attempt to get him to quit. He would defend himself by listening to his wife's increasing attacks, try to deny that he had a problem, and eventually agree that she was right—he was worthless. His denial continued until his family asked him to leave the home in an attempt to motivate him to get help. Even after two inpatient programs His desire for help lasted only for short periods of time, and he began using drugs again. He truly did not believe that he could be helped. Unfortunately, his use of drugs progressed until the downward spiral cost him his job and his family. Many times clients have to hit "rock bottom" before reaching the level of desperation required to motivate them to seriously seek the help they need.

In Joshua Chapter 9, the Hivites of Gibeon were subtle in their dealings with the Israelites. They convinced the Israelites that they were to be trusted as friends. In the same way, the Hivite giants of today present themselves as our friends. It is only later that we learn the dangers involved in inviting them into our lives. Some counselors believe that sexual addiction can be one of the most difficult to treat. It many times has all the traits of a drug addiction because the pornography, fantasy, and masturbation trigger endorphins and adrenaline in the body.

Michael was only 22 but was so addicted to Internet sex that he stated, "If I even see a computer, I know that I will shortly be looking at pornography. It's like the devil has a hook in my nose." His father had been delivered from heavy drug use and had become a pastor. He spent so much time at church that he had no time for his family. As Michael's addiction progressed, he isolated himself from others and spent all his free time viewing Internet pornography. One day when he visited a "chat room," a man invited him to meet with him to have group sex with the man and his wife. The man even paid for the airline ticket. Mike was progressing deeper and deeper into the depths of ever-increasing perversion. His best hope for recovery was to embrace God, Who he believed was responsible for taking his father away from him. This was very difficult for him to do.

Understanding Addictions

The giants of addiction are the result of what the Bible calls the lust of the flesh. As I have already stated, the average codependent has at least two addictions. Whether alcohol, drugs, sex, relationships, eating, buying things, gambling, or even workaholism, the process is the same. Let us look at the story of Samson, who became a sex and relationship addict. Judges Chapters 13-16 reveals this all-too-prevalent psychological problem.

1. <u>Even Christians who are called, anointed, and come from good Christian homes can have problems with addictions</u>. As we look at the story of Samson, it is very clear by the visitations of the angel that he was particularly chosen to deliver Israel from the Philistines. Philistia means "sojourners or aliens" which stand for the forces of evil and Satan in this world.

2. <u>The underlying root of addictions is codependency or an addictive personality</u>. This modern term, which I have defined as "excessive dependence or independence on people or things," has already been extensively discussed in the previous chapters. Codependency is a dysfunctional means of coping with life, which is passed from generation to generation. Another term for codependency is an addictive personality. A number of the symptoms of codependency are clear in this account of the story of Samson:

   a. Manoah, Samson's father, was angry (Zorah means "to shout or cry out"), judgmental (Dan means "to judge") and withdrawn (Manoah means "rest"). He did not believe what his wife told him and did not feel adequate to carry out the directions of the angel without further instruction. He asked God to send the angel to repeat the message. His legalistic attitude (which is a sign of insecurity) is seen in his belief that because he had seen God, he would die. The bondage of the law is an important factor in the addictive process. When we are forbidden to do something, we are naturally tempted to do it and often rely on only our own strength to avoid it. Later, we will see that Manoah did little to influence Samson to do what was right. In fact, he even enabled Samson's addiction. On the other hand, he did pray and he had faith enough to ask the angel whom to give credit to when the prophecy came to pass. He offered burnt offerings and a meat offering unto God. The irony of this story is that these sacrifices represent the very things required in the process of addiction recovery, repentance and dedication to God.
   b. Manoah's wife was living in shame (she was barren, which was a great disgrace at that time), seemed very passive, but was less legalistic than her husband. Unfortunately, she also became an enabler of Samson's addiction.
   c. God warned the parents to keep Samson away from wine or strong drink. Nazarites were not even allowed to eat anything from the grapevine. He was never to cut his hair (his faith) or eat anything unclean (a type of sin).

3. <u>A Christian can have everything going for him and still become addicted</u>. Samson means "distinguished and strong" from a word that means "sunlight." His miraculous birth and filling by the Spirit indicates that he represents someone who is saved. He was to be a light to his world just as each Christian is to be a light to the world (Matthew 5:16). He was blessed of God and was moved upon by the Spirit of God.

4. <u>Wrong choices provide the initial opening for an addiction to begin</u>. Samson seemed to have inherited some of his father's traits of judgmentalism (Dan) and anger (shouting out). Yet, he seemed receptive to the Spirit of God. We can only guess why Samson was strongly attracted to heathen women. Rigid codependent families usually lack intimacy. Relationship addiction and sexual addiction are found more often in families that lack intimacy, have an extremely negative view of sex, or in which sexual abuse has occurred. Lust looks at the outward appearance in order to get its desires met. Samson went where he should not have been and he saw a woman from Timnath. Israelites were forbidden

to marry people that were not Israelites. In lust, the thrill is higher if the action is forbidden or dangerous because adrenaline is added to the power of the endorphin released by the brain during sex. He chose to meet his own needs in spite of his values and God's direction.

5. <u>The addict is blinded to his own motivation and often excuses his behavior</u>. Samson justified marrying the heathen woman, because he was using the marriage as a means to offend the Philistines. Even after his parents objected, he still insisted on the illicit marriage. This is similar to the mistake of thinking that drinking with non-Christian friends will give an opportunity to witness to them. Even if our motivation is right, using an addictive substance can still lead to an addiction, or it simply may be justifying our wrong actions. Using something external in an attempt to meet internal needs provides the ground for an addiction to develop.

6. <u>Codependents want to please others so much that they will actually assist the addict in his addiction</u>. Although Samson's parents initially objected to his marriage to a non-Israelite, they eventually accompanied him to Timnath to assist him in arranging the marriage.

7. <u>In the initial stages of an addiction, the addict usually still has power over the compulsion</u>. Samson easily tore apart the young lion (Satan) that tried to attack him. He did not tell his parents about this. He knew that there was danger in what he was doing but chose to continue. Addictions begin with a choice of short-term pleasure and a denial of long-term consequences.

8. <u>Addictions do initially bring pleasure and relief to the addict</u>. The Bible says that "sin has pleasure for a season" (Hebrews 11:25). The danger for the addict is that, according to the laws of operant conditioning, if he does something that produces immediate, positive results, he will want to do it more often. This is the principle that turns a desire into a lust. The first step toward addiction occurs when we choose to meet our needs through the flesh rather than by trusting and obeying God.

9. <u>The addict convinces himself that he can have the pleasure of doing wrong without receiving the consequences</u>. This is the meaning of the parable of the lion and the honey that pervades Samson's story (Judges 14:8): Can a person really take honey (pleasurable things) from a dead lion (Satan) and not get stung (by the bees)? The addict initially thinks that he can. This initial denial is only the beginning of the addict's increasing attempts to avoid his shame and deny that he is actually addicted. In taking honey from the lion, Samson violated his Nazarite vow, which included the requirement to avoid touching anything that was dead.

10. <u>The addict will draw others into his problem</u>. Samson, who, as a Nazarite, was not to touch anything dead (Numbers 6:6), not only defiled himself, but also gave some of the defiled honey to his parents. (Judges 14:9) In doing so, he caused his parents to sin; because they did not know that the honey came from a dead animal. According to Jewish law, if a person touched anything that had been in contact with something dead, the person was required to purify himself. (Leviticus 11:27) Numerous addicts run bars, deal drugs, or get others involved in their addictions.

11. <u>The addict truly believes that he can escape the consequences of his addiction and sometimes even becomes proud of it</u>. Samson challenged his wedding guests to figure out the secret concerning his addiction—that he could do it and get away with it. Whoever figured out the riddle would be richly rewarded. If what Samson believed was actually true, then all of us could live for Satan and indulge in worldly pleasure and yet escape the consequences of our sin. If this could be done, we could sin with impunity, in order to reap rich worldly rewards. This clearly violates God's law of reaping what we sow.

12. <u>When the addict experiences the consequences of his addiction, he blames others for his problems</u>. When the wedding guests answered his riddle (after threatening his wife in order to find out the answer), he had to pay the consequences. An addict's mate is almost always codependent (this is where the word originated). Therefore, it is hardly surprising that the wedding guests were able to

manipulate his wife, and it is hardly surprising that Samson gave in to her manipulations. He had only himself to blame, but the addict clings to his belief that his consequences are caused by others, especially those close to him like his wife. He was not willing to admit that what happened was a natural result of his own choices.

13. <u>As consequences mount up, the addict lashes out and eventually destroys his own family</u>. Instead of accepting the consequences of his game and paying for the garments, he made others pay by killing 30 Philistines and taking their clothes. Consequently, his wife was given to his best man. Because of this, he burned the Philistine's fields. In response, they burned his wife and her family. This kind of out-of-control cycle of boundary violations usually continues until decisive action is taken to stop it.

14. <u>Eventually, the addict becomes so destructive that even the church is forced to turn against him</u>. Samson eventually became like a wild animal and became so isolated that he went to live on the top of a rock. The name of the rock was Etam, which means "lair of wild beasts." The Israelites bound him and turned him over to the Philistines. I believe that this is a type of the church turning the unrepentant addict over to Satan for the destruction of the flesh. (1 Corinthians 5:5) Tough love is the only thing that can help an addict at this point in his addiction. A staged confrontation with boss, pastor, family, and friends can sometimes get the addict to face his addiction, but more often his family and church may have to ask him to leave until he gets help. Unfortunately, this seldom is done in families or churches until the problem is totally out of control.

15. <u>Sometimes, bringing the addict under authority and accountability, and refocusing on his calling can bring relief</u>. I believe that the cords that Samson was bound with by the Israelites represent authority and accountability. After being helped off the rock of wild animals by the church, he recovered enough of his strength to kill a thousand men with a jawbone (preaching) of an ass (burden-bearer or Christ's anointing). I have observed that addicts who totally focus on their calling can sometimes temporarily control their addiction. Samson's needs were met by a spring of water called "Enhakkore" which means "spring of one calling." The addict's emptiness is temporarily filled by his accomplishments. I believe that this change of focus works because God's call is outwardly directed while addictions are inwardly focused.

16. <u>If the addict relapses, he will continue his addiction at the intensity level where he left off, and because of an increased tolerance for the drug, will go even deeper into the addiction</u>. Samson's relapse this time was with a prostitute. This is a level deeper into sexual addiction. He went into the city of Gaza, which was the Philistine's stronghold. He put his life in jeopardy just to satisfy his addiction. When strongly addicted, the addict will do anything to get his lust met, without regard for danger or possible consequences. I had a client who was so addicted to crack that she broke into her own house to steal her own television, so she could pawn it without her husband knowing that she did it. It is also common for addicts to meet their need for drugs through prostitution.

17. <u>Addictions do not immediately negate all spiritual power in an addict's life</u>. Although Samson had fallen farther into sin and was depressed (midnight), he still was able to take the doors (his will) and posts (shame and denial) of the city gate (Satan's authority) and carry them to a hill near Hebron (association) (Judges 16:3). I believe that this tells us that if an addict can exercise his will enough to get help from others, recovery is still possible. Support groups are among the most effective means of helping addicts.

18. <u>As the addiction progresses, it becomes stronger and the addict becomes weaker, but as long as he holds onto his faith, he cannot ultimately be defeated</u>. Delilah means "feeble, longing, and dainty." She was from Sorek, which means "vines." Here, I believe that vines represent codependent relationships, which entangle people. Samson was to eat nothing that came from the vine.

The Philistines or forces of Satan enlisted Delilah to entice Samson by offering to pay her 1100 pieces of silver. Silver is the price of redemption and eleven is a combination of six (man's sufficiency) combined with five (man's failure and weakness). The addict acts strong on the outside, but is very insecure. Delilah asked him where his strength came from three times. Each time he lied to her. His lies give us the list of things that cannot, in themselves, defeat a Christian's faith. The man of God operating in faith cannot be defeated by problems of the soul (green withs never dried), new schemes of the devil (new ropes never occupied), or attempts to undermine and confuse his faith (hair woven in seven locks).

19. <u>Without faith in God, the addict is powerless in his own strength</u>. Samson's codependency finally overwhelmed him and he gave up his hair (faith) to get Delilah's "love." He chose to trust her, instead of God, to meet his needs (the root problem of addictions). Samson's complete submission to Delilah is clear when he slept on her knees after telling her the secret of his strength.

20. <u>Eventually, the addiction will overwhelm the addict's values, faith, and walk with God</u>. When Samson awoke, the "Lord was departed from him." Romans 8:9 tells us that if we have not the Spirit, we do not belong to God. **Either our faith will overcome our addiction or our addiction will overcome our faith!** This battle between an addiction and one's faith is an extremely serious matter. It will be discussed in more detail later in this chapter. It is possible that the addict will not even notice when the Spirit of God is no longer present (as was the case with Samson in Judges 16:20).

21. <u>Addiction eventually results in the loss of spiritual insight, bondage by toxic shame, and subservience to Satan</u>. The Bible tells us that we are slaves to the one we obey. (Romans 6:16) Samson's eyes were put out (spiritual sight), he was put in chains of brass (judgment, guilt, and shame), and he was made a slave to grind in the Philistine (Satan's realm) prison house like an ox.

Faith is the Answer!

1. <u>The most important factor in recovery from an addiction is faith! Samson's hair (faith) began to grow again</u>. Since the addict, by this point, is totally overwhelmed by his lust; he is incapable of helping himself in his own strength. The best predictor of whether an addict will actually recover is whether he believes that with the help of God he can recover. (McGee, 1990)

2. <u>The real issue underlying an addiction is the choice by the addict of which god he will trust to meet his needs</u>. The god of the Philistines was Dagon, the fish-god of fertility or sex. Dagon represents Samson's addictions to sex and relationships with women in whom he had trusted. He was brought to the temple of Dagon by the Philistines "to make sport of him." Satan will use the Christian addict to bring disgrace on Christianity just as Samson was brought out by the Philistines to demonstrate that Dagon was more powerful than Jehovah.

3. <u>Unfortunately, most addicts have to come to the end of themselves and hit "rock bottom" before they turn to God for help</u>. Samson finally put his trust back in God, out of the very anguish of his heart, as he grieved the loss of his eyes (spiritual sight).

4. <u>The addict must push down the pillars of denial and toxic shame that support his addiction</u>. Samson pushed over the two pillars that held up the temple of Dagon (the god of his addiction) through his faith in God. The addict must come to believe that his addictive personality and the power of his addiction were crucified with Christ. The power of Christ within him can be relied upon to meet his needs, overcome his shame, and give him the strength to face life without his addiction.

5. <u>The addict must be willing to die to his own self-gratification in order to successfully recover</u>. Pulling down the temple of his addiction cost Samson his own life. The cost of recovery to the addict is the loss of "his best friend" (his drug). This is the price required for coming out of an addiction and only the desperate are willing to pay it. The addict must believe that God is going to meet his needs

even without his addictive substance. Dying to the self means delaying gratification; in order to be willing to delay gratification, we must believe that our needs will eventually be met.

6. <u>Recovery through faith is a great victory for God</u>. Samson slew more in his destruction of the temple of Dagon than in everything else he did during his life. (Judges 16:30) Recovery from an addiction is a great victory over one of Satan's most formidable psychological giants. When accomplished through faith, God gets the credit. In spite of all his failures, Samson is still listed as one of the heroes of faith. (Hebrews 1:32) Through God, everything—even recovery from addiction—is possible.

7. <u>Even though the addict may recover, his addiction will still cost him something</u>. Samson was buried after judging Israel for only twenty years. He forfeited half of what was the normal length of a successful reign of a judge or king of Israel. Although an addict may recover, many times the damage that has been done to his body during the addiction lasts for the remainder of the addict's life. In addition, because of the lust that is developed through addiction, the addict will always have to be on guard against relapse.

Addictions are Serious Problems

Addictions of all types are very serious problems. Alcoholism is the most widespread addiction in our society. According to *Taking Control* (1988) by Minirth, Meier, Fink, Byrd, and Hawkins, 70 percent of our society drinks—the largest percent ever—and consumes an average of 30 gallons of alcohol each year. Ten percent are heavy drinkers and seven percent are problem drinkers or alcoholics. Alcoholism is the third leading cause of death in America and is responsible for 50 percent of highway deaths. It is also a major factor in suicide. In the church, 81 percent of Catholics and 64 percent of Protestants drink at least socially.

Although the most comprehensive information concerning addictions in the Bible is found in the story of Samson's life, a number of other addictions are mentioned in the Bible. Nabal possibly died of an alcoholic seizure. King Saul was addicted to rage and domestic violence. Solomon was addicted to work, sex, and possibly alcohol. Eglon and Eli were most likely addicted to food, and Lot struggled with homosexuality. In addition, the Bible deals with drug addictions under the more inclusive name of sorcery.

In 1st Corinthians Chapter 6, we find a list of addictions that can separate us from the Kingdom of God. As with most of present tense Greek in the New Testament, I believe that these verses should be interpreted as continuous action. As an example, it is not getting drunk once that keeps a person from inheriting the kingdom of God, but continually being drunk over a period of time. This is substantiated by the verses that follow this list. As we have already seen in the story of Samson's life, **either our faith will destroy our addictive behavior, or our addiction will destroy our faith.** The good news is that, even though the power of an addiction can be great, each and every addiction—including homosexuality—can be and has been overcome through a deep faith-filled relationship with Christ. Paul, however, strongly advises that we should do everything possible to avoid these behaviors so that we will not be brought under their power.

1 Co 6:9 Know ye not that the unrighteous shall not inherit the kingdom of God? Be not deceived: neither <u>fornicators</u>, nor <u>idolaters</u>, nor <u>adulterers</u>, nor <u>effeminate</u>, <u>nor abusers of themselves with mankind,</u>

10 Nor <u>thieves</u>, nor <u>covetous</u>, nor <u>drunkards</u>, nor <u>revilers</u>, nor <u>extortioners</u>, shall inherit the kingdom of God.

11 And such were some of you: but ye are washed, but ye are sanctified, but ye are justified in the name of the Lord Jesus, and by the Spirit of our God.

12 All things are lawful unto me, but all things are not expedient: all things are lawful for me, but <u>I will not be brought under the power of any</u>.

13 Meats for the belly, and the belly for meats: but God shall destroy both it and them. Now the body [is] not for fornication, but for the Lord; and the Lord for the body.

The Gangrene Model of Addiction

A way to understand addictions is to consider the analogy of a person who has gangrene in his arm. He does not want to admit that he has a sickness that is poisoning his whole body, so he covers it with a bandage and takes a painkiller so he cannot feel the pain. Similarly, the addict often feels badly about himself due to toxic shame that has piled up throughout his life and most often dates back to his childhood. Rather than deal with this emotional pain, he attempts to deny its existence and tries to kill the pain of it through some type of drug. External things cannot fix internal problems! As an example, how much food will a woman who tries to medicate her feelings of worthlessness have to eat before she feels good about herself? The problem is that the more she eats, the heavier she gets and the worse she feels about herself. Consequently, all the food in the world will not suffice. Therefore, the harder the addict tries to fix the internal problem, the worse it gets. The denial is the bandage and the painkiller is the alcohol, drugs, sex, work, food or codependent relationship. The addict continues to avoid dealing with the problem even when it gets worse. This is because he does not see or feel like he has a problem. He knows that in order to get help, he will have to give up the painkiller, rip off the bandage and expose the wound. He believes that this emotional pain would be too great to bear. As he becomes more powerless over the addiction and his life becomes progressively more unmanageable, the addict begins to believe that he is so worthless and so addicted that he cannot be helped. His problem is either not really that bad or the problem has progressed so far that recovery is impossible. Consequently, many addicts go to their graves without ever seeking help.

The Law of Sin and Death

On the following page, the reader will find a chart labeled "The Law of Sin and Death" which summarizes the addictive process. When our basic internal needs for love, security, worth, and significance are not met, we are motivated to do something about it. We select a method of meeting our own needs based on our prior experiences. If we reach our goal through the flesh, these methods provide temporary partial satisfaction along with condemnation (if we believe that what we have done is wrong or sinful). Operant conditioning suggests that if we do something and it results in immediate gratification, we will be disposed to do it more often. This is how desire for something turns into lust. If we choose to protect ourselves by hiding our shame, our guilt or shame ("I did something bad") turns into toxic shame ("I am a bad person"). This is how in the long run the initial feelings of worthlessness increase. These short-term gains, which result in long-term shame, set the process of addiction into motion. After one complete loop of this chart, we have: 1. Increased the desire for the substance. 2. Increased the level of toxic shame and internal neediness. 3. Increased the level of denial about being addicted. After each use, all three of these results increase until toxic shame pervades the addict's life, his lust is so strong that it overrides his values, and his denial blinds him to his problem. At this point, when the addict "tries harder to quit," his failure to stop only adds to his shame. Finally, out of extreme despair, he may even turn to self-destructive behavior or suicide to relieve himself of his intense level of internal emotional pain. This is the point where most addicts are willing to enter recovery. However, many go on to their deaths through medical complications or suicide. These individuals are frequently convinced that they are already too bad, they cannot recover or there is no way out.

The Law of the Spirit of Life

On the second diagram following this page, the reader will find a chart labeled the Law of the Spirit of Life. It depicts the biblical method of recovery from addictions. This chart contains three separate circles of flow that end in very different results. By making two critical choices, we determine the consequences for our life. The choice to believe God to meet our needs through the Spirit results in a process that increases our faith and our desire for the spirit-led life. It also decreases our selfishness and dependence on the addictive process. The end of this circle is love, which results in actual need satisfaction. The choice to trust in the flesh to meet our needs results in sin, shame, and the development of a lust for the addictive agent. If we choose to admit our sin and trust God for forgiveness, our shame or guilt is removed so that it does not

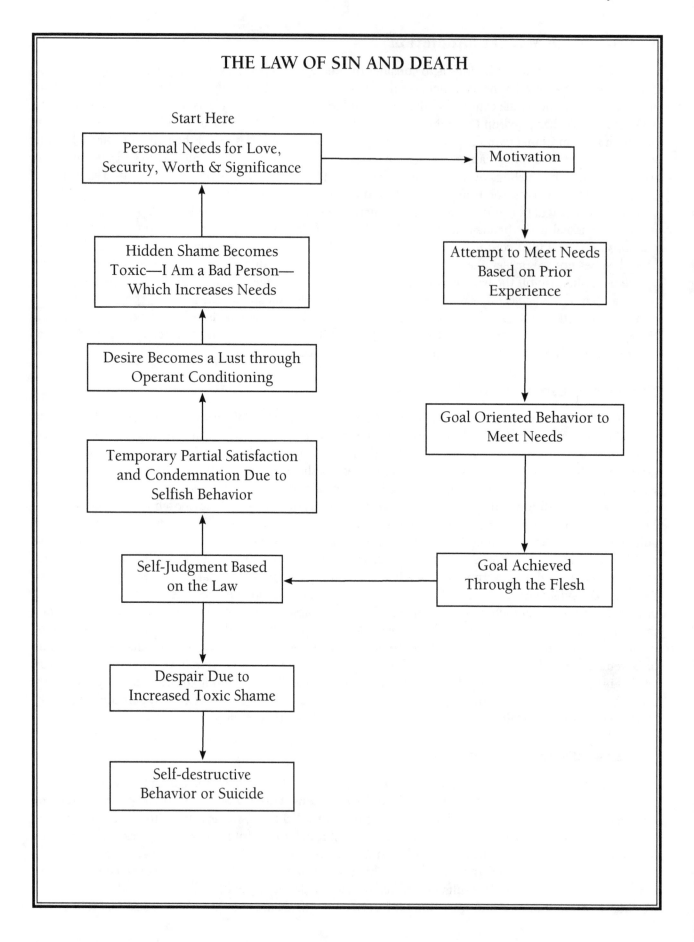

THE LAW OF SIN AND DEATH

Start Here

Personal Needs for Love, Security, Worth & Significance

Motivation

Attempt to Meet Needs Based on Prior Experience

Hidden Shame Becomes Toxic—I Am a Bad Person—Which Increases Needs

Desire Becomes a Lust through Operant Conditioning

Goal Oriented Behavior to Meet Needs

Temporary Partial Satisfaction and Condemnation Due to Selfish Behavior

Self-Judgment Based on the Law

Goal Achieved Through the Flesh

Despair Due to Increased Toxic Shame

Self-destructive Behavior or Suicide

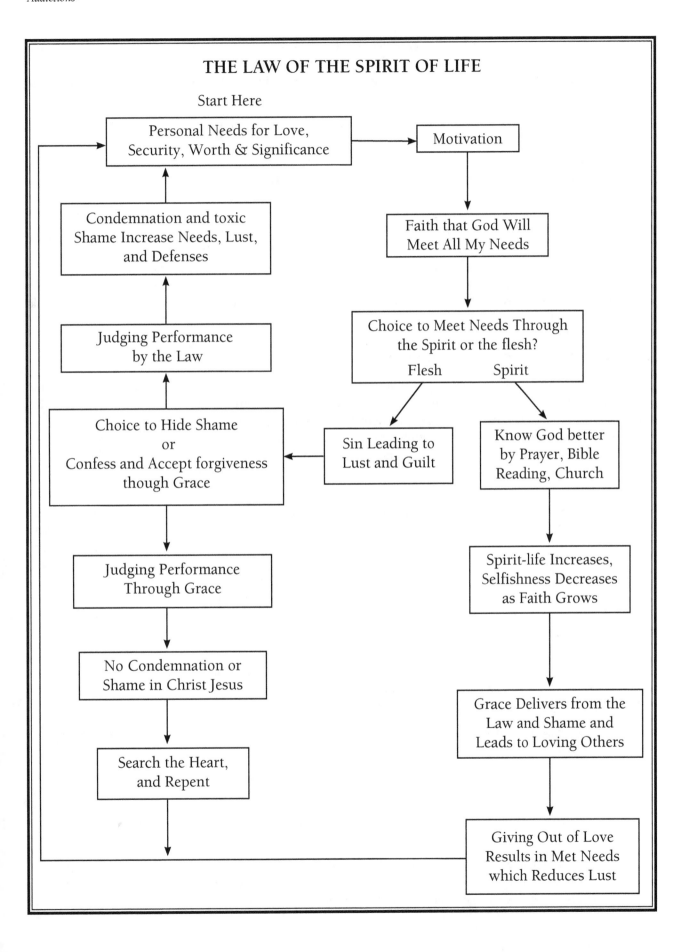

THE LAW OF THE SPIRIT OF LIFE

Start Here

Personal Needs for Love, Security, Worth & Significance

Motivation

Faith that God Will Meet All My Needs

Choice to Meet Needs Through the Spirit or the flesh?

Flesh   Spirit

Condemnation and toxic Shame Increase Needs, Lust, and Defenses

Judging Performance by the Law

Choice to Hide Shame or Confess and Accept forgiveness though Grace

Sin Leading to Lust and Guilt

Know God better by Prayer, Bible Reading, Church

Judging Performance Through Grace

No Condemnation or Shame in Christ Jesus

Search the Heart, and Repent

Spirit-life Increases, Selfishness Decreases as Faith Grows

Grace Delivers from the Law and Shame and Leads to Loving Others

Giving Out of Love Results in Met Needs which Reduces Lust

become toxic shame. This process is called grace. If we choose to hide our shame, we enter a circle exactly like the Law of Sin and Death that for the Christian is called legalism. Toxic shame leads to increased need, strengthened lust, and our defenses hide our ever-increasing addiction. This explains why Christians can become or remain addicted.

The two critical questions that each of us answer every time we are tempted are: 1. Whether we will choose to walk in the Spirit or the flesh, and 2. Whether or not we choose to hide or confess our sin. How we answer these questions will be determined by our faith in God. At the first decision point, if we truly trust God to meet all of our needs, we will rely on His Spirit to fulfill our emptiness. If we do not, we will rely on ourselves and the flesh to meet our needs. At the second decision point, our choice will be based on whether we believe that God still loves us in spite of our sin, will forgive us, and will restore us to Himself. If we do not believe this, we will attempt to cover up our sin and fall into the trap of legalism. Without trusting in Christ for the power to make the right choices, an addiction cannot usually be overcome. It is important to realize that this chart presupposes that the client is a Christian and that he believes that the power of his addiction (the old man) has been crucified with Christ and that the power of Jesus' resurrection is available to him through the new birth (becoming a new man). This subject is explained in more depth in the book of Romans.

The Ultimate Answer from Romans

Romans Chapters 6-8 provide what I believe is the most biblical, effective, and rapid deliverance from addictions for Bible-oriented Christians. Nonetheless, these Chapters are "the meat and not the milk" of the Word of God. Therefore, they require an excellent foundation in the Word of God. I am making a distinction here because for those with little Bible knowledge or for new believers a Christian 12-step program is simpler to understand, although deliverance may take longer. I usually teach the Roman method of deliverance in five steps.

1. <u>In Christ, the addict is free to choose what he will do</u>. This is very enlightening to addicts because by the time they seek help they have usually reached the conclusion that they are powerless to quit. They are, but Christ has done something that restores their ability to choose to overcome every temptation! Romans 6 begins by telling us that although we, as people, have a selfish sin nature and are powerless over it, Jesus, by dying on the cross, destroyed the power of the sin nature. Because we who are saved are "in Christ" and the spiritual realm exists outside of natural time, we were in Christ when He was crucified. Since Christ died on the cross, we died with Him to our old sin nature. Dead men cannot sin. Through Christ's resurrection, we have now been given power over our sin.

    Ro 6:6 Knowing this, that our old man is crucified with [him], that the body of sin might be destroyed, that henceforth we should not serve sin.

    7 For he that is dead is freed from sin.

    11 Likewise reckon ye also yourselves to be dead indeed unto sin, but alive unto God through Jesus Christ our Lord.

    Our part is to believe and "reckon" it so. The Greek word translated as reckon, *logizomai,* in this verse means "to count, compute, or calculate that something is true." The fact that we can now choose not to fall to temptation must become a reality. In 1st Corinthians Chapter 10, the Bible states:

    1 Co 10:13 There hath no temptation taken you but such as is common to man: but God [is] faithful, who will not suffer you to be tempted above that ye are able; but will with the temptation also make a way to escape, that ye may be able to bear [it].

Understanding exactly how this is done is critical. I teach addicts to go to God immediately in prayer every time they are tempted. They need to admit that they will fail for sure if they try to resist the temptation in their own strength, claim 1st Corinthians 10:13 that God will provide a way of escape, and trust God in faith to provide the escape from that temptation. They are instructed to then go about their work trusting God for their victory. Each time they are able to successfully overcome the temptation with God's help, their faith in God grows. Over a period of time, they eventually become convinced that anytime they choose to call on and trust God, they will not fail to have victory over the temptation.

2. <u>He must exercise his will to call on God</u>. It is not enough for the addict to realize that through Jesus, he now has a choice; he must exercise his will in order to choose to be delivered. He must decide that he is "not going to live in his addiction any longer" no matter how desperate the emotional pain. If he is overcome by his compulsion and does not choose to trust in God to deliver him from a temptation, he will relapse. Romans puts it this way:

Ro 6:12 Let not sin therefore reign in your mortal body, that ye should obey it in the lusts thereof.

13 Neither yield ye your members [as] instruments of unrighteousness unto sin: but yield yourselves unto God, as those that are alive from the dead, and your members [as] instruments of righteousness unto God.

3. <u>He must not attempt to do any of this in his own strength</u>. Romans warns us concerning the trap of the law. When people are told not to do something, one of two reactions is almost automatic. Either they rebel and do not want to do what they are told or they attempt to do what they are told in their own strength. Either way leads to failure since sin and addictions cannot be overcome in one's own strength; but only by grace (the unmerited favor and power of God). In fact, the first sign of a coming relapse is when the addict believes he again has control over his addiction. Romans puts it this way:

Ro 6:14 For sin shall not have dominion over you: for ye are not under the law, but under grace.

7:11 For sin, taking occasion by the commandment, deceived me, and by it slew [me].

15 For that which I do I allow not: for what I would, that do I not; but what I hate, that do I.

18 For I know that in me (that is, in my flesh,) dwelleth no good thing: for to will is present with me; but [how] to perform that which is good I find not.

19 For the good that I (in my strength) would I do not: but the evil which I (in my strength) would not, that I do

4. <u>He must also trust God to make him willing to quit relying on his addiction</u>. My experience is that willingness is a critical factor in overcoming addictions. The good news is that God also provides us an answer based on His ability, not ours. It is our job to choose and to obey, but He also provides the resources to do both. We find this most clearly stated in the book of Philippians.

Php 2:12 Wherefore, my beloved, as ye have always obeyed…work out your own salvation with fear and trembling.

13 For it is <u>God which worketh in you both to will and to do of</u> [his] good pleasure.

If an addict is struggling with willingness, I instruct him to again call on God, admit his inability to even be willing, and to trust God to make him willing. I sometimes suggest that they pray, "God,

I am willing for you to make me willing to be willing (as many 'to be willings as needed to be truthful) to do your will."

5. <u>He must learn to consistently walk according to the Spirit</u>. In assisting addicts, I have found that even willingness and faith are not enough. Even after a victory over an addiction has been gained, the devil will begin eroding the recovering addict's willingness and finally cause a relapse if the client does not continue to walk according to the Spirit. This is not surprising since spirits operate primarily through influencing a person's will. If a person walks according to or is under the influence of the Spirit of God, he will consistently want and choose to do God's will. We find this answer in Romans Chapter 8.

Ro 8:3 For what the law could not do, in that it was weak through the flesh, God sending his own Son in the likeness of sinful flesh, and for sin, condemned sin in the flesh:

4 That the righteousness of the law might be fulfilled in us, who walk not after the flesh, but after the Spirit.

5 For they that are after the flesh do mind the things of the flesh; but they that are after the Spirit the things of the Spirit.

6 For to be carnally minded [is] death; but to be spiritually minded [is] life and peace.

13 For if ye live after the flesh, ye shall die: but if ye through the Spirit do mortify the deeds of the body, ye shall live.

In summary, the final answer for addictions is faith in Christ, reliance on Him to do the work, and a transformation through the Spirit as we walk with Him and become like Him.

Ro 8:29 For whom he did foreknow, he also did predestinate [to be] conformed to the image of his Son, that he might be the firstborn among many brethren.

30 Moreover whom he did predestinate, them he also called: and whom he called, them he also justified: and whom he justified, them he also glorified.

37 Nay, in all these things we are more than conquerors through him that loved us.

38 For I am persuaded, that neither death, nor life, nor angels, nor principalities, nor powers, nor things present, nor things to come,

39 Nor height, nor depth, nor any other creature, shall be able to separate us from the love of God, which is in Christ Jesus our Lord.

As a resource for recovery from chemical dependency, I use *Conquering Chemical Dependency* (1994) by McGee and McCleskey. For Christians with a deeper understanding of the Bible, I sometimes use *Freedom From Addiction* (1996) by Anderson and Quarles. For a basic understanding of romance, relationship, and sexual addiction, I assign *Addicted to "Love"* (1991) by Arterburn. In dealing with sexual addiction, I use *At the Altar of Sexual Idolatry* (2000) by Gallagher, *Rapha's Step Studies for Overcoming Sexual Addiction* (undated) by McGee and Yost, or the *Faithful and True: Sexual Integrity in a Fallen World* workbook (1996) by Laaser.

Steps for Overcoming Addictions

1. Understand that the underlying problem is trying to meet deep personal needs through something other than God.

2. The client must overcome his belief that he can meet his needs through sin and not suffer the consequences.

3. He must understand that an addiction results in increased lust, denial, and neediness thus making the problem worse, not better.

4. The client must understand that he is powerless over his addiction and that the harder he tries to stop out of his own strength, the more addicted he will become.

5. He should realize that either his addiction will eventually destroy his faith in God, or his faith in God will destroy his addiction.

6. It is the client's choice to meet his needs either through God or through his addiction.

7. The client must be willing to build his faith, die to his self-life and overcome his denial and shame.

Eating Disorders
(Eli)

One of the most common types of addictions in this country involves eating either too much or too little. Most people in our society are overweight while our society applauds a youthful, slim figure. This paradox has resulted in the problems of overeating, anorexia, and bulimia, though there are often other more serious factors involved.

Marjorie had been overweight ever since she could remember. She had been brought up in a very codependent family. She felt like a failure since all of her brothers and sisters had gone on to have "good" families and jobs. She was divorced from her first husband who had been a "crack" addict. Although she had a close relationship with the Lord and started to progress in a good job, she could not stop her overeating. She saw life as too difficult for her to face. She deserved a break and when she took a break, she turned to eating. She had tried almost every diet. Although these diets worked for a while, she rebounded after each diet and gained even more weight than she had lost. She wondered why God had done so much in her life, but in this area, He continued to fail her. In counseling, she realized that she was protecting herself by remaining heavy. She did not have to worry about men being interested in her as long as she was overweight; and if men were not interested, she did not have to face her fears of rejection and another failed relationship. As long as she was not willing to face these fears, there was little hope that she would ever successfully lose weight.

For some reason, our society discounts the significance of eating addictions except when they result in very significant health problems. Many churches have even exasperated the problem by encouraging overeating through numerous social events that promote eating and fellowship. The Bible calls overeating gluttony and associates it with drunkenness and rebellion.

De 21:20 And they shall say unto the elders of his city, This our son is stubborn and rebellious, he will not obey our voice; he is a <u>glutton</u>, and a drunkard.

These problems again find their origin in an addictive personality or codependency. As with other addictions, the client is making food or body size the integrating force of their life, or their God. This is clearly stated in the story of Eli, the priest, the grandson of Aaron, who judged Israel after Samson, beginning in 1st Samuel Chapter 1.

1. <u>The addict usually comes from some sort of difficult or dysfunctional heritage.</u> Eli means "to ascent" or "my God." His father was Ithamar, the youngest son of Aaron. Ithamar means "palm coast or palm island." According to Wilson (1957), palm trees stand for living the Christian life under adverse circumstances. Both of his brothers were killed for offering wild fire before the Lord. He was born either under the yoke of slavery in Egypt or in the wilderness. Aaron (Ithamar's father) had not been allowed to enter the Promised Land, because he and Moses had disobeyed God at Meribah. (Deuteronomy 32:51,52)

2. <u>The addict is trying to control his own life, cope with the emotional pain within and somehow meet his own emotional needs</u>. Eli's name (my God or ascent) could possibly suggest that he had become his own god, or he was trying to improve or make himself into somebody important.

3. <u>Addictions distort the client's ability to see things objectively</u>. Eli interpreted Hannah's emotional pain as drunkenness. Since he had a problem with eating and drinking himself, he must have thought that she had a similar problem. This story is in the first chapter of 1ˢᵗ Samuel. The person with an eating disorder many times has a very distorted view of life. Those with anorexia and bulimia usually see themselves as much heavier than they actually are. They also believe that eating (or not eating) is the most important thing in their lives or that if they are not thin, they will be rejected and are worthless.

4. <u>Addictions affect the entire family</u>. Our children reflect who we are. Eli's sons were named Hophni (boxer) and Phinehas (mouth of brass). They were characterized by fist fighting and being judgmental. These behaviors are usually related to struggles with low self-image. They were also immoral, as seen by their actions (of sleeping with the women who came to the temple and extorting from the people parts of the offering that priests were not allowed to eat). Their desperation to obtain the fat of the offering suggests they depended more on eating than on God to meet their needs, and probably had an eating disorder. (A description of their lives is in 1ˢᵗ Samuel Chapters 2-4).

5. <u>The addict will do whatever it takes to get their needs met</u>. Eli and his sons were taking part of the offering that was to be sacrificed and Eli refused to discipline his sons. His shame concerning his own weight may have made him sympathetic to his sons' abusive behavior. The following verse suggests both Eli and his sons were making themselves fat. Consequently, God warned Eli that his actions were unacceptable.

    1 Sa 2:29 Wherefore kick ye at my sacrifice and at mine offering, which I have commanded in my habitation; and honourest thy sons above me, to <u>make yourselves fat</u> with the chiefest of all the offerings of Israel my people?

6. <u>God will honor those who honor Him in the way they live their lives</u>. This includes every aspect of their lives; including eating.

    1 Sa 2:30 Wherefore the LORD God of Israel saith, I said indeed that thy house, and the house of thy father, should walk before me for ever: but now the LORD saith, Be it far from me; for them that honour me I will honour, and they that despise me shall be lightly esteemed.

7. <u>If the client will not deal with his addiction, God warns him that judgment will fall not only him, but on his children</u>. Eating addictions and problems of weight affect generation after generation. A list of the consequences that accompany eating addictions are found in the following verses:

    1 Sa 1:31 Behold, the days come, that I will cut off thine arm, and the arm of thy father's house, that there shall not be an old man in thine house.

    32 And thou shalt <u>see an enemy in my habitation</u>, in all the wealth which God shall give Israel: and there shall not be an old man in thine house for ever.

    33 And the man of thine, whom I shall not cut off from mine altar, shall be to consume thine eyes, and to grieve thine heart: and all the increase of thine house shall die in the flower of their age.

1. Premature death.
2. Providing a foothold for Satan in a person's life.
3. It limits the blessings of God.
4. It affects the children's salvation and walk with God.
5. It destroys spiritual insight and body image.
6. It grieves the person's heart.
7. It causes the person's children to die prematurely.

These are the direct effects of an eating addiction. In addition, heaviness leads to a sedentary lifestyle, which is related to problems like high blood pressure and diabetes. Anorexia and bulimia can lead to early death due to malnutrition and vitamin deficiencies. Putting the things of this world ahead of God, to meet our needs, gives a foothold to Satan in our lives and may lead to other addictions. The quality of our lives and our blessings are greatly diminished by overeating, anorexia and bulimia. Demonstrating hypocrisy and a lack of full commitment to God in our lives provides our children a poor example to follow. Our spiritual insight is limited by our love for the things of this world. The Bible tells us that "there was no open vision" in the time of Eli (1 Samuel 3:1b). It took Eli three times before he realized that God was trying to speak to Samuel. We also find in verse 2 that Eli's "eyes waxed dim." Physical loss of sight can also be a result of diabetes. The domination of food or the obsession with having a slim figure can grieve our hearts because we know that these things have become more important to us than God, and that what we are doing is sin. Eating addictions tend to be continued from generation to generation and will have the same consequences in the generations that follow.

8. <u>The addict may have difficulty doing what is right in other areas of his life, including parental discipline</u>. When God spoke to Samuel about Eli, he cited Eli's failure to restrain his sons from continuing to do evil.

   1 Sa 3:13 For I have told him that I will judge his house for ever for the iniquity which he knoweth; because his sons made themselves vile, and he restrained them not.

   14 And therefore I have sworn unto the house of Eli, that the iniquity of Eli's house shall not be purged with sacrifice nor offering for ever.

9. <u>After a while the addict believes that he cannot change even when he knows that the consequences are catastrophic</u>. When a person has an eating addiction, even the numerous warnings of a trusted medical doctor may go unheeded. Notice Eli's passive response after Samuel told him what the Lord said was going to happen.

   1 Sa 3:17 And he said, What is the thing that the LORD hath said unto thee? I pray thee hide it not from me: God do so to thee, and more also, if thou hide any thing from me of all the things that he said unto thee.

   18 And Samuel told him every whit, and hid nothing from him. And he said, It is the LORD: let him do what seemeth him good.

10. <u>The psychological weakness provided by the addiction will eventually lead to an all out attack on the believer</u>. The Philistines (satanic forces) attacked Israel in full force. The Israelites lost four thousand men. Four stands for God's government of men on the earth. This suggests that God had taken His hand of protection off the addict to allow him to learn from his consequences. They had pitched at Ebenezer, which means "stone of help"; but God did not help them.

1 Sa 4:1 And the word of Samuel came to all Israel. Now Israel went out against the Philistines to battle, and pitched beside Ebenezer: and the Philistines pitched in Aphek.

2 And the Philistines put themselves in array against Israel: and when they joined battle, Israel was smitten before the Philistines: and they slew of the army in the field about four thousand men.

11. <u>The addict must realize from his failures that only God can deliver him</u>. The Israelites realized that without God they could not beat the Philistines. The answer to addictions is faith in God, but the client must do his part.

1 Sa 4:3 And when the people were come into the camp, the elders of Israel said, Wherefore hath the LORD smitten us to day before the Philistines? Let us fetch the ark of the covenant of the LORD out of Shiloh unto us, that, when it cometh among us, it may save us out of the hand of our enemies.

12. <u>Without repentance, even relying on the very presence of God will not defeat the addiction</u>. Either the client will repent, do whatever it takes, and trust God for his deliverance or his addiction will eventually overcome his faith and take away his salvation (the Ark of God). Without repentance, Hophni and Phinehas were killed along with 30,000 Israelites, and the Ark of God was captured.

1 Sa 4:10 And the Philistines fought, and Israel was smitten, and they fled every man into his tent: and there was a very great slaughter; for there fell of Israel thirty thousand footmen.

11 And the ark of God was taken; and the two sons of Eli, Hophni and Phinehas, were slain.

13. <u>The consequences of not dealing with an addiction will suddenly take its toll</u>. A man from Benjamin (son of the right hand) delivered the message to Eli. Eli fell backwards and broke his neck. It was his over-weight body that killed him!

1 Sa 4:17 And the messenger answered and said, Israel is fled before the Philistines, and there hath been also a great slaughter among the people, and thy two sons also, Hophni and Phinehas, are dead, and the ark of God is taken.

18 And it came to pass, when he made mention of the ark of God, that he fell from off the seat backward by the side of the gate, and his neck brake, and he died: for he was an old man, and heavy. And he had judged Israel forty years.

14. <u>The final end of the unrepentant addict is the loss of the presence of God in his life</u>. As she was dying, Phinehas's wife gave birth to a son and named him Ichabod. Ichabod means "the presence of God has departed." The message is again clear, either the client will serve and trust God for his needs, or his faith in his addiction will overwhelm the very presence of God in his life.

1 Sa 4:21 And she named the child Ichabod, saying, The glory is departed from Israel: because the ark of God was taken, and because of her father in law and her husband.

These should be sobering thoughts concerning an addiction that our society tolerates and which churches rarely confront. This story clearly illustrates that the consequences of an addiction—any addiction—can be catastrophic to the person, their family and their spiritual life. The answer is also clear. The addict must repent of his idolatry and reliance on the things of the world and turn his trust to God to meet his emotional needs. Counseling or support groups are usually required. The principles for recovery from addictions that have been discussed in the previous chapter apply.

However, even if the client is able to overcome his desire to medicate his emotions through eating, how is he to lose or gain weight in order to achieve a normal healthy weight? Diets alone do not seem to be the answer because most persons quickly return at least to their pre-diet weight. We must help the client develop faith that they will be able to successfully change their weight and help them modify their "set point" which fights any change in weight. If a client needs to lose or gain a significant amount of weight, I first address the underlying issues. As additional resources for helping clients deal with the addictive portion of their problem, I use *The Thin Disguise* (1992) by Pam Vredevelt, et. al. and *Conquering Eating Disorders* by McGee and Mountcastle (1993). I then suggest a simple experiment. They are to set a goal of changing their weight by no more than ten pounds and ask God to help them achieve it. They are to fast, diet, or make life-style changes in order to achieve the goal. They are to weigh daily and if they have gained or lost beyond their goal they are to do what is necessary to maintain that weight for at least one month. Maintaining this new weight for a significant period of time will change their set point. Now their body will fight to maintain this new weight instead of fighting them to return to their old weight. Each time they succeed their faith grows that with God's help they can eventually successfully achieve a healthy weight.

Steps for Overcoming Eating Addictions

1. Understand that the underlying problem is a family history that has led to emotional pain and a need to feel in control.

2. The addict is trying to control his own life and meet his own emotional needs through eating or external appearance. Eating or how he or she looks has become a god to meet these needs.

3. God sees eating disorders as serious problems and expects everyone to honor Him and their bodies in the way they eat.

4. Eating addictions result in serious consequences including premature death, serious medical problems, loss of spiritual insight, and give Satan a stronghold in the client's life.

5. Eating disorders also affect the addict's children and will bring similar consequences to them if they do not deal with the problem. God holds everyone responsible for dealing with these issues in the lives of their children.

6. The client must repent, face his emotional pain, obey God in his eating, and choose to meet his deepest needs through God; or judgment will come.

7. The client must be willing to die to himself, put his faith in God and do his part to overcome his addiction.

8. Without repentance, the end result of the addict will be the loss of the presence of God and a defeat in his life at the hands of Satan.

Chapter 20

Homosexuality

Understanding Homosexuality

One of the most prominent addictions listed in 1st Corinthians 6:9; and potentially, one of the most powerful addictions of our day is that of homosexuality. Because of political correctness, some have tried to rename homosexuality as an alternate lifestyle. It is an extremely powerful addiction and difficult for many to deal with because it combines two powerful problems: identity confusion and sexual addiction. Both can go back to early childhood. Out of the many self-serving theories that have been proposed concerning the etiology of homosexuality (especially in the wake of homosexual agenda today), I have found only one that both explains this problem and is consistent with what the Bible has to say.

Identity Confusion

This prominent theory of the origin of homosexuality suggests that the problem begins with identity confusion at around three years of age. I believe that the early onset of this problem accounts for the fact that many homosexuals believe they have always had homosexual tendencies. Around this age, the male child begins to develop a gender identity by transferring his allegiance from the nurturing mother to the father. A number of factors can lead to a child rejecting his gender identity. The father may reject him or be distant or cold. The mother may attempt to meet her emotional needs through the child (this is called "emotional incest"). As a consequence, the child does not really feel a part of the male gender, yet knows that he is not a woman. A quest for identity or connection then begins that can last a lifetime. A reparative drive that motivates each of us to try to resolve our problems drives the growing child to attempt to find his lost identity by connecting with males. Because women do not make this transfer of allegiance, fewer lesbians exist in the population. Many times a girl becomes a lesbian as a result of the rejection of a distant or alcoholic mother or rejecting father. Because the identity-rejecting female child is without a gender identity, a desperate search for identity again occurs. (For more on the etiology and treatment of homosexuality see Nicolosi, 1997)

Sexual Addiction

Because of the rejection and dysfunction in the families mentioned in the first part of this section of the book, feelings of worthlessness and inadequacy provide the groundwork for addiction. When the resulting codependency is combined with a lack of intimacy, sexual abuse, a shameful attitude about sex or early childhood sexual experience, all the factors for sexual addiction are present. Consequently, when intimacy with the same gender is attempted as a result of the reparative drive, sexualization occurs. However, because the connection meets both the need for identity and triggers the sexual endorphin, it becomes a stronger and harder type of addiction to break.

It is important to realize that many men who call themselves "homosexuals" really are not; and that most studies concerning the numbers of homosexuals in our society are flawed because of this difference.

A true homosexual struggles with both identity confusion and sexual addiction. A sexual addict may develop a preference for sex with the same gender or even children through masturbation or sexual experiences.

Jim's father had his own sexual problems and perversions. As Jim grew older, he was afraid to bring his friends home for fear of what his father might do. When he feels rejected, the reparative drive to connect with his father leads to cruising the parks and adult bookstores looking for another man. He just wants to be close. He performs sexually in order to find someone to meet his deep emotional needs, and then feels dirty afterward. Jim has not fallen to the lie of the homosexual lifestyle in order to find an identity. He knows that what he is doing is wrong; but when he feels rejected, especially by someone in authority, he is driven to connect to somebody, anybody. He holds a good job, goes to a good church, and very few of his acquaintances realize he has a problem. When he goes "cruising" he fears that he might get caught, but the fear is not enough to stop his behavior. At this time, it is impossible for him to even think of having a healthy relationship with a woman.

Escaping the Homosexual Lifestyle (Lot)

Nowhere else in the Bible is the struggle to overcome the pull and influence of homosexuality as clearly portrayed as in the story of Lot, which begins in Genesis Chapter 11. Let me provide a brief understanding of the principles presented in this story as a foundation for dealing with the problem of homosexuality.

1. The roots of homosexuality go back to the family of origin. Lot means "something veiled, covered, or hidden inside." His father's name, Haran, means "childhood or cessation," indicating that something was not right in childhood. Lot's father died before his grandfather Terah (delay) in Ur of the Chaldess, a place known for its soothsayers and spirits. It is not absolutely clear, but Lot's father may have died when Lot was still a child and the resulting problem became internalized or hidden.

2. Yielding to homosexual tendencies is a choice of lust and bondage. In Genesis Chapter 13, when Abraham and Lot's flocks became too large, Lot chose to "pitch his tent (or desires) toward Sodom." Sodom means "burning" (desire) and Gomorrah means "submersion due to binding" (something under the surface causing a bondage). Zoar, another city that was to be destroyed, means "insignificance" (one of the underlying feelings of the homosexual). Lot chose this area of land because it was well-watered, therefore, it showed promise to meet his needs.

3. God sees homosexuality as an exceedingly great sin. This is true, because, at its root, homosexuality is a rejection of God's unconditional love (Romans 1:21-32); and it results in the destruction not only of individuals but whole societies. Genesis 13:13 states, "But the men of Sodom [were] wicked and sinners before the LORD exceedingly."

4. Without repentance, the homosexual lifestyle will eventually lead to judgment. God sent the angels to rescue Lot and destroy Sodom and the surrounding cities. By now, Lot lived in the city and was one of its leaders. This shows how even Christians can be drawn into accepting the homosexual lifestyle. It is clear that Lot knew what was going on in the city, because he tried so strongly to persuade the angels to stay at his house in order to protect them. The fact that he baked unleavened bread for the angels, I believe, indicates that Lot had not yet acted on his homosexual tendencies. Leaven usually stands for sin, and unleavened bread for the absence of sin. It is also clear that Lot still believed that at least homosexual rape was wrong, since he admonished the people of Sodom to "do not do so wickedly." (Genesis 19: 3-7)

5. Homosexuality is an aggressive, selfish, seductive spirit. Homosexual lust many times becomes increasingly perverted until the homosexual even attempts to force his views and lifestyle on others. This is manifested today in homosexual political action groups like ACTUP, which has been known to

actually attack churches that oppose the homosexual agenda. In Sodom, the homosexuals attempted to knock down Lot's door in an attempt to rape the angels. When he resisted them, they accused him of judging them (homophobia). Lot had become so influenced by the perversion of Sodom that he offered his daughters to be raped instead. Even after the angels blinded the homosexuals, they still continued to try to find the door! (Genesis 19:11)

6. <u>Homosexuality blinds those who are surrounded by it</u>. Lot's sons-in-law had become so blinded to the sin of homosexuality that they thought Lot's warning of a coming judgment against homosexuality was a joke.

7. <u>The homosexual struggler must escape while there is still time</u>. The angels warned Lot that his only hope was to escape immediately. The pull of homosexuality was so strong that the angels had to physically take Lot and his wife by the hand in order to get them to leave. In the same way, it many times takes significant outside influence to help the homosexual struggler to choose to leave his lifestyle.

8. <u>After leaving the influence of the gay lifestyle, even looking back can lead to destruction</u>. Lot still did not want to leave the influence of the homosexual lifestyle but begged to remain in Zoar (insignificant). This shows how the homosexual believes that his needs will not be met without his homosexuality. He is still holding onto his feelings of insignificance. Even when leaving, he still desires what little bit he can get away with. His wife, however, looked back and was turned into a pillar of salt. The word for salt means "to dissipate." Homosexuality is a dissipation or waste of real life and destroys the potential of the person's life.

9. <u>Intercession by others is important in the process of deliverance from homosexuality</u>. Abraham had previously interceded with God to spare Sodom. (Genesis 18:17-33) The Bible tells us in Genesis 19:29, that God "sent Lot out of the midst of the overthrow" because "God remembered Abraham."

10. <u>Just because a Christian escapes homosexuality does not necessarily mean he will escape all the consequences of the homosexual lifestyle</u>. Lot's daughters had become so perverted during their years in Sodom that they chose to commit incest with Lot in order to have children. Their descendants represent the aftermath of playing around with homosexuality. Moab, the son of the firstborn daughter by incest, symbolizes lust and Ammon, the son by incest of Lot's youngest daughter, stands for selfish desires. The children reaped what the father had sown. The Moabites and Ammonites became known for their strong lust and selfish cruelty.

Overcoming Identity Confusion (Ruth)

So far, we have learned that prayer and help from others is essential in helping the homosexual to decide to quit. Next, we need an answer for overcoming the underlying lust and identity confusion.

The key to discovering an answer for the healing of identity confusion comes through Lot's son by incest, Moab. As previously stated, Moab stands for "lust." In the story of Ruth (in the book of Ruth), Naomi and her family moved to Moab (or lust). One of Naomi's Israelite sons married Ruth, a Moabite. This is a clear case of identity confusion. Ruth gave up her Moabite identity for her husband's Israelite identity. When her husband died, she no longer had an identity and had to choose which identity she would have. This is the case of the homosexual. She has rejected her birth identity and is seeking another. We have in this same story of Ruth both parts of homosexuality—lust and identity confusion.

1. <u>Choosing lust over your Christian identity leads to spiritual death</u>. Due to a famine in the land (needs not met), Elimelech, which means "my God is King," (indicating he is saved) moved his family to Moab (lust). The result was that he and his two sons died (as a result of lust), and Naomi (pleas-

antness or joy), his wife, was left helpless in a foreign land. She had two daughters-in-law, Orpah (youthful freshness) and Ruth (friendship). As a result, they experienced identity confusion since they were Moabites by birth and Israelites by marriage to their now-deceased husbands.

2. <u>The homosexual must clearly choose his identity</u>. I am not necessarily implying that Ruth or Orpah were lesbians, although I believe that they most likely had a problem with sexual lust (since they were Moabites). Naomi gave her daughters-in-laws a choice to return to Israel with her or return to their Moabite identity. She made it clear that doing so would not be easy. Ruth clearly chose the Israelite identity when she said in Ruth 1: 16-17, "...for whither thou goest, I will go; and where thou lodgest, I will lodge: thy people [shall be] my people, and thy God my God: Where thou diest, will I die, and there will I be buried: the LORD do so to me, and more also, [if ought] but death part thee and me."

3. <u>The struggler must seek Jesus as the first step toward establishing his new identity</u>. In Israel, only a kinsman redeemer was allowed to marry a widow so that the land and inheritance would remain in the family. Boaz means "strength." He was an ancestor of Christ and is a type of Christ. Ruth took the first step of building a relationship with Boaz when she chose his fields in which to follow the harvesters picking up grain for herself and her mother-in-law Naomi. When she did this, she found favor with him. Jesus is looking for those who would seek to find their identity in Him.

4. <u>Fellowship with other believers is important</u>. Boaz chose to elevate Ruth by allowing her to eat with the servants and glean even among the sheaves without reproach. He had them "accidentally" drop handfuls for her to pick up. Healthy, nonsexual, same-sex relationships are essential for homosexual recovery. The homosexual needs and desires connection to the same sex, but needs to learn how to connect in a "correct" healthy way.

5. <u>The homosexual must seek out and ask for redemption</u>. Ruth had to go to the threshing floor and symbolically ask Boaz to "spread therefore thy skirt over thine handmaid" or give her his identity. (Ruth 3:6-9) Boaz graciously did what was needed, just as Christ has already done all that is needed for us to receive His identity. In today's Exodus International Movement, which attempts to help homosexuals escape from homosexuality, the main emphasis is on a relationship with God, the Father. God must become the replacement, or Righteous Father, in place of the parent that the homosexual rejected many years earlier.

6. <u>With a new identity, the ex-homosexual can be fruitful and bear children</u>. The blessing of the people at Ruth's wedding was that Ruth's house would be like that of Pharez (bursting forth). Pharez was the son of Judah and Tamar (who prostituted herself with Judah in order to receive the family identity, which she was denied when her husband died). (Genesis 38:6-30) Tamar and Ruth are both in the lineage of Christ! Ruth's son Obed was the father of Jesse and the grandfather of David. This shows how in spite of their sexual struggles of the past, just like Tamar and Ruth, former homosexuals are fully accepted by God into the body of Christ.

7. <u>The former homosexual can learn to be a servant and a blessing to others</u>. Through Ruth, Naomi, who had chosen to go to Moab along with her husband and sons and lost almost everything, was blessed and restored. The selfishness of homosexuality must be replaced with a giving, servant's spirit. Ruth's son was named Obed, which means "servant."

Ruth 4:17 And the women her neighbours gave it a name, saying, There is a son born to Naomi; and they called his name Obed (servant): he [is] the father of Jesse, the father of David.

Dealing with Homosexuality in the Church (Benjamin)

The last issue to be dealt with is how we are to address the problem of homosexuality within the church itself. With the advent of the "homosexual church" and even the ordination of homosexual pastors in some denominations, this is an important issue.

Dan was a very successful, talented, and charismatic pastor. I received a call from his district supervisor. He wanted me to meet with Dan because he had learned that Dan was a practicing homosexual. After hearing of Dan's dysfunctional relationship with his father, the major role he played at a homosexual bar, and his series of hundreds of homosexual encounters, I asked him if he wanted to be free. He looked me square in the eyes and said "no." I said, "Can I ask you that question another way? If you could be free from your homosexuality and still have your needs met, would you want to quit?" He said, "Oh, yes." Unfortunately, he did not believe that this was possible, resigned from his church and recently contracted AIDS.

In Judges Chapter 20, we find the story of the rape of the concubine of a man from Bethlehem-Judah by the homosexuals in Gibeah. They had initially demanded to have sex with him, but settled with raping his concubine all night until she died. (Judges 19:22-29)

1. <u>The homosexual act cuts a person to pieces and kills his spirit</u>. After the death of his concubine, the man from Bethlehem-Judah cut her in pieces and sent the pieces to the tribes of Israel. The previous act of attempted homosexuality and the rape of the concubine are labeled as "wickedness."

2. <u>The homosexual must be confronted and given a chance to repent</u>. The advice and counsel was that one tenth of the Israeli soldiers were to confront Gibeah, where the offense had occurred. Remember that Gibeah was the Hivite city that tricked the Israelites into a treaty. I believe that this selection of one out of ten represents the elders of the church. They were "knit together as one man." The elders must be unified in purpose.

3. <u>Not only the unrepentant homosexuals, but those that defended them had to be cut off from Israel</u>. Just as the Israelites swore that they would not give their daughters to a Benjamite, so the church is called not to closely associate with the sexually immoral who call themselves Christians. Confronting the homosexuals who raped the concubine did not turn out to be an easy task but resulted in the loss of many lives. Confronting homosexuality in the church is not usually easy (The battle with the Benjamites took three days) and can result in the loss of church members (thousands of Israelites died fighting the Benjamites), but it was and is clearly the will of God (they inquired of God three times). If it is not swiftly dealt with, the strong homosexual spirit will invade the church and bring destruction to many people. In 1st Corinthians Chapter 5, we find a similar story where the Apostle Paul directed that an incest perpetrator be excluded from the church "for the destruction of the flesh." After repentance, he was later restored. (2 Corinthians 2:6-8)

4. <u>The church must use wisdom in dealing with homosexuality in the church</u>. The Benjamites had to be drawn out of the city before being defeated. The homosexual community labels those who object to homosexuality as homophobic and tries to justify homosexuality from the scriptures. These defenses need to be destroyed through God's Word before the homosexual spirit can be defeated.

5. <u>Those that do repent can be restored again to fruitfulness</u>. Only 600 of the Benjamites (2.4%) fled to the rock of Rimmon (pomegranate which symbolizes fruitfulness). These were the only members of that tribe to survive. The Israelites were sent to make peace with them. Unfortunately, because homosexuality is such a strong delusion, many who are confronted will not repent and instead leave the church.

6. <u>Those that do repent are to be welcomed back and befriended by the church</u>. Even though the Israelites had a difficult time finding mates for the remnant of the Benjamites who remained, they helped them. The church must be careful not to ostracize the recovering ex-homosexual and should attempt

to provide assistance in his struggle. Dealing with identity confusion requires the development of healthy heterosexual relationships, and the healthiest of these are to be found in the church.

Victory over Lust and Addictions

God has given us the answers for dealing with lust and addictions. We are promised complete victory over lust (Moab) and selfish desires (Ammon).

Zep 2:9 Therefore [as] I live, saith the LORD of hosts, the God of Israel, Surely Moab (lust) shall be as Sodom, and the children of Ammon as Gomorrah, [even] the breeding of nettles, and saltpits, and a perpetual desolation: the residue of my people shall spoil them, and the remnant of my people shall possess them.

Development of an addiction is very similar to the development of faith (but in the wrong thing). The Bible clearly sums up the answer for lust and addictions:

1 Jo 2:15 Love not the world, neither the things [that are] in the world. If any man love the world, the love of the Father is not in him.

16 For all that [is] in the world, the lust of the flesh, and the lust of the eyes, and the pride of life, is not of the Father, but is of the world.

17 And the world passeth away, and the lust thereof: but he that doeth the will of God abideth for ever.

For additional resources dealing with homosexuality, see *Pursuing Sexual Wholeness* (1989) and its associated workbook by Comiskey, *Homosexual No More* (1991) by Consiglio, or *Out of Egypt* (1988) by Howard (for lesbians). For another approach that deals with lust, see the Model of Ehud in my book, *Faith Therapy* (2005).

Steps for Overcoming Homosexuality

1. Understand that homosexuality is a combination of identity confusion and sexual addiction that usually begins with feelings of parental rejection at about three years of age.

2. However, choice is still a major factor. Not everyone who feels rejected at an early age becomes a homosexual and many who are tempted to have a homosexual relationship do not chose to act according to that temptation.

3. The underlying basis of homosexuality is a rejection of what God intended the person to be and of God as the source of love and protection. This rejection of God leads the client to try to meet his needs for gender identity and love through lust.

4. Homosexuality is accompanied by an aggressive, selfish, seductive spirit, which requires determined efforts to escape.

5. The homosexual must repent, or he must be put out of the church until he does.

6. He should realize that either his faith in God will result in his recovery or his homosexuality will destroy his faith

7. The homosexual must choose to abandon his false identity, accept his Godly identity, and build a relationship with God his Father.

8. The client must deal with his sexual addiction and trust in God to meet his needs and accept his new identity in Christ.

PART IX

The Girgashite Giants Dominating Emotions

Chapter 21

Bitterness
Hurts, Wounds, and Scars
(John Mark)

The name Girgashite means literally "dwelling on a clayey soil" or "one who turns back." I believe this is equivalent to "being stuck in the mud." In many cases, it is our dominating emotions that hold us back from going on or forward in life. In this chapter, I will deal with the emotional problems that result in the bitterness that is frequently caused by hurts, emotional wounds, and psychological scars. Although this problem is a common one, when it results in deep feelings of bitterness, it can become a complex problem that pervades the client's entire life. If clients do not overcome the bitterness in their lives, it can scar them permanently. It can significantly destroy the quality of their lives and the lives of everyone around them. To a bitter person, nothing in life, except possibly revenge, tastes sweet.

Probably the greatest impact on our feelings of love and attachment are caused by the negative experiences of our lives and the hurts, wounds, and scars that remain from our interpersonal experiences. For those of us who have accepted the world's system of evaluating our worth by how others view us, these hurts, wounds, and scars can also have a significant effect on how we view our self-worth. When we take offenses personally and apply them to our self-worth, they become wounds; and if we fail to deal with them correctly, they become scars that continue to affect us for the rest of our lives. Correctly perceiving the events of our lives from God's point of view, and processing them through forgiveness and reconciliation can bring healing.

John and Margie had been married for forty-seven years. They had weathered the storms of life together, but, in doing so, had grown far apart. After retirement, John spent most of his time in front of the television set. Margie was frustrated that he did not do more, and finally prodded him into coming to counseling. She was angry and wanted him to know why. "Didn't he remember what he had done on their honeymoon?" In truth, he did not remember and was amazed that she had never said that he had offended her. As they were walking down the street, he had forgotten his change in marital status and had whistled at a pretty girl as she walked by. The bitterness from that initial wound had permeated the marriage, and it had never been resolved. She felt rejected, and he did not even remember that he had done it! This was the beginning of a series of attachment wounds and scars that eventually convinced her that he really did not love her. Instead of taking it personally, if they had been willing to talk about it and trust God to work it all for good, many years of marital strife could have been avoided.

The Model of John Mark

In order to understand these concepts in a clearer way, let us examine this process in the lives of John Mark and the Apostle Paul. Most of us would agree that, with the exception of Jesus Himself, the Apostle Paul probably suffered more for the Gospel and experienced more hurts, wounds and scars at the hands of other people than anyone else in the Bible. This story provides us with a clear illustration of how we are to deal with our inevitable hurts so that they do not become wounds or scars. Hopefully, it will provide insight so that our negative experiences will not become an emotional table of contents for our future. In the Greek, John means "Jehovah is a gracious giver," and Mark is interpreted "a defense." We have to choose what we will believe about the events of our lives. Is God a gracious giver who will meet all of our needs in spite of what others do to us, or is the world a dangerous place where we have to look out for and defend ourselves?

Even a great man like the Apostle Paul can struggle with issues of self-worth and offenses in his life. In this story, we can see how taking things personally can affect our lives in negative ways. This is especially true if we allow what happens to us to affect our self-image. Correctly interpreting what happens to us from God's point of view is the key to handling the offenses of life. We should understand that initially even the Apostle Paul took the events of his life as a personal affront; but later was able, by changing his perspective, to see them from God's point of view and restore his relationship with John Mark.

1. <u>John Mark came from a good family and had even experienced miracles</u>. He seemed like the perfect person for the Apostle Paul to disciple as a future missionary. Paul at this time went by the name of Saul that means "asked or desired." This may suggest that all he wanted was to do whatever God asked or desired of him.

    Ac 12:12 And when he had considered the thing, he came to the house of Mary the mother of John, whose surname was Mark; where many were gathered together praying.

    17 But he, beckoning unto them with the hand to hold their peace, declared unto them how the Lord had brought him out of the prison. And he said, Go shew these things unto James, and to the brethren. And he departed, and went into another place.

    25 And Barnabas and Saul returned from Jerusalem, when they had fulfilled their ministry, and took with them John, whose surname was Mark.

2. <u>John Mark was asked to be an assistant to a great missionary venture</u>. God had called Barnabas, his cousin, and Saul to lead the first missionary trip of the early church. Barnabas asked John to go along as an assistant. Things seemed to be going John's way.

    Ac 13:2 As they ministered to the Lord, and fasted, the Holy Ghost said, Separate me Barnabas and Saul for the work whereunto I have called them.

    3 And when they had fasted and prayed, and laid their hands on them, they sent them away.

    4 So they, being sent forth by the Holy Ghost, departed unto Seleucia; and from thence they sailed to Cyprus.

    5 And when they were at Salamis, they preached the word of God in the synagogues of the Jews: and <u>they had also John to their minister</u>.

3. <u>At Paphos something seems to have happened that changed the overall character of the missionary trip</u>. God used Saul to confront and blind the sorcerer Barjesus when he attempted to resist the gospel. This experience appears to have changed Saul's self-image and the overall character of the mission-ary trip itself. After this time, Saul began to refer to himself as Paul. Paul means "little." Possibly, when God used him to do a miracle, he took it to heart, and in order to deal with his pride, began referring to himself as Paul. Later, Paul's "thorn in the flesh" is related to his struggle with pride (2 Corinthians 12:7). It also appears that he supplanted Mark's uncle Barnabas as leader of the mis-sionary trip. This is clear when we compare verse 7 which reads "Barnabus and Saul" with verse 13 which reads "Paul and his company." This significant change in order of Paul and Barnabas's names continues throughout the remainder of the references to this missionary trip. Historically this trip it is now known as "Paul's first missionary trip."

    Ac 13:6 And when they had gone through the isle unto Paphos, they found a certain sorcerer, a false prophet, a Jew, whose name was Barjesus (son of Jesus or Joshua):

7 Which was with the deputy of the country, Sergius (earth borne, wonderer) Paulus (small or little), a prudent man; who called for <u>Barnabas and Saul</u>, and desired to hear the word of God.

8 But Elymas (a wise man) the sorcerer (for so is his name by interpretation) withstood them, seeking to turn away the deputy from the faith.

9 Then Saul, (who also is called Paul), filled with the Holy Ghost, set his eyes on him,

10 And said, O full of all subtilty and all mischief, thou child of the devil, thou enemy of all righteousness, wilt thou not cease to pervert the right ways of the Lord?

11 And now, behold, the hand of the Lord is upon thee, and thou shalt be blind, not seeing the sun for a season. And immediately there fell on him a mist and a darkness; and he went about seeking some to lead him by the hand.

12 Then the deputy, when he saw what was done, believed, being astonished at the doctrine of the Lord.

4. <u>John Mark left the missionary venture in Pamphylia and returned to Jerusalem</u>. He may have taken the change of leadership and Paul's new attitude personally, been offended and returned to Jerusalem (his home town; it means "peace"). It also appears that Paul became very sick at Pamphylia. Pamphylia was known for a particularly virulent form of recurring malarial fever, which caused excruciating headaches, described like "a red-hot bar thrust through the forehead." (Barklay, 1976, Vol. 7, p. 102.) The fact that he was sick is clear from his later comment to the Galatians, their next stop on the trip. John Mark may have feared the next part of the journey that required traveling on one of the most difficult and dangerous roads in the world. (P. 101) Whatever the reason, John Mark deserted his post at a most inopportune time without much notice.

Ac 13:13 Now when <u>Paul and his company</u> loosed from Paphos, they came to Perga in Pamphylia: and John departing from them returned to Jerusalem.

Ga 4:13 Ye know how through infirmity of the flesh I preached the gospel unto you at the first.

14 And my temptation which was in my flesh ye despised not, nor rejected; but received me as an angel of God, even as Christ Jesus.

15 Where is then the blessedness ye spake of? for I bear you record, that, if it had been possible, ye would have plucked out your own eyes, and have given them to me.

5. <u>Paul seems to have taken John Mark's desertion, when he was needed most, personally and refused to take him on the next missionary trip</u>. Barnabas whose name means "son of consolation" clearly forgave and reconciled with his cousin Mark. Paul did not, and it led to such a conflict that Paul and Barnabas parted company. People struggling with low self-worth and pride are prone to taking everything personally, and this is part of their downfall. When we perceive others as personally offending us, it is easy to see this as additional evidence that we must be inadequate in some way or that it is not safe to attach with or depend on them.

Ac 15:36 And some days after Paul said unto Barnabas, Let us go again and visit our brethren in every city where we have preached the word of the Lord, and see how they do.

37 And Barnabas determined to take with them John, whose surname was Mark.

38 But Paul thought not good to take him with them, who departed from them from Pamphylia, and went not with them to the work.

39 And the contention was so sharp between them, that they departed asunder one from the other: and so Barnabas took Mark, and sailed unto Cyprus;

40 And Paul chose Silas, and departed, being recommended by the brethren unto the grace of God.

Overcoming Hurts, Wounds, and Scars

As Paul continued to struggled with his self-worth and his conflict with John Mark, he was finally able to achieve victory over them. Through his letters and actions, he provides us with the principles for overcoming these problems in our own lives. When our perceptions about others and ourselves change, so do our emotions and our willingness to reconcile our relationships.

1. <u>We must believe that God works everything for our good—even our mistakes, other's offenses, and the attacks of Satan</u>. God has a plan for our lives that includes being conformed to the image of His son Jesus. It is our job simply to submit to His plan and believe that everything will eventually work out for good. Therefore, it is clear that the events of our life have nothing to do with our worth as a person.

    Ro 8:28 And we know that all things work together for good to them that love God, to them who are the called according to his purpose.

    29 For whom he did foreknow, he also did predestinate to be conformed to the image of his Son, that he might be the firstborn among many brethren.

    30 Moreover whom he did predestinate, them he also called: and whom he called, them he also justified: and whom he justified, them he also glorified.

2. <u>We must believe that God is for us and that He will not condemn us for our failures</u>. Consequently, we should not condemn ourselves or apply negative, or even positive, experiences to our worth as a person.

    Ro 8:31 What shall we then say to these things? If God be for us, who can be against us?

    32 He that spared not his own Son, but delivered him up for us all, how shall he not with him also freely give us all things?

    33 Who shall lay any thing to the charge of God's elect? It is God that justifieth.

    34 Who is he that condemneth? It is Christ that died, yea rather, that is risen again, who is even at the right hand of God, who also maketh intercession for us.

3. <u>We are to interpret even the most negative experiences as simply challenges to be overcome and opportunities for God to demonstrate His power through us</u>.

    Ro 8:35 Who shall separate us from the love of Christ? shall tribulation, or distress, or persecution, or famine, or nakedness, or peril, or sword?

    36 As it is written, For thy sake we are killed all the day long; we are accounted as sheep for the slaughter.

    37 Nay, in all these things we are more than conquerors through him that loved us.

4. <u>Our worth is to be based on God's unconditional and unending love for us, which cannot be affected in any way by the circumstances, enemies, or events of our lives</u>.

    Ro 8:38 For I am persuaded, that neither death, nor life, nor angels, nor principalities, nor powers, nor things present, nor things to come,

    39 Nor height, nor depth, nor any other creature, shall be able to separate us from the love of God, which is in Christ Jesus our Lord.

5. <u>We must deal with our pride as the Apostle Paul did, so that God will get the glory, not us</u>.

2 Co 12:5 Of such an one will I glory: yet of myself I will not glory, but in mine infirmities.

6 For though I would desire to glory, I shall not be a fool; for I will say the truth: but now I forbear, lest any man should think of me above that which he seeth me to be, or that he heareth of me.

7 And lest I should be exalted above measure through the abundance of the revelations, there was given to me a thorn in the flesh, the messenger of Satan to buffet me, lest I should be exalted above measure.

8 For this thing I besought the Lord thrice, that it might depart from me.

9 And he said unto me, My grace is sufficient for thee: for my strength is made perfect in weakness. Most gladly therefore will I rather glory in my infirmities, that the power of Christ may rest upon me.

10 Therefore I take pleasure in infirmities, in reproaches, in necessities, in persecutions, in distresses for Christ's sake: for when I am weak, then am I strong.

6. <u>We need to see other people and the events of life from an eternal perspective</u>. Other people are just like us. We are all of equal value to God even though we all have problems and make mistakes. We all have a specific race to run and are not in competition with each other. We all need to focus on Jesus as our great example and pattern for life.

Heb 12:1 Wherefore seeing we also are compassed about with so great a cloud of witnesses, let us lay aside every weight, and the sin which doth so easily beset us, and let us run with patience the race that is set before us,

2 Looking unto Jesus the author and finisher of our faith; who for the joy that was set before him endured the cross, despising the shame, and is set down at the right hand of the throne of God.

3 For consider him that endured such contradiction of sinners against himself, lest ye be wearied and faint in your minds.

4 Ye have not yet resisted unto blood, striving against sin.

7. <u>We need to see our problems as stepping stones for the development of our character, not threats to our self-worth</u>.

Ro 5:3 And not only so, but we glory in tribulations also: knowing that tribulation worketh patience;

4 And patience, experience; and experience, hope:

5 And hope maketh not ashamed; because the love of God is shed abroad in our hearts by the Holy Ghost which is given unto us.

8. <u>Sometimes negative events in our lives are for our correction so that we do not fail in our character or in fulfilling our ministry</u>.

Heb 12:5 And ye have forgotten the exhortation which speaketh unto you as unto children, My son, despise not thou the chastening of the Lord, nor faint when thou art rebuked of him:

6 For whom the Lord loveth he chasteneth, and scourgeth every son whom he receiveth.

7 If ye endure chastening, God dealeth with you as with sons; for what son is he whom the father chasteneth not?

8 But if ye be without chastisement, whereof all are partakers, then are ye bastards, and not sons.

9 Furthermore we have had fathers of our flesh which corrected us, and we gave them reverence: shall we not much rather be in subjection unto the Father of spirits, and live?

10 For they verily for a few days chastened us after their own pleasure; but he for our profit, that we might be partakers of his holiness.

11 Now no chastening for the present seemeth to be joyous, but grievous: nevertheless afterward it yieldeth the peaceable fruit of righteousness unto them which are exercised thereby.

12 Wherefore lift up the hands which hang down, and the feeble knees;

13 And make straight paths for your feet, lest that which is lame be turned out of the way; but let it rather be healed.

14 Follow peace with all men, and holiness, without which no man shall see the Lord:

9. <u>We must both accept God's grace and give it to others to avoid bitterness</u>. Our emotions are simply thermometers reflecting how we perceive our world. Once Paul began to see that even the failures of others and the attacks of Satan were used by God for his good, his feelings about the situation with John Mark began to change. Here, he warned against developing a root of bitterness and suggested that God would comfort us no matter what the circumstances were. When we see the hand of God working in our lives in spite of everything that may happen, we begin to feel more confident, especially concerning our value to God.

    Heb 12:15 Looking diligently lest any man fail of the grace of God; lest any root of bitterness springing up trouble you, and thereby many be defiled;

    2 Co 1:4 Who comforteth us in all our tribulation, that we may be able to comfort them which are in any trouble, by the comfort wherewith we ourselves are comforted of God.

10. <u>We need to expect that God will work even the negative events of our lives for our good</u>. Paul had replaced John Mark with Timothy. If John Mark had not deserted Paul, Timothy would probably not have had the opportunity to be discipled by Paul. Timothy became one of the greatest pastors of the early church. Silas, who was recruited to replace Barnabas on the second missionary trip, also became a great man of God.

    Ac 16:1 Then came he to Derbe and Lystra: and, behold, a certain disciple was there, named Timotheus, the son of a certain woman, which was a Jewess, and believed; but his father was a Greek:

    2 Which was well reported of by the brethren that were at Lystra and Iconium (little image).

    3 Him would Paul have to go forth with him; and took and circumcised him because of the Jews which were in those quarters: for they knew all that his father was a Greek.

    4 And as they went through the cities, they delivered them the decrees for to keep, that were ordained of the apostles and elders which were at Jerusalem.

    5 And so were the churches established in the faith, and increased in number daily.

11. <u>We must forgive and do our part to resolve any offenses</u>. It is not enough to change how we perceive the events of our lives and to emotionally understand our value to God; we need to begin to act according to our new outlook. Paul finally reached the conclusion that John Mark was useful to him in his ministry and asked Luke to bring Mark to him so that he could be restored to the ministry. It appears that Paul had already forgiven John Mark and that John Mark had already proven himself

after he had been given a second chance. Paul wrote numerous verses on the subject of forgiveness. He believed that God is the only one that is to judge other people, and that we are to trust Him to vindicate us.

2 Ti 4:11 Only Luke is with me. Take Mark, and bring him with thee: for he is profitable to me for the ministry.

Mt 6:14 For if ye forgive men their trespasses, your heavenly Father will also forgive you:

15 But if ye forgive not men their trespasses, neither will your Father forgive your trespasses.

12. <u>We need to refocus on the things that really count—the Kingdom of God</u>. The Apostle Paul makes it very clear that the negative events of life are to be put behind us and not allowed to affect our self-worth so that we can fully focus on what God has called us to do. We are not to base our worth on our own acts of righteousness but on our faith in God's love for us. We should expect to experience suffering and always be careful not to think that we have become somebody by our own effort.

Php 3:7 But what things were gain to me, those I counted loss for Christ.

8 Yea doubtless, and I count all things but loss for the excellency of the knowledge of Christ Jesus my Lord: for whom I have suffered the loss of all things, and do count them but dung, that I may win Christ,

9 And be found in him, not having mine own righteousness, which is of the law, but that which is through the faith of Christ, the righteousness which is of God by faith:

10 That I may know him, and the power of his resurrection, and the fellowship of his sufferings, being made conformable unto his death;

11 If by any means I might attain unto the resurrection of the dead.

12 Not as though I had already attained, either were already perfect: but I follow after, if that I may apprehend that for which also I am apprehended of Christ Jesus.

13 Brethren, I count not myself to have apprehended: but this one thing I do, forgetting those things which are behind, and reaching forth unto those things which are before,

14 I press toward the mark for the prize of the high calling of God in Christ Jesus.

In order to more easily summarize the issues discussed in this Chapter, I have provided a flow chart of this process on the following page.

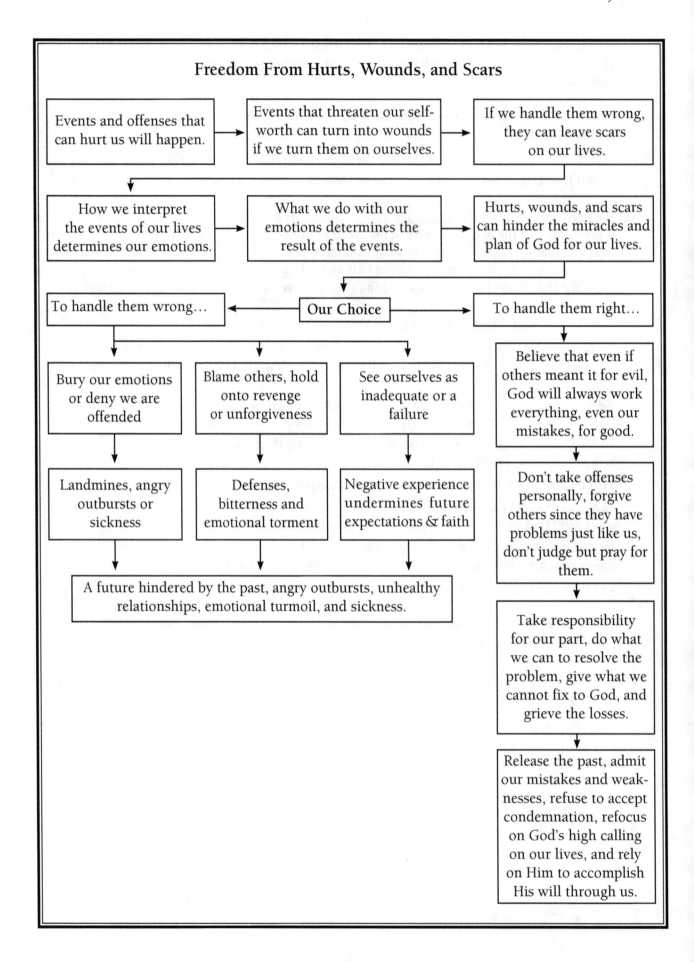

Freedom From Hurts, Wounds, and Scars

Events and offenses that can hurt us will happen. → Events that threaten our self-worth can turn into wounds if we turn them on ourselves. → If we handle them wrong, they can leave scars on our lives.

How we interpret the events of our lives determines our emotions. → What we do with our emotions determines the result of the events. → Hurts, wounds, and scars can hinder the miracles and plan of God for our lives.

To handle them wrong… ← **Our Choice** → To handle them right…

To handle them wrong…

- Bury our emotions or deny we are offended
- Blame others, hold onto revenge or unforgiveness
- See ourselves as inadequate or a failure

↓

- Landmines, angry outbursts or sickness
- Defenses, bitterness and emotional torment
- Negative experience undermines future expectations & faith

↓

A future hindered by the past, angry outbursts, unhealthy relationships, emotional turmoil, and sickness.

To handle them right…

Believe that even if others meant it for evil, God will always work everything, even our mistakes, for good.

↓

Don't take offenses personally, forgive others since they have problems just like us, don't judge but pray for them.

↓

Take responsibility for our part, do what we can to resolve the problem, give what we cannot fix to God, and grieve the losses.

↓

Release the past, admit our mistakes and weaknesses, refuse to accept condemnation, refocus on God's high calling on our lives, and rely on Him to accomplish His will through us.

Overcoming Hurts, Wounds, and Scars

1. Events and offenses will happen, but they do not have to turn into hurts, wounds, and scars.

2. If we make the mistake of taking what happens to us personally, it hurts us. If we apply it to our worth as a person, it becomes a wound; if we handle our wounds incorrectly, they can become a scar.

3. We handle our wounds incorrectly if we bury our emotions, blame others, or let them affect how we perceive ourselves. This can result in a future hindered by the past, angry outbursts, unhealthy relationships, emotional turmoil, and sickness.

4. We must believe that even if others meant it for evil, God will always work everything, even our mistakes, for our good.

5. We must forgive others since they have problems just like us, refuse to judge others, pray for them and not take offenses personally.

6. We should take responsibility for our part, do what we can to resolve the problem, give what we cannot fix to God, and grieve our losses.

7. We are to release the past, admit our mistakes and weaknesses, refuse to accept condemnation, refocus on God's high calling for our lives, and rely on God to accomplish His will through us.

Chapter 22

Depression
(Elijah)

One of the most prevalent psychological giants of our age is depression. Today, it is treated largely with medication; and in many cases, this is justified. Low levels of certain neurotransmitters can result in clinical depression, which so affects the brain that therapy is of limited use. However, in most cases, therapy is equally effective if it is begun before a clinical level of depression occurs. Research suggests that medication, in addition to counseling, is the most effective approach for significant levels of depression.

Bill was the senior pastor of a moderately sized church. He was so depressed that he could no longer function in the church. At the slightest conflict, he would become desperate and hopeless, and question whether he should remain in the ministry. His perception was that any conflict in the church meant that he had failed as its pastor. Worse yet, conflict meant that the ministry was too hard, God had failed him and, therefore, life was hopeless. He felt like he was carrying the weight of the world, dreading when the next conflict would occur, and his response to it. In actuality, although a little insecure, he was well liked and a reasonably successful pastor with many years of experience in a prominent denomination.

As we search the Bible, the most detailed model of depression (and maybe burnout) in the Bible is included in the life of Elijah. It is also possible that he was suffering from bipolar disorder since he seemed to have a very elevated mood and energy level shortly before becoming depressed. Our story begins in 1ˢᵗ Kings Chapters 18-19.

1. Depression many times follows periods of great accomplishment, failure, loss, or expenditure of energy. Elijah (Jehovah is God) was a prophet of God during the reign of Ahab and Jezebel. Jezebel (Baal exalts, Baal is my husband, unchaste) killed the prophets of God and promoted the fertility god, Baal. After a three-year famine, Elijah confronted Ahab and the prophets of Baal and proved to the people that Jehovah was God, by bringing down fire from heaven that consumed the sacrifice, stones and even the water around the altar. He then killed 400 prophets of Baal, prayed for rain (which resulted in a deluge), and out-raced Ahab's chariot back to Jezreel. Elijah's high energy level in facing all of Israel and then out-racing Ahab's chariot could be explained either as God's supernatural enablement or as the manic phase of a bipolar disorder.

2. When depression suddenly appears, it is important to determine what occurred or changed about that same time. When Ahab told Jezebel what had happened, she sent a message threatening Elijah's life. He so feared Jezebel, that he ran for his life to Beersheba (the edge of Israel). Beersheba means "well of oath or well of seven." Possibly this indicates that Elijah was struggling with the oath he took to serve God or that he was looking for God's complete provision (this is the meaning of the number seven).

3. Depression is like living in a dried up wilderness, without water and food, and wanting to die. Elijah took a day's journey into the wilderness and sat under a juniper tree. *Wilson's Dictionary of Bible Types* suggests that this type of dry bush represents, "a defeated spirit, a disappointed life, and a depressed

soul." (p. 273) Depression made Elijah feel like dying. Today, depression is strongly correlated with suicidal intent.

4. Depression, as well as our other emotions, are usually determined by how we look at the events in our lives. 1st Kings 19:3 states, "And when he saw [that], he arose, and went for his life…" It was the way he "saw" what happened that motivated him to run for his life. It is important to investigate the depressed individual's perception of the events just prior to the depression. These perceptions are usually one of the most important issues to be dealt with in therapy. It is also possible that the client is turning anger inward, which is causing the depression. In verse 4, Elijah clearly states how he sees things: "It is enough; now, O LORD, take away my life; for I [am] not better than my fathers." He had hoped that the great miracle of bringing down fire from heaven would turn the nation to God. All it accomplished was to have the queen seek his life. In his eyes, he had failed!

5. When the body is physically depleted, it is difficult to see life clearly. While Elijah slept an angel prepared a cake baked on coals for him to eat and gave him a container of water to drink. Sometimes taking care of physical needs is all that is required to snap out of depression. At least, caring for the client's physical needs will help him to rationally evaluate his perceptions. Symbolically, this verse also suggests the need to be filled again with God's Word and His Spirit.

6. The depressed person needs to exercise and then reevaluate his view of his life. After sleeping and eating again, Elijah traveled 40 (testing of human life) days and nights to Mount Horeb, the sight of most of God's Old Testament revelations to humanity. Studies have indicated that exercise can be as effective as medication in reducing depression. Elijah needed a new way of looking at his situation in the middle of his testing.

7. In their misery and circumstances, depressed individuals must be challenged to reevaluate their situation from God's point of view. God asked Elijah how he got himself in this situation, because the perceptions of the depressed person are many times the cause of the depression. Since emotions are controlled by how the person perceives a situation, if he sees the situation as God sees it; he will be set free.

8. The depressed person is locked into his way of looking at life and feels alone. When questioned, Elijah repeats his litany, "I have been very jealous for the LORD God of hosts: for the children of Israel have forsaken thy covenant, thrown down thine altars, and slain thy prophets with the sword; and I, [even] I only, am left; and they seek my life, to take it away." (1 Kings 19:14)

9. They need to be brought to the realization that God is not limited by, nor operates through man's circumstances or methods. There was a great wind on the mountain, then an earthquake and finally a fire; but God was not in any of these. We expect God to accomplish His will in spectacular ways, but He usually chooses to operate behind the scenes in almost undetectable ways. In this case, God spoke in a still, small voice.

10. The depressed person's view of life must be challenged and shown to be incorrect. The suicidal person needs to be shown that there are other ways out of his situation rather than suicide. God showed him that he was not alone. God still had 7000 other people in Israel that had never worshiped Baal. (1 Kings 19:18)

11. What the depressed person needs is a rekindled faith in God and new direction for his life. God is the one to provide this, but the client, like Elijah, must meet with God.

12. The depressed person usually feels over-responsible for his situation and needs to recognize his true position in life. God told Elijah exactly what to do and God's solution did not rely on Elijah as much as he had thought. He was simply to anoint new kings for Syria and Israel, and a new prophet to replace himself. God would use these people to accomplish what Elijah could not do. Many times

the client feels that his failures or successes are more important than they actually are. He needs to be reminded that the world is not dependent on him alone.

13. <u>After a new vision for life, the depressed person must choose to act according to that direction</u>. Elijah called Elisha as the next prophet, and anointed new kings over Syria and Israel who were to overthrow Ahab and Jezebel, the very thing Elijah had failed to do. Restoration is complete when the depressed person again has the energy to invest in a renewed life and vision. Elijah was set free as he acted according to God's will and began to disciple Elisha.

Sometimes depression is caused by how the client is viewing the unresolved events of the past. Recently a Christian method for the healing of emotions called "Theophostic Ministry" was developed by Dr. Ed Smith. The basic theory of this method is that since emotions are determined by how a person views a life experience, emotions from the past can by modified by changing the incorrect view of the situation into truth. Past experiences are "stirred up" until the lie seems real. At that point, the Lord Jesus is called upon to reveal the truth about the event to the client. When Jesus is revealed in the experience, His presence is felt or newfound truths are revealed, the perception of the event is changed. When the client sees the event from God's point of view, the emotions connected to the event are healed. The result is that current emotional problems, which are an echo of the past, no longer affect the client in the same way. (Smith, 1996)

Treatment of bipolar almost always requires medication to control the associated emotional swings. In addition, the manic phase must be challenged in counseling because if the client believes he is more worthwhile because of what he can do, he must also believe he is of less worth if he fails. As a resource for unipolar depression, I use *The Freedom from Depression Workbook* (1995) by Carter and Minirth, and concentrate primarily on the client's perceptions of life and faith in God for his future. Depression is also a primary symptom of the grief process, which I will discuss in more detail in the next chapter.

Steps for Overcoming Depression

1. Depression many times follows periods of accomplishment, stress, failure or loss. It may also be caused by anger turned inward.

2. All emotions, including depression, are determined by how the client perceives the events of his life. If past events are strongly involved, a healing of emotions may be required in order to deal with present circumstances.

3. The first step to recovery is to get adequate sleep, nourishment, and exercise. If this is not possible, medication may be temporarily required. The client must also rebuild his spiritual life.

4. The depressed person must be challenged to reevaluate his view of his circumstances from God's point of view.

5. The client must rekindle his faith and hope in God's ability to work everything for good. He must learn to thank God that He will use even these circumstances for the client's good.

6. He must realize that God loves him and is not limited by the methods or the circumstances of his life.

7. The client must obtain a new vision for his life from God and take action to fulfill it.

Chapter 23

Grief
(Job)

In each person's lifetime, he will be forced to deal with grief in some form. Everyone will eventually experience losses in their lives. Sometimes, going through grief can become extremely difficult, and if the client becomes "stuck" in the process of grief, he could even resort to self-destructive behavior or suicide.

Jimmy clearly remembered the day that his mother told him to leave the house and never come back. He had not seen her for over 40 years. Even though he had a very conflicted and traumatic relationship with his mother even before she had "kicked him out of the house," he still hoped to see her again. He received a call from a nursing home where she was in the last stages of dying from Alzheimer's disease. Although she never recognized him, he attended to her needs until, after several months, she died in his arms. He never recovered. He turned to drugs and alcohol for comfort and refused to go to counseling. In his despair, he abandoned his family. His wife finally divorced him. His son became involved in a gang and eventually went to prison. Dealing with grief is usually more difficult after an ambivalent relationship filled with both very bad and some good experiences.

I believe that God directly gave me this model for grief therapy. I had been counseling a young Christian woman who was grieving a recent divorce. She was angry at God. Nothing I tried seemed to help. She was even hospitalized by her doctor for being suicidal. One day as she was leaving after an especially frustrating session, God spoke these words to my spirit: "You are just one of Job's helpers." Several times in past years, I had tried to make sense out of the book of Job with little success. When I finally recognized it as a model for grief therapy, everything fell into place. It is interesting to note that Elisabeth Kubler-Ross's well-known five stagers of grief (Denial, anger, bargaining, depression, and acceptance) are clearly differentiated in this biblical model. (*On Grief and Grieving*, 2005) In the next session, we began a study of the book of Job; and eventually she completely recovered. Let me share what I learned.

1. Grief is the natural response to a significant loss. Job had everything, at least from a worldly viewpoint: Wife and children, wealth, honor, possessions, and good health. He lost it all, except for his wife who was also so devastated that she advised him to, "curse God and die." Grief is the natural response to all types of losses.

2. The grief response is intensified if the client has a wrong view about what is to be expected in life. Job believed that if he did his very best to do good works, he should only experience blessings and should never experience any great losses or disasters in his life. However, I believe that Job secretly knew that life was not that simple. Unfortunately, even today, many Christians seem to believe that because they have accepted Christ; they should no longer experience problems, struggles, and losses in their lives.

3. A valid biblical view of life will assist the aggrieved person as he progresses through the grief process. From the glimpses into heaven in the book of Job, we learn that although God puts a hedge around His people, because we are not perfect, Satan can use our sins as an opening to attack us. Job

believed that because of his good works he should be protected. Unfortunately, none of us is perfect enough for this to happen. It was Job's fear that provided an opening for Satan's attack. Deep within, Job feared that he could never be good enough to deserve complete protection from all the losses in life.

Job 3:25 For the thing which I greatly feared is come upon me, and that which I was afraid of is come unto me.

26 I was not in safety, neither had I rest, neither was I quiet; yet trouble came.

Fortunately, for us, our protection no longer depends on our performance or good works but on the finished work of Christ. To the degree we rely on Him we are protected. (For more on the principles of protection from catastrophe see my book, *Faith Therapy*)

4. <u>Many grieving people feel hated and persecuted, and blame others for their loss</u>. Job's name means "hated and persecuted." He saw himself as a righteous, God-fearing man. He saw his possessions and family as blessings from God. If this is true, then how had he deserved all of the calamity that had come upon him? It was not fair. Therefore, God or someone other than himself must be responsible for what happened.

5. <u>The aggrieved person usually feels that God "allowed it</u>." Here, the Christian must understand that just because God is all-powerful does not necessarily make him responsible for everything. Just because I have the capability to stop a car accident in front of my house if it occurred at two A.M. in the morning, does not mean that I am responsible to stay up every night and barricade my street in order to prevent one. God has given us dominion over our world and has given us everything through faith that is necessary for our lives. According to James, God never does evil, nor is He even tempted to do evil. However, in the middle of what we see as an unfair world, it is hard emotionally to see and believe this. Even if Job felt that God had allowed it, he did not "charge God foolishly." (Job 1:22)

6. <u>The first phase of the grief experience is usually shock and denial</u>. We are not emotionally prepared for what happens so we shut it out. It seems unreal. In order to show how he felt, Job tore his mantle (authority to control his life), shaved his head (his faith was shaken), and fell upon the ground (humbled himself). His denial of his emotions is captured in Job 1:21, "Naked came I out of my mother's womb, and naked shall I return thither: the LORD gave, and the LORD hath taken away; blessed be the name of the LORD." This noble saying is typical of the initial minimization of the emotional pain that normally occurs at the time of a great loss.

7. <u>It is Satan's purpose to mess up the client's walk, and his mind, make him feel worthless, and get him into a pity-party in the midst of the ashes of his life</u>. Satan attacked Job in his feet (affected his walk) and his head (his thinking). Job scraped himself with broken pottery (feelings of worthlessness) and sat in the ashes (shameful remains of his life).

8. <u>Friends and counselors seldom handle grief appropriately</u>. Unless we have experienced a similar situation, we have not really understood the emotional issues or struggle that come with the pain of loss. **My experience is that most Christians do exactly the wrong things—minimize the situation and defend God.**

9. <u>Do not try to tell him that because God is correcting him for his sins that it is for his good</u>. Job's three friends are examples of how <u>not</u> to counsel grief! Eliphaz means "God is dispenser." He argued that calamity only comes from God as correction for, or as a consequence of our sins. We reap what we sow. He was a Temamite, which means "south, soft or warm." According to Eliphaz, since Job needed to be corrected for his sins he should realize that what happened to him was for his good. Eliphaz concludes:

Job 5:17 Behold, happy [is] the man whom God correcteth: therefore despise not thou the chastening of the Almighty:

27 Lo this, we have searched it, so it [is]; hear it, and know thou [it] for thy good.

I do not believe that God brings this level of calamity on his children to "correct them." Except, in the most extreme circumstances, this would be considered abuse. Jesus made it clear that it is only through God's grace (which is not based on works), that Christians are spared from catastrophe as they repent and trust in Him,

Lu 13:2 And Jesus answering said unto them, Suppose ye that these Galilaeans were sinners above all the Galilaeans, because they suffered such things?

3 I tell you, Nay: but, except ye repent, ye shall all likewise perish.

4 Or those eighteen, upon whom the tower in Siloam fell, and slew them, think ye that they were sinners above all men that dwelt in Jerusalem?

5 I tell you, Nay: but, except ye repent, ye shall all likewise perish.

10. Do not suggest that the tragedy is "punishment" for his sin. Bildad means "son of contention." He was a Shuhite, which means "depression." Trying to blame the client only increases his depression. He reasoned that since tragedy had happened—and only bad things happen to bad people—it was clear that Job must have committed some dire sin. This aggressive approach that tries to defend God only leads to more contention. If the client has sinned or the tragedy is a direct consequence of his actions, he will eventually face this fact as his recovery progresses; but initially he will only defend himself when confronted. Since Jesus died for us, we are forgiven, not punished for our sins. If tragedy came as punishment for our sin it would happen to all of us, for we all sin. The disciples believed that tragedy was punishment for sin, but Jesus denied that this was true in the case of the man born blind from his birth. In this case, there was another reason, that God might use the tragedy to demonstrate his love for him. God is not the author of tragedies, but even turns what Satan authors for the good of them that love Him and are willing to do things His way. (Romans 8:28)

Jo 9:1 And as Jesus passed by, he saw a man which was blind from his birth.

2 And his disciples asked him, saying, Master, who did sin, this man, or his parents, that he was born blind?

3 Jesus answered, Neither hath this man sinned, nor his parents: but that the works of God should be made manifest in him.

11. Do not tell him "to just get over it." Zophar means "hairy or worldly." He is a Naamathite, which means "pleasantness." He argued that since we all sin, bad things happen to all of us. In fact, Job has gotten less than what he deserved (Job 11:6), so why not just accept it, put it behind him, and go on. Job should quit complaining, accept his lot in life, and try harder next time. This is a fatalistic approach to life. It dooms the person to a life of fear concerning what might happen next. It also ignores the fact that going through the process of grief is essential for emotional recovery. If the client buries his grief, it will reappear at another time in another way.

12. We are to empathize with the client's emotional pain. His friends wept, tore their mantles, and sprinkled dust (feelings of insignificance) upon their heads. They sat there for seven days (completeness) "for they saw that [his] grief was very great." (Job 2:12,13)

13. All clients have a certain amount of fear that some calamity will come upon them. The problem is that down deep, everyone knows that he is powerless over his circumstances and can never achieve

total control of his life through his own actions. A person's own goodness can never guarantee his safety. Only faith in God provides a guarantee. Job declares:

Job 3:25 For the thing which I greatly feared is come upon me, and that which I was afraid of is come unto me.

26 I was not in safety, neither had I rest, neither was I quiet; yet trouble came.

14. <u>The second phase of grief is anger at almost everyone and everything</u>. Job cursed the day he was born, the fact that he was not stillborn, and life itself. He felt that death would be easier than enduring his grief. (Job 3:3-16)

15. <u>The client is also many times angry with God</u>. Job points this out in Chapter 6:14 "To him that is afflicted pity [should be shewed] from his friend; but he forsaketh the fear of the Almighty." Blaming God seems to be natural, because we do not want to take responsibility for what has happened, and because we feel that God could have prevented it. As already discussed, it is important to remember that there is a big difference between having the power to do something about a situation and being responsible to do it. God provided all we need for life and godliness through His promises and gave the responsibility to us for their use.

16. <u>The next phase of grief is what some have called bargaining</u>. Throughout these chapters, Job is constantly trying to get God to "hear his case," and "bargain" with him. We see this in Chapter 13:

Job 13:20 Only do not two [things] unto me: then will I not hide myself from thee.

21 Withdraw thine hand far from me: and let not thy dread make me afraid.

22 Then call thou, and I will answer: or let me speak, and answer thou me.

17. <u>The next phase of grief is depression, which is the result of a loss of hope</u>. In Job 7:6 he writes, "My days are swifter than a weaver's shuttle, and are spent without hope."

18. <u>Defending God is not helpful for the grieved person</u>. It seems natural to us that when the client going through grief, complains to God, that it is our job to defend God. This is not the correct approach since these words are an expression of the anguish of the soul and spirit and are part of the healing process. God is able to adequately defend Himself. Job says,

Job 7:11 Therefore I will not refrain my mouth; I will speak in the anguish of my spirit; I will complain in the bitterness of my soul.

13:7 Will ye speak wickedly for God? and talk deceitfully for him?

8 Will ye accept his person? will ye contend for God?

13 Hold your peace, let me alone, that I may speak, and let come on me what [will]."

19. <u>The client's discussion with God is a means of trying to sort out his responsibility and bring order to his confusing world</u>. Job states,

Job 13:18 Behold now, I have ordered [my] cause; I know that I shall be justified.

19 Who [is] he [that] will plead with me? for now, if I hold my tongue, I shall give up the ghost.

23 How many [are] mine iniquities and sins? make me to know my transgression and my sin.

20. <u>During the depression phase of grief, the client primarily needs emotional support</u>. I remember at a seminar hearing a counselor suggest a better approach than attempting to defend God. When a client came in "angry at what God had done to him," he sat down beside him and said, "If God did that to you, I'm angry at God too." By the end of the session, the client, through just being allowed to talk, reached the conclusion that God had not been responsible for his calamity. Job tells us what he needs:

    Job 16:2 I have heard many such things: miserable comforters [are] ye all.

    5 [But] I would strengthen you with my mouth, and the moving of my lips should assuage [your grief]."

21. <u>We should take the client's side by interceding for them</u>. In Job 16:21, Job pleads for this, "O that one might plead for a man with God, as a man [pleadeth] for his neighbour!"

22. <u>It takes faith in God to help him out of his self-pity</u>. We finally see faith beginning to return in Job's life in Chapter 19:

    Job 19:21 Have pity upon me, have pity upon me, O ye my friends; for the hand of God hath touched me.

    22 Why do ye persecute me as God, and are not satisfied with my flesh?

    25 For I know [that] my redeemer liveth, and [that] he shall stand at the latter [day] upon the earth:

    26 And [though] after my skin [worms] destroy this [body], yet in my flesh shall I see God:

    27 Whom I shall see for myself, and mine eyes shall behold, and not another; [though] my reins be consumed within me.

23. <u>One of the things that usually bothers the aggrieved person the most is that he seems unable to hear from God</u>. This happens even to many Christians who have previously been close to God and had consistently heard God's voice in the past. I believe this loss of contact with God occurs because the faith foundation of the relationship has been shaken. In John Chapter 14, Jesus explained that when He returns only those willing to obey (act on their faith) would be able to see Him. Job complains:

    Job 23:3 Oh that I knew where I might find him! [that] I might come [even] to his seat!

    4 I would order [my] cause before him, and fill my mouth with arguments.

    5 I would know the words [which] he would answer me, and understand what he would say unto me."

24. <u>The counselor's job is to speak for God and build the client's faith until he can again hear from God for himself</u>. If we closely examine these verses, we realize that only three friends came to speak to Job; but finally a fourth person speaks. Elihu (God Himself), the son of Barachel (blessed of God), tells us in Job 33:6, "Behold, I [am] according to thy wish in God's stead." He goes on to explain that God has no obligation to "give account of any of his matters." He explains in verse 17 that God allows struggles: "That he may withdraw man [from his] purpose, and hide pride from man," but that He is on the person's side and will deliver him if he will respond to God in faith. In Job 34:10, Elihu makes it clear that God is never responsible for evil: "Therefore hearken unto me, ye men of understanding: far be it from God, [that he should do] wickedness; and [from] the Almighty, [that he should commit] iniquity." Consequently, God was not responsible for Job's calamity. It is important for the client to get to the place where he can thank God in his situation, because he knows

that somehow God will use even this for his good. (Romans 8:28) According to Job Chapter 35, the problem is that the client has relied on his own ideas rather than trusting that God loves him and always has his best interests in mind.

Job 35:2 Thinkest thou this to be right, [that] thou saidst, My righteousness [is] more than God's?

5 Look unto the heavens, and see; and behold the clouds [which] are higher than thou.

14 Although thou sayest thou shalt not see him, [yet] judgment [is] before him; therefore trust thou in him.

25. During the acceptance phase of grief, the client's faith finally recovers to the point where he can again hear from God. At this point, God Himself can deal with any remaining issues better than any counselor. In Chapter 38, Job finally heard from God again and God asked him,

Job 38:2 Who [is] this that darkeneth counsel by words without knowledge?

3 Gird up now thy loins like a man; for I will demand of thee, and answer thou me.

4 Where wast thou when I laid the foundations of the earth? declare, if thou hast understanding...

40:2 Shall he that contendeth with the Almighty instruct [him]? he that reproveth God, let him answer it."

26. When the client's pride and ego defenses have been dealt with and he accepts what has happened to him, he is finally in a position to have his relationship with God restored. This is an essential step in the acceptance phase of the grief process.

Job 40:3 Then Job answered the LORD, and said,

4 Behold, I am vile; what shall I answer thee? I will lay mine hand upon my mouth.

27. God makes the problem clear; the aggrieved person has been trying to escape personal responsibility by blaming God and others. God asks in Job 40:8, "Wilt thou also disannul my judgment? wilt thou condemn me, that thou mayest be righteous?" The client must decide if he is going to trust God again or rely on his own understanding and logic. God does not feel obligated to explain everything to him. He just wants the client to trust that He does have his best interests in mind.

28. The client should repent, realizing how ridiculous his accusations against God and other people have been, and take responsibility for his own actions.

Job 42:2 I know that thou canst do every [thing], and [that] no thought can be withholden from thee.

3 Who [is] he that hideth counsel without knowledge? therefore have I uttered that I understood not; things too wonderful for me, which I knew not.

29. The ultimate answer in grief recovery is personally knowing God through faith.

Job 42:5 I have heard of thee by the hearing of the ear: but now mine eye seeth thee. Wherefore I abhor [myself], and repent in dust and ashes.

30. <u>The final step of grief is complete when the client again has energy to invest in others</u>. This is many times expressed by praying for the needs of other people.

Job 42:10 And the LORD turned the captivity of Job, when he prayed for his friends: also the LORD gave Job twice as much as he had before.

31. <u>The client should realize that grief has an important part in his life, and is actually a beautiful process of restoration</u>. We see this in the names of Job's beautiful daughters,

Job 42:14 And he called the name of the first, Jemima (day by day or it takes time); and the name of the second, Kezia (spice like cinnamon—it makes life fragrant again); and the name of the third, Kerenhappuch (horn of antimony or eye paint or makeup—it makes life seem good again).

15 And in all the land were no women found [so] fair as the daughters of Job: and their father gave them inheritance among their brethren."

In dealing with grief, in addition to just listening and giving emotional support, I attempt to educate the client on the grief process. Sometimes I use the book, *Mourning Into Dancing* (1992) by Walter Wangerin, Jr. As a resource on how to help people through grief see *Helping People Through Grief* (1987) by Kuenning. I also directly address the loss and teach the principles of protection from catastrophe when appropriate. (A useful chart entitled "Principles for Protection From Catasptrophe" can be found in my book *Faith Therapy.*) Of course, rebuilding faith is my most important task.

Steps for Helping a Client through Grief

1. Grief is the natural, automatic response to the perception of a significant loss.

2. The aggrieved person feels unfairly treated and usually blames themselves, God or others for the loss.

3. He goes through stages of denial, anger, bargaining, depression and acceptance.

4. The counselor should not attempt to give explanations or immediately challenge the client's wrong thinking or emotional reaction, but listen and provide emotional support.

5. The grief process, which requires time for the sorting out of responsibility, emotional healing and overcoming fears, should neither be rushed nor allowed to stagnate.

6. The counselor should not attempt to defend God but try to slowly rebuild the client's faith.

7. Recovery results in acceptance when the loss has finally been processed. Faith in God will help in overcoming the client's fears and he again becomes concerned about the needs of other people.

Chapter 24

Suicide
(Judas and Peter)

The suicide of a person we love is probably the most devastating event in anyone's life. Unfortunately, suicides are not uncommon in the United States. They are the third leading cause of death among teenagers (Comer, 1995. p. 366).

Billy was the teenage son of a police lieutenant. They attended church regularly and Billy was a regular member of the youth group. Billy and his dad had ongoing arguments. Billy felt he could never live up to his father's expectations. He was never good enough. He just wanted his dad to leave him alone and let him do whatever he wanted. His dad refused. One day during an argument, Billy demanded to have his way. If he did not, he said he would kill himself. Although this is not an unusual teenage threat, Billy took it a step further. He pulled his father's police revolver from where his Dad kept it and pointed it at his head. No one will ever know if he intended to kill himself, or if he accidentally pulled the trigger of the gun. As his father watched, flesh and blood covered the ceiling; and Billy died instantly. His family was so devastated that his father resigned from the police force, and the family moved to another part of the United States, so they would not be reminded of the most terrible incident in their entire lives.

Although a lot has been written on this topic, let us examine what the Bible has to say about it in the well-known story of Judas Iscariot. Judas means "praise" and Iscariot means "a man from Kerioth," a town of Moab. As you might remember, Moab stands for lust. He was the son of Simon, which means "a stone or rock." This seems to say he had the potential to be a man whose life would be a praise and honor to God, one who could become solid like a rock (like Simon Peter), but who struggled with lust (Moab). Judas was selected to be one of Jesus' original twelve disciples and the treasurer of the group. Possibly, he was chosen because he was one of the most educated and initially, one of the most trustworthy in the group. He, like the other twelve disciples, was sent forth to preach the gospel, heal the sick, and cast out demons. It would also appear that he was at least as successful as the rest in their earlier ministry endeavors.

1. <u>Thoughts of suicide are usually an indication of deep depression and low self-image</u>. It is not unusual for addicts to have suicidal thoughts after failing over and over again. This is especially true when they have hidden their inner shame until it has turned to toxic shame. To be forgiven they would have to confess their sin and they perceive that they would feel even worse and may even be rejected. They fear doing the very thing that is most necessary. Judas was hiding the fact that he was stealing from Jesus and the disciples. Judas' lust problem was that of covetousness or a greed for money.

2. <u>The person contemplating suicide tends to either bury his problems or project them on others</u>. The key to Judas' betrayal is clear in each gospel. Immediately before he went to the priests to offer to betray Jesus, Mary broke the bottle of expensive perfume and washed Jesus' feet with it. Judas objected that it should have been sold and given to the poor. In John, we are told that his comment was motivated by his own greed, so he could have the opportunity to take some of the money.

Jo 12:3 Then took Mary a pound of ointment of spikenard, very costly, and anointed the feet of Jesus, and wiped his feet with her hair: and the house was filled with the odour of the ointment.

5 Why was not this ointment sold for three hundred pence, and given to the poor?

6 This he (Judas) said, not that he cared for the poor; but because he was a thief, and had the bag, and bare what was put therein.

3. <u>Many times the suicidal person feels rejected and not part of the group</u>. In the same story in Matthew, Jesus responded with a fairly strong rebuke. Persons with low self-image are usually extremely sensitive to criticism and take it as rejection.

    Mt 26: 10 When Jesus understood it, he said unto them, Why trouble ye the woman? for she hath wrought a good work upon me.

    11 For ye have the poor always with you; but me ye have not always.

    12 For in that she hath poured this ointment on my body, she did it for my burial.

    13 Verily I say unto you, Wheresoever this gospel shall be preached in the whole world, there shall also this, that this woman hath done, be told for a memorial of her.

4. <u>When a person feels rejected, he tends to want to strike back</u>. In the next verse, we see the result. He offered to betray Jesus for 30 pieces of silver, the price of an ordinary slave. I believe Judas was attempting to bring Jesus down to the level of worth he felt about himself. This is not an unusual reaction for someone who has deeply personalized a feeling of rejection.

    Mt 26:14 Then one of the twelve, called Judas Iscariot, went unto the chief priests,

    15 And said unto them, What will ye give me, and I will deliver him unto you? And they covenanted with him for thirty pieces of silver.

    16 And from that time he sought opportunity to betray him.

5. <u>When a person is closed or sees others as against him, he will not accept gestures of love or attempts to help him</u>. Judas was invited to the last supper with the other disciples even though Jesus knew his intentions. Jesus washed his feet along with the others showing great humility and love. He also gave Judas a sop (meat on a stick) which was a sign of special honor. Then Jesus set a boundary. It was not right for a disciple to betray his master. The consequence would be great—it would be better for him if he had not been born (Matthew 26:24)—but Jesus would not stop him if he insisted on betraying Him. Jesus did all he could to win back Judas, but to no avail. Sometimes the only option is to take a suicidal person to the nearest emergency room for hospitalization.

    Jo 13:2 And supper being ended, the devil having now put into the heart of Judas Iscariot, Simon's son, to betray him;

    3 Jesus knowing that the Father had given all things into his hands, and that he was come from God, and went to God;

    4 He riseth from supper, and laid aside his garments; and took a towel, and girded himself.

    5 After that he poureth water into a bason, and began to wash the disciples' feet, and to wipe them with the towel wherewith he was girded.

    Mt 26:21 When Jesus had thus said, he was troubled in spirit, and testified, and said, Verily, verily, I say unto you, that one of you shall betray me.

26 Jesus answered, He it is, to whom I shall give a sop, when I have dipped it. And when he had dipped the sop, he gave it to Judas Iscariot, the son of Simon.

27And after the sop Satan entered into him. Then said Jesus unto him, That thou doest, do quickly.

6. <u>The suicidal person's own actions compound his problems</u>. Judas not only told his enemies where Jesus would be, but he led the soldiers to him and betrayed him with a kiss of friendship in front of the other disciples. By doing this he not only clearly broke off all possibility of a relationship with those he had been friends with for three years but did everything he could to make the hurt worse by contemptuously kissing Jesus. He was cutting himself off from any possibility of reconciliation. What seems to be hatred and revenge is many times just the opposite side of a deeply entrenched feeling of rejection.

    Mt 26:47 And while he yet spake, lo, Judas, one of the twelve, came, and with him a great multitude with swords and staves, from the chief priests and elders of the people.

    48 Now he that betrayed him gave them a sign, saying, Whomsoever I shall kiss, that same is he: hold him fast.

    49 And forthwith he came to Jesus, and said, Hail, master; and <u>kissed him</u>.

    50 And Jesus said unto him, <u>Friend, wherefore art thou come</u>? Then came they, and laid hands on Jesus, and took him.

7. <u>After he sees himself as a failure and remorse set in; he may even regret what he has done</u>. If he believes that there is nothing he can do to succeed or redress the wrong, he may begin to contemplate suicide. He has no options.

    Mt 27:3 Then Judas, which had betrayed him, when he saw that he was condemned, repented himself, and brought again the thirty pieces of silver to the chief priests and elders,

    4 Saying, I have sinned in that I have betrayed the innocent blood. And they said, What is that to us? see thou to that.

8. <u>Suicide becomes an option when a person loses faith that life can ever become worth living again and believes that there is no hope for the future</u>. Suicide is like being in a room with only one door and no windows. As Judas saw it, through his blatant betrayal, he had cut himself off from Jesus and all his friends. His new allies, the priests, had also rudely rejected his attempt to repent; and he believed that there was nowhere to turn. Even when a person has not done anything as evil as Judus did, they may still become so depressed due to adverse circumstances that they consider suicide. Women are more apt to become depressed and attempt suicide, but men are more lethal in their attempt, because they more often use more deadly and irreversible means.

    Mt 27:5 And he cast down the pieces of silver in the temple, and departed, and went and hanged himself

9. <u>The suicidal person is in extreme emotional pain and sees suicide as the only way to stop the pain</u>. In the book of Acts, we are told that when he hung himself, his bowels gushed out. Bowels in the Bible signify the deepest of emotions.

    Acts 1:16 Men and brethren, this scripture must needs have been fulfilled, which the Holy Ghost by the mouth of David spake before concerning Judas, which was guide to them that took Jesus.

17 For he was numbered with us, and had obtained part of this ministry.

18 Now this man purchased a field with the reward of iniquity; and falling headlong, he burst asunder in the midst, and all his bowels gushed out.

19 And it was known unto all the dwellers at Jerusalem; insomuch as that field is called in their proper tongue, Aceldama, that is to say, The field of blood.

Steps to Recovery for Those Contemplating Suicide

In order to understand the steps for recovery for a person tempted to commit suicide, we will turn to the story of Simon Peter. He also had the potential of being a rock. Just like Judas, he also was strongly rebuked by Jesus for what he said. In addition, he had denied Jesus three times after strongly declaring that he would even die with Jesus. The Bible says he was also extremely distraught over his denial (a type of betrayal) of Jesus. With Peter's personality (one person has suggested he may have been ADHD), he probably was also a prime candidate for suicide.

1. <u>Thoughts of suicide many times accompany deep feelings of failure or loss</u>. When Peter saw Jesus, he realized what he had just done. He had failed by doing the very thing he had promised he would never do. His worth as a person was immediately devastated, and he wept bitterly.

    Lu 22:61 And the Lord turned, and looked upon Peter. And Peter remembered the word of the Lord, how he had said unto him, Before the cock crow, thou shalt deny me thrice.

    62 And Peter went out, and wept bitterly.

2. <u>The key factors in helping a suicidal person are providing a support system of friends and hope for the future</u>. This is where a counselor and someone to befriend the suicidal person is important. The suicidal person needs someone to talk to and to give them hope that they still have a worthwhile future. They need to know that the room has at least another window or door that leads to life. **At this point, I usually ask them to make an anti-suicide contract with me.** I explain that I can help them only if they will give me time, but if they actually kill themselves, my work would be wasted. I ask them to commit to not attempting suicide for a particular length of time and to call me if they are tempted. Many suicidal people want to put everything in order before they die and may call even if they have already decided to kill themselves. If they do call, it provides at least one more chance to help them.

3. <u>Some of the signs of a potential suicide are giving up important plans for the future, ending relationships, selling treasured objects, or quitting work</u>. Peter was so devastated by his failure that even after Jesus rose from the dead, he decided to go back to being a fisherman and asked several of the other disciples to join him. This is significant because Jesus had called them from fishing for fish to become fishers of men. Peter saw no hope for the future with Jesus for a failure like him. Fortunately, he at least had enough hope to return to his old trade of fishing.

    Jo 21:3 Simon Peter saith unto them, I go a fishing. They say unto him, We also go with thee. They went forth, and entered into a ship immediately; and that night they caught nothing.

4. <u>The suicidal person needs to quit trying to make his life work in his own efforts and trust God to give him a future and a hope</u>. After fishing all night, Jesus came to the shore where they were fishing and suggested that they throw the net on the right side, reminiscent of when Jesus had first called Peter. This time, however, the nets did not break, and they caught 153 fish. Jesus was illustrating for them that if they relied on themselves, they would fail; but if they relied on Him, they could do great things for God. It is when we fail and wish to give up on life that we have the opportunity to turn to God and trust Him to overcome our inadequacies.

Jo 21:6 And he said unto them, Cast the net on the right side of the ship, and ye shall find. They cast therefore, and now they were not able to draw it for the multitude of fishes.

11 Simon Peter went up, and drew the net to land full of great fishes, an hundred and fifty and three: and for all there were so many, yet was not the net broken.

5.   <u>The suicidal person needs someone who cares enough to accept them where they are and yet believe that they have a future.</u> Jesus confronted Peter about his denial by asking him if he loved Him three times. When Jesus initially asked Peter if he was fully committed to him (agape), Peter could only answer that he was fond of Jesus (phileo). Each time Jesus asked Peter to return to the work of the Gospel. When Jesus finally asked if Peter was only fond but not fully committed to him, Peter agreed. He had been so devastated by his earlier self-confident declaration that he would even die for Jesus, and his subsequent denial of Christ, that he felt he could not promise to do anything for Jesus again. Jesus responded that he had so much confidence in Peter that he was still calling Peter to be a pastor of God's flock.

Jo 21:15 So when they had dined, Jesus saith to Simon Peter, Simon, son of Jonas, lovest (agape) thou me more than these? He saith unto him, Yea, Lord; thou knowest that I love (phileo) thee. He saith unto him, Feed my lambs.

16 He saith to him again the second time, Simon, son of Jonas, lovest (agape) thou me? He saith unto him, Yea, Lord; thou knowest that I love (phileo) thee. He saith unto him, Feed my sheep.

17 He saith unto him the third time, Simon, son of Jonas, lovest (phileo) thou me? Peter was grieved because he said unto him the third time, Lovest (phileo) thou me? And he said unto him, Lord, thou knowest all things; thou knowest that I love (phileo) thee. Jesus saith unto him, Feed my sheep.

6.   <u>The suicidal person must understand that suicide is murder and that because Jesus has bought him with the price of His death on the cross, no one has a right to take his own life.</u> He is to serve God and if necessary give his life for God. Jesus even predicted that instead of selfishly going back to fishing, Peter would, in the end, sacrifice his life in the service of Christ on a cross. Sometimes, I will confront the client and tell them that they do not look like a murderer to me. They are usually shocked, because they do not realize that to kill themselves is murder in God's eyes, since they were created and redeemed to serve Him.

Jo 21:18 Verily, verily, I say unto thee, When thou wast young, thou girdedst thyself, and walkedst whither thou wouldest: but when thou shalt be old, thou shalt stretch forth thy hands, and another shall gird thee, and carry thee whither thou wouldest not.

19 This spake he, signifying by what death he should glorify God. And when he had spoken this, he saith unto him, Follow me.

It is critical that when counseling someone who you believe may be suicidal, that you do everything possible to prevent them from actually committing suicide. Because many suicidal people want to meet all of their obligations before they die, it is standard practice to ask the client to call you if he is ever again tempted to kill himself. Hopefully, if they do call, this will give you another chance to talk them out of committing suicide. At least the phone call may provide a chance of locating them so that you can send emergency personnel in order to attempt to save their life. Counselors are obligated to prevent suicide, homicide, and to report child and elder abuse. On the following chart, I have summarized the steps that a counselor or friend should take if they truly believe that the person may attempt suicide.

Steps for Preventing Suicide

1. Suicide attempts usually occur when a person is in deep emotional pain, has suffered a great loss or failure, or when they are deeply depressed about life.

2. The suicidal person believes that they have no future worth living for and that they have no other options. It is like a person in a room with only one door and no windows.

3.   If you really believe they are suicidal and will kill themselves and you cannot dissuade them, ask them if they have a plan and if they do, make sure they are watched at all times, take them to the nearest emergency room, or call 911.

4. Try to show them that they do have other options that lead to life and help them turn to God for help with their inadequacies. Help them to understand that both you and God love and accept them and will assist them to find a new life in Christ.

5. Suggest that they make an anti-suicide contract with you to give you time to help them recover. They should agree not to attempt suicide for a specific length of time and call you if tempted.

6. Help them understand that they do not have a right to take their own life, because Jesus died to redeem them and their lives are to be dedicated to obey and follow Him.

7. Express your belief that, in spite of the past failure or loss, they will recover to an even better and fuller life in Christ Jesus. If they are not sure they are saved, lead them to accept Christ or rededicate their lives, making Him Lord of their life.

PART X

Application

Chapter 25

A Case Study

The vast majority of client cases cited in this book have been counseled to a successful conclusion using the methods discussed so far in this book. We must remember, however, that we, as counselors, are not responsible for the complete wholeness or salvation of each client. It is the Holy Spirit that orchestrates the process of salvation in each person and it is He that brings the client to us for a specific purpose. As we understand where the client is in the process of salvation, we are to help him deal with the current problems that are blocking this process and help to build his faith in order to take the next step toward conquering the land of God's promises. We must be careful not to take the client's responsibility to "work out his own salvation" (Philippians 2:12b) or make choices for him. The Holy Spirit, Himself, will not ever override a client's free choice even to get a person saved. Each client must be set free to take responsibility for his life, make his own choices, and learn from his own consequences.

In this chapter, I will demonstrate the application of the overall biblical counseling method described in this book in the lives of Dan and Randi Davis. They first came to counseling because their new marriage was in desperate trouble. A counselor they had seen previously had advised that they just get divorced. The steps of the counseling method illustrated in this case study correlate with those on the chart entitled "A Biblical Plan for Christian Counseling" at the end of Chapter 4.

1. <u>Determine the problem</u>. After explaining that it was not my job to "fix" them or make their decisions for them, I asked them each to describe their perception of the problem. Randi spoke first. She had recently gone through a bad divorce, and their new blended family was becoming chaotic. When a problem arose in the marriage, she expected Dan to resolve it; but the more she wanted to talk about it, the more he would withdraw. Sometimes he would get to the point where he would push her to create some distance between them. To her, he was simply not taking the leadership of this family; and she was afraid this marriage would fail like her previous marriage. Dan had a different point of view. He was beginning to believe his wife was an emotional "basket case" because of her extreme actions and emotional outbursts. He blamed the failure of his business on her debts. He had never been married and did not expect it to be like this. She was very much like his mom—demanding more than he could do. He remembered cowering in the corner, as his mother demanded he somehow fix her current complaint. He said that, at times, Randi pursued him day and night for days with her demands. He admitted that sometimes he did push her in order to stop the pursuit or get away. As they continued to talk, the problem became clear. They were both overly dependent on each other to meet their needs, and they were blaming each other for their problems. It was a typical case of codependency.

2. <u>Demonstrate that what the client is doing will not solve his problems or meet his needs and build hope that his problems can be overcome through Christ</u>. Clearly, trying to demand that their mate should meet all their needs and blaming the other for the chaos in their lives was not working. The more they tried and failed, the more they became insecure about their marriage, and the more they

became insecure, the worse the situation looked. They were trying to make the other into a god that would "meet all their needs according to his riches in glory." They needed to build real trust in God and learn His ways in order to have a good relationship. Trying to control another person results in more rebellion, which requires more control. This normally leads to escalation until, frequently, the relationship becomes physically violent. Their methods clearly were leading to the destruction of their marriage. I challenged them to be open to trust in God and learn His ways of dealing with relationships. I assured them that if they did, Jesus could bring healing to their marriage. At this point, I suggested that they begin attending one of our Codependent Support Groups to deal with that part of the problem. I identified Dan as a responsibility avoidant. He avoided his family responsibilities out of fear that he could never really please Randi. I determined she was a codependent dependent rescuer. She had taken responsibility to make this family and her husband what she needed them to be.

3. <u>Use the biblical model to help the client understand the problem from a biblical perspective</u>. I used the models for a codependent dependent rescuer and a codependent responsibility avoidant to help them understand that they were looking too much to their spouse to solve all of their problems and not trusting God for their marriage. As long as they were trying to make their mate into a god to meet all their needs, their marriage would continue to be a series of fights and conflicts. I explained that on this earth they could never expect anyone to make them happy or to be as perfect as they wished. I had them read *Love is a Choice* by Hemfelt, Minirth, and Meier to help them get an overview of the codependent recovery process.

4. <u>Determine where the client is in the process of salvation and, if appropriate, lead him to accept Christ, be baptized, yield the control of his life to God, and help him get established in a good church</u>. Dan and Randi said that they had previously committed their lives to God, had been baptized, and were doing their best to serve Him. To verify that they were truly saved, I reviewed and explained the three requirements of Romans 10:9. Yes, they both believed that Jesus was the Son of God, that He had risen from the dead, and each had openly confessed Him. Both were attempting to yield to Him as Lord of their lives and were convinced that if they died they would go to Heaven due to their personal faith and relationship with Christ. They were already established in a good church. However, they had not yet set aside their worldly ways of coping. We must remember that although the children of Israel had left Egypt, as they entered the wilderness, they were still relying on what they had learned in Egypt to meet their needs. It is in the wilderness that we are to build our faith in God and find deliverance from our worldly ways. This deliverance is almost always accomplished through the process of making choices and learning from our consequences.

5. <u>Help the client take responsibility for his own actions, do everything as unto God, and not blame others or react to what they do</u>. As long as clients react emotionally to each other, relationship problems will escalate. This is one of the inherent problems with codependency. I explained that as long as they blamed each other, they could not be helped. They could change only themselves. In fact, it was not their job, but it was God's job to deal with their mate. When they stood before God, God was not going to ask them what their mate had done, only how they had responded to their mate's actions. One of their ongoing fights was over Randi's weight. When they were married she happened to be at an all-time low and had gained weight since their marriage. Dan felt he had been deceived. He eventually realized that he could not fix her weight problem and that it was her personal problem. Unless she became so heavy that it greatly affected their marriage or her health, he needed to allow Randi and God to be responsible for her weight loss.

6. <u>Help the client grow in his personal relationship with Christ and build faith that, with God's help, he can overcome the problem</u>. In one session, Dan painted a picture of feeling trapped on a ladder with Randi at the bottom holding a pitchfork demanding he do more than he could do, and the devil on the top with a pitchfork representing his fear of failure. Dan needed help in trusting God

so he could understand his responsibilities and obtain the strength to carry them out. It was not his job, necessarily, to please Randi, but to accept his rightful responsibility for the marriage and do everything he could to acknowledge God as his boss. In order to do this and overcome the insecurity that was at the root of the problem, they both needed to grow in their personal relationship with Christ. Consequently, they needed to learn to trust Him for the strength to overcome their fears. To do this they needed to spend more time in God's Word, pray, and read biographies of how others have overcome their marital difficulties.

7. <u>Assist the client in receiving the empowerment of the baptism of the Holy Spirit if he chooses to do so</u>. Both Dan and Randi had already received the baptism of the Holy Spirit.

8. <u>Help the client apply the biblical principles or model to overcome the identified psychological problem</u>. The complex underlying problems of a dysfunctional marriage and codependency were dealt with one by one. Using the quick reference on Healing Dysfunctional Families at the end of Chapter 10, after getting both of them to take responsibility for their own lives, I taught them communication and problem solving skills and helped them establish mutual boundary agreements. They were to stop demanding that problems be immediately resolved, making angry outbursts, and pushing each other physically. According to these models, abusive relationships are resolved through the use of boundaries (e.g. Jacob and Laban established a boundary between them at Mizpah to resolve their conflict). Randi eventually set boundaries that if Dan ever pushed her in anger again she would take $100 from their checking account to spend as she wished; and if he ever hit her she would take $1000. After a pushing incident, she withdrew and spent $100 on herself. That was the last time that Dan ever touched Randi when he was angry.

We soon discovered that another stronghold in Randi's life was fairness. One ongoing argument had to do with the fan in their bedroom. Dan was always too hot, and she was too cold. He would just turn the fan on without asking her. She saw this as unfair. Fairness was important to her because she had experienced unfairness in her family growing up. In fact, the fan became such a major issue that we had to meet for counseling as often as three times a week just to keep the marriage together. As I attempted to help them understand each other's point of view, the problem became clear. Because he had lost his business mainly due to the debts Randi had made before the marriage, he felt she owed him something. Since he saw the entire marriage as a debt she owed him, he saw nothing wrong with getting a few special benefits from time to time for himself. Randi, of course, did not see it that way at all. She looked at each individual situation to determine if it was fair, and consequently saw him as selfish and uncaring. They finally brought an end to the win/lose games they had been playing when they agreed that all future decisions would be made on a win/win basis without any coercion or pressure. Dan's perception of the marriage eventually changed as Randi's home business began to make more profit than his job. It became apparent that she was exceptionally intelligent; and, at one time, she even had her own citywide radio program. She was definitely not a "basket case" as he had originally perceived her.

9. <u>Determine the root cause of the difficulty and assist the client in developing faith to overcome this root problem</u>. The real underlying problem in both of their lives was insecurity and fear that their needs would not be met. Unless this fear could be overcome, they would probably relapse into old patterns following the termination of counseling. Dan's fear was that he could not resolve issues to Randi's satisfaction, just as he could never meet his mother's expectations. The basic principal here is that fear is overcome by faith, as a person succeeds in slowly overcoming the problem. After helping them resolve some of their problems in counseling sessions, they were assigned to try to resolve problems themselves at home. If they became angry, they were to take an anger break of about 30 minutes to cool off and then try again. If on the second try they ended up in a fight again, they were to put the problem on a list and bring it to counseling for assistance in finding a resolution. In another session, I asked Randi if she reacted at work the way she did at home. She said, "oh no."

I questioned how things were different at work. At work, she had procedures to handle every kind of problem. That helped her feel more secure. Consequently, she was given the task of developing procedures for the family. She even developed an "error report" to fill out if Dan blew up. The results were dramatic. She no longer lost it emotionally.

As Dan faced his fear of resolving issues, he became more confident and took more responsibility for the family. As Randi realized that as a team they could resolve their issues, her fears that the marriage might fail subsided. She no longer had to codependently rescue and fix him. He no longer had to always meet her expectations to keep her happy but could do what he believed was right in his service to God. Each learned to set the other mate free to make their own decisions and learn from their own consequences. They used boundary agreements to insure that the one making the decision was the one who received the consequences.

As they grew in God and they took on greater challenges, their faith grew so that they could do everything that He had called them to do. They finally reached the point where they again believed that their mate did have their best interest in mind. After this turning point, as they began to trust each other more, the grace and love began again to flow into their marriage. They had learned how to effectively provide boundaries for their own family, and now they applied it to doing foster care with highly disturbed children. As Dan and Randi were able to work out their own problems, I saw them less frequently in counseling until they would call only if they could not resolve an issue themselves. At one point, it almost became a joke between us since they would call because they could not deal with some issue in their lives, then they would often call again to cancel the appointment, after being successful in resolving it.

10. <u>Release them again to the care of the Holy Spirit to continue orchestrating this growth process of salvation in their lives.</u> I have seen Dan and Randi only a few times in the last several years to help them work out issues with their growing children and some of the foster children they have helped. They continued as exemplary members of their church and have worked together in children's ministry. Most of their codependent ways of coping have been replaced by a life of faith, they have learned to work as a team toward win/win solutions, and have developed reasonably good personal boundaries in their lives. Although recently, after a series of major setbacks in their lives, they again had to face some significant problems and get some help, they currently seem to be doing well and have been released to continue to grow in the Lord as the Holy Spirit guides them toward the plans that He has for their lives.

Jesus is indeed the answer to all the problems in our lives and God has promised to bring each and every one of us into the wonder of His abundant life if we will submit to His process of salvation for our lives. As counselors, He allows us to participate in certain aspects of this process, but all the glory for what is accomplished is His alone.

Conclusion

In this book, I have discussed the need that exists today for a simple, solidly biblical counseling plan and in-depth biblical answers to many of life's difficult, long-term problems. I believe that the lack of these answers has resulted in an over-reliance on secular psychology. I believe that this lack of answers is also at the core of the ongoing controversy within the Christian counseling community, and has led to the confusing array of what is today called Christian counseling.

In this book, I have attempted to develop a straightforward, concretely biblical method for counseling many of the hardest problems encountered in the church today. Through the use of a types and shadows interpretation of the Bible, I have developed a narrative method for Christian counseling. From the tribes of the land of Canaan, I have provided a basic biblical categorization of common psychological problems. Using the lives of Bible characters that were transformed by faith, I have suggested detailed narrative models that provide what I believe are biblical answers for many of these complex problems. Nevertheless, God has provided all that is needed through His Word; and it is He, through the Holy Spirit, the Chief Counselor, who is responsible for the overall development and orchestration of this counseling process. He alone deserves all the credit.

Even if you, the reader, still question the validity of some of the details presented, I challenge you to continue to consider the basic concepts that I have presented. I also request that you do what you can to help all of us to better understand and apply them in actual pastoral, counseling, and support group situations. I, in no way, claim to have the final answers or revelation on any of the subjects presented, but I do believe that they provide the basis for a more effective, uncomplicated, biblically-based methodology for counseling.

The time has come for the church to demonstrate that it has the answers to life's problems, even the more deeply rooted and psychological ones. Although we have claimed to have the answers, too often people have been blocked from receiving the fullness of their Christian heritage because of the psychological strategies of the devil. Too often it has been unresolved mental and emotional problems that have made spiritual victories much more difficult and sometimes impossible. Too often, we have given pat answers for serious problems and have seen only meager results. We have a great opportunity to retake the psychological ground that we have lost.

At Word of Life Church, Word of Life Counseling Center and Word of Life Institute, we are continuing to develop and to apply these concepts. I take no credit for what we are doing, because God has led myself and others in a step-by-step, revelation by revelation manner, in order to understand these concepts. However, I do take total responsibility for any and all mistakes, errors, misconceptions, and lack of insight contained in this book. I have only just begun to understand the impact of what the Lord has been trying to help us understand. As we do so, He is providing greater effectiveness in our efforts to help our clients find the transformation that He promised when He said that He came to heal the broken hearted and set the captive free. (Luke 4:18b)

Codependent Inventory

Name _____ Date _____

To determine your overall type of codependency circle the number of the questions that are generally more true than false as they apply to you during your entire lifetime, or to determine your current level of codependency place an X on the number of the questions based on how they currently apply to you. If you wish, you may do both.

1. Others in my family or relatives have had problems with codependency or abuse.
2. Most of the time I take on more tasks than I should.
3. Some of my close relatives have had problems with alcohol, drugs, sex, or workaholism.
4. I have a very hard time accepting criticism without getting angry and defending myself.
5. Many times I do not let others know how I really feel.
6. Many times I do not feel I can measure up to all that God and others demand of me.
7. I tend to feel guilty when others are not pleased with me.
8. I have been abandoned, adopted, one of my parents died during childhood, a person in my family is severely handicapped, or one of my parents has had two or more marriages.
9. My mother, father or step parents were excessively controlling or did not express love.
10. I have extreme emotional highs and lows.

If you circled 3 or more of these questions you are probably codependent. Answer the next 15 questions with the same markings to determine which predominant type you were/are.

11. Other people are my biggest problem.
12. Most of the time I feel driven to get things done.
13. I have a hard time opening up to people and letting them know what I am really like.
14. I am competitive in most of the things that I do.
15. People are valuable to me primarily because of what they can do.
16. I tend to feel very guilty when others are not pleased with me.
17. Close relationships are the most important part of my life.
18. When somebody else is hurt, I feel almost as emotionally hurt as they do.
19. I tend to blame myself when things go wrong in my close relationships.
20. I desire a mate that will take care of me and meet all my needs.
21. I would rather play it safe, even if it means that my needs go unmet.
22. Deep down I feel extremely inadequate to meet the challenges of my life.
23. I am reluctant to take personal risks to engage in new activities or relationships.
24. Instead of doing it myself, I want others to do it for me.
25. I tend to avoid jobs where I feel I might fail or be rejected.

If you circled more questions numbered 11-15 you are probably codependent independent or a dependent rescuer, Go to questions 26-35 to determine your type. If you circled more questions numbered 16-20 you are probably codependent dependent, Go to questions 36-45 to determine your type of codependent dependence. If you circled more questions numbered 21-25 you are probably codependent avoidant, Go to questions 46-55 to determine your type of codependent avoidance.

26. I am probably too focused on work/projects and sometimes neglect my family.
27. Both myself and others see me as very successful.
28. I almost never feel inferior to others.
29. I like to lead and am a leader in almost everything I am involved in.
30. I get extremely frustrated with incompetent people.
31. Although I don't like to admit it, I see myself as a failure in many aspects of my life.

32. I want to be a leader but I get anxious when I have too much responsibility.
33. I switch back and forth from feeling prideful and superior to others, to feeling inferior.
34. I get extremely angry at people who disrespect me or interfere with my success.
35. Many times I become jealous or envious of others who are more successful than I am.

If you circled more questions on numbers 26-30 and you would rather be the leader than follow a good leader, you are probably a codependent independent worldly success. If you would rather follow a good leader, continue to questions 36–45. If you circled more questions on numbers 31-35 you are probably a codependent independent worldly failure.

36. I will do almost anything to keep others happy and avoid making them angry.
37. I tend to overreact to criticism by my mate and significant others and blame myself.
38. Keeping good relationships with people is more important to me than accomplishments.
39. I seldom notice when others take advantage of me.
40. I am able to relax and enjoy life even when I am not doing anything important.
41. Many times I allow others to take advantage of me and do more than I should for them.
42. I am driven to be the very best at everything that I do and I am probably a perfectionist.
43. I am overwhelmed with all my responsibilities and get angry that I am asked to do so much.
44. I tend to feel over-responsible for other people and try to fix, rescue, or enable them.
45. Although I usually take charge of things, I do it because no one else will.

If you circled more questions on numbers 36-40 you are probably a codependent dependent passive. If you circled more questions on numbers 41-45 you are probably a codependent dependent rescuer.

46. I try to avoid responsibility except in situations in which I know I can succeed.
47. I have a big problem procrastinating or not finishing things I start.
48. People expect too much of me.
49. Many times, I get others to do something for me by simply not doing it myself.
50. Consistently, I forget or don't do the things I am supposed to do.
51. I tend to get very attached to my pets.
52. I am unwilling to get involved with people unless I am certain of being liked.
53. I am angry and wish someone would protect me and bring justice to my abusers.
54. Many times, I dwell on what has happened to me and feel like a victim.
55. I find it hard to forgive what has been done to me.

If you circled more questions numbered 46-50 you are probably codependent responsibility avoidant. If you circled more questions numbered 51-55 you are probably a codependent relationship avoidant. If you wish, complete the remaining questions and summarize your results so that you can compare your lifetime and current characteristics for each type below. The greater the number of positive responses to these questions, the more codependent you are. An overall score of 10 or higher indicates you have significant codependent characteristics that need to be addressed. The greater the number of positive responses for each codependent type the more you tend to manifest that type. A decrease of positive responses to these questions from lifetime to current reflects your progress in overcoming your codependency.

Lifetime	Current	
_____	_____	Total of questions 1-10. General Codependency Scale.
_____	_____	Total of questions 11-15 and 26-30. Independent Worldly Success Score.
_____	_____	Total of questions 11-15 and 31-35. Independent Worldly Failure Score.
_____	_____	Total of questions 16-20 and 36-40. Dependent Passive Score.
_____	_____	Total of questions 12, 13, 16, 28, 30 and 41-45. Dependent Rescuer Score.
_____	_____	Total of questions 21-25 and 46-50. Responsibility Avoidant Score.
_____	_____	Total of questions 21-25 and 51-55. Relationship Avoidant Score.

References

Adams, Jay (1973). <u>The Christian Counselor's Manual</u>. Zondervan Publishing, Grand Rapids, Michigan.

Allender, Dan B. (1990). <u>The Wounded Heart</u>. NAVPRESS, Colorado Springs, Colorado.

Alsdurf, James & Alsdurf, Phyllis (1989). <u>Battered into Submission</u>. Intervarsity Press, Downers Grove, Illinois.

American Psychiatric Association (1994). <u>Diagnostic and Statistical Manual of Mental Disorders</u> (4th ed.). Washington D.C.

Anderson, Neil T., and Quarles, Mike and Julia (1996). <u>Freedom From Addiction</u>. Regal Books, Ventura, California.

Arterburn, Stephen (1991). <u>Addicted to "Love."</u> Servant Publications, Ann Arbor, Michigan.

Barclay, William (1978). <u>The Daily Study Bible, Revised Edition</u>. The Westminister Press, Philadelphia, Pennslavania.

Blackaby, Henry T., and King, Claude V. (1990). <u>Experiencing God: Knowing and Doing the Will of God</u>. Lifeway Press, Nashville, Tennessee.

Bufford, Rodger K. (1988). <u>Counseling the Demonic</u>. Word Publishing, Dallas, Texas.

Cameron, Lee. (2001). The Postmodern Turn in Family Therapy. <u>Christian Counseling Today</u>, Vol 9 No. 3, American Association of Christian Counseling, Glen Ellyn, Illinois.

Carter, Les, Minirth, Frank (1995). <u>The Anger Workbook</u>. Thomas Nelson Publishers, Nashville, Tennessee.

Carter, Les, Minirth, Frank (1995). <u>The Freedom from Depression Workbook</u>. Thomas Nelson Publishers, Nashville, Tennessee.

Cline, Foster, and Fay, Jim. (1992). <u>Parenting Teens with Love and Logic</u>. Pinion Press, Colorado Springs, Colorado.

Clinton, Tim (1999). <u>Before a Bad Goodbye</u>. Word Publishing, Nashville, Tennessee.

Cloud, Henry, and Townsend, John (1992). <u>Boundaries</u>. Zondervan Publishing House, Grand Rapids, Michigan.

Cloud, Henry, and Townsend, John (1995). <u>Boundaries Workbook</u>. Zondervan Publishing House, Grand Rapids, Michigan.

Cloud, Dr. Henry, and Townsend, Dr. John (1998). <u>Boundaries with Kids</u>. Zondervan Publishing House, Grand Rapids, Michigan.

Cloud, Dr. Henry, and Townsend, Dr. John (1999). <u>Boundaries in Marriage</u>. Zondervan Publishing House, Grand Rapids, Michigan.

Comer, Ronald J. (1995). <u>Abnormal Psychology</u>. W. H. Freeman and Company, New York.

Comiskey, Andrew (1989). <u>Pursuing Sexual Wholeness</u>. Creation Books, Lake Mary, Florida.

Comiskey, Andrew (1988). <u>Pursuing Sexual Wholeness Workbook</u>. Creation House, Lake Mary, Florida.

Consiglio, Dr. William (1991). <u>Homosexual No More</u>. Victor Books, Wheaton, Illinois.

Cox, Wade (2000). <u>Moses and the Gods of Egypt</u> (No. 105). Christian Churches of God, Woden Act, Australia.

Eggerichs, Emerson (2004). <u>Love & Respect</u>. Integrity Publishers, Nashville, Tennessee.

Gallagher, Steve (2000). <u>At the Altar of Sexual Idolatry</u>. Pure Life Ministries, Dry Ridge, Kentucky.

Hagin, Kenneth E. (1993). <u>The Triumphant Church</u>. Rhema Bible Church, Tulsa, Oklahoma.

Hart, Archibald D. and Morris, Sharon Hart (2003). <u>Safe Haven Marriage</u>. Thomas Nelson Publishers, Nashville, Tennessee.

Heitritter, Lynn, Vought, Jeanette (1989). <u>Helping Victims of Sexual Abuse</u>. Bethany House, Minneapolis, Minnesota.

Hemfelt, Robert, Minirth, Frank, and Meier, Paul (1989). <u>Love is a Choice: Recovery for Codependent Relationships</u>. Thomas Nelson Publishers, Nashville, Tennessee.

Hemfelt, Robert, Minirth, Frank, and Meier, Paul, Newman, Deborah, Newman, Brian (1991). <u>Love is a Choice Workbook</u>. Thomas Nelson Publishers, Nashville, Tennessee.

Hemfelt, Robert, Minirth, Frank, and Meier, Paul (1991). <u>We Are Driven</u>. Thomas Nelson Publishers, Nashville, Tennessee.

Henslin, Earl R. (1991). <u>The Way Out of the Wilderness or Forgiven and Free</u>. Thomas Nelson, Nashville, Tennessee.

Howard, Jeanette (1991). <u>Out of Egypt</u>. Monarch, Tunbridge Wells, Kentucky.

Ketterman, Dr. Grace (1992). <u>Verbal Abuse: Healing the Hidden Wound</u>. Servant Publications, Ann Arbor, Michigan.

Klimionok, Reginald (1982). <u>Giants or Grasshoppers</u>. Assembly Press Pty, Ltd., Queensland, Australia.

Kubler-Ross, Elisabeth and Kessler, David.(2005). <u>On Grief and Grieving: Finding the Meaning of Grief Though the Five Stages of Loss.</u> Simon and Schuster Publishers, New York.

Kuenning, Delores (1987). <u>Helping People Through Grief</u>. Bethany House Publishers, Minneapolis, Minnesota.

Laaser, Mark R., Ph. D. (1996). <u>Faithful and True: Sexual Integrity in a Fallen World</u> (Workbook). Lifeway Press, Nashville, Tennessee.

LaHaye, Tim (1982). <u>Anger is a Choice</u>. Zondervan Publishing, Grand Rapids, Michigan.

McGee, Robert S. and McCleskey, Dale W. (1994). <u>Conquering Chemical Dependency: A Christ-Centered 12-Step Process</u>. Lifeway Press, Nashville, Tennessee.

McGee, Robert S., Mountcastle, William (1993). <u>Conquering Eating Disorders</u>. Lifeway Press, Nashville, Tennessee.

McGee, Robert S., Morrison, Rujon (1997). <u>From Head to Heart</u>. Servant Publications, Ann Arbor, Michigan.

McGee, Robert S., Springle, Pat, and Joiner, Susan (1990). <u>Overcoming Chemical Dependency</u>. RAPHA Publishing/Word, Inc., Houston and Dallas, Texas.

McGee, Robert S., Yost, Russell (undated). <u>Rapha's Step Studies for Overcoming Sexual Addiction</u>. Rapha Resources, Inc., Houston, Texas.

McGee, Robert S. (1990). <u>The Search for Significance</u>. Rapha Publishing, Houston, Texas.

Minirth, Frank, Meier, Paul, Fink, Siegfried, Byrd, Walter, and Hawkins, Don (1988). <u>Taking Control</u>. Baker House Publishing, Grand Rapids, Michigan.

Missler, Chuck (2000). The Invisible War: Against the Gods of Egypt. <u>Personal Update News Journal</u>, July 2000, Koinonia House, Wheaton, Illinois.

Morris, Charles G. (1996). <u>Psychology, An Introduction</u>. Prentice Hall, Upper Saddle River, New Jersey.

Nicolosi, Joseph (1997). <u>Reparative Therapy of Male Homosexuality: A Clinical Approach</u>. Jason Aronson, Lanhan, Maryland.

Paymar, Michael (1993). <u>Violent No More</u>. Hunter House, Alameda, California.

Piehl, Robert O. (2001). Narrative Therapy and the Christian Counselor. <u>Christian Counseling Today</u>, Vol 9 No. 3, American Association of Christian Counseling, Glen Ellyn, Illinois.

Pierce, Larry (1996). <u>The Online Bible for Windows</u>. Larry Pierce, Winterbourne, Ontario.

Reiner, Troy D. (2005). <u>Faith Therapy</u>. Pleasant Word Publishing, Enumclaw, Washington.

Reiner, Troy D. (2005). <u>Revelations That will Set You Free</u>. Pleasant Word Publishing, Enumclaw, Washington.

Reiner, Troy D. (2005), <u>Principles for Life</u>. Pleasant Word Publishing, Enumclaw, Washington.

Salter, Anna C. (1988). <u>Treating Child Sex Offenders and Victims</u>. Sage Publishing, Newbury Park, California.

Slemming, C. W. (1974). <u>Made According to Pattern</u>. Christian Literature Crusade, Fort Washington, Pennsylvania.

Smalley, Gary (1988). <u>Hidden Keys of a Loving Lasting Marriage</u>. Zondervan Publishing, Grand Rapids, Michigan.

Smith, Malcom (Undated). <u>The Search for Self-worth</u> (An audio tape series). Malcom Smith Ministries, San Antonio, Texas.

Smith, Ed M. (1996). <u>Beyond Tolerable Recovery</u>. Family Care Ministers, Campbellsville, Kentucky.

Springle, Pat (1993). <u>Conquering Codependency</u>. Lifeway Press, Nashville, Tennessee.

Stoop, David, Ph. D. (1995). <u>What's He So Angry About</u>. Moorings, Nashville, Tennessee.

Strom, Kay Marshall (1986). <u>In the Name of Submission</u>. Multnomah Press, Portland, Oregon.

Strong, James (1890). <u>The Exhaustive Concordance of the Bible</u>. Abington Press, Nashville, Tennessee.

Trench, Richard Chenevix (1961). <u>Notes on the Parables of our Lord</u>. Baker Book House, Grand Rapids, Michigan.

Vredevelt, Pam, Newman, Deborah, Beverly, Harry, Minirth, Frank (1992). <u>The Thin Disguise</u>. Thomas Nelson Publishers, Nashville, Tennessee.

Wangerin, Walter Jr. (1992). <u>Mourning into Dancing</u>. Zondervan Publishing, Grand Rapids, Michigan.

Wilson, Walter Lewis (1957). <u>Wilson's Dictionary of Bible Types</u>. Eerdmans Printing Company, Grand Rapids, Michigan.

CPSIA information can be obtained
at www.ICGtesting.com
Printed in the USA
BVHW051210061019
560015BV00011B/4/P